DATE DUE

JUL 2 0 2004		

Demco

THE GYPSY TRAIL

AN ANTHOLOGY FOR CAMPERS

Under the roof-tree of the world
We keep the gypsy calendar,
As the revolving seasons rise
Above the tree-tops, star by star.
                    Bliss Carman

THE GYPSY TRAIL

AN ANTHOLOGY FOR CAMPERS

COMPILED BY

PAULINE GOLDMARK

AND

MARY HOPKINS

VOLUME I

Granger Poetry Library

GRANGER BOOK CO., INC.
GREAT NECK, N.Y.

FIRST PUBLISHED 1914
REPRINTED 1979

INTERNATIONAL STANDARD BOOK NUMBER
0-89609-135-X

LIBRARY OF CONGRESS CATALOG NUMBER
78-74817

PRINTED IN THE UNITED STATES OF AMERICA

To
Comrades of the Trail

ACKNOWLEDGMENT

The editors acknowledge their indebtedness to the following authors and publishers for the use of copyright poems. "Golden Shoes," by Miss Josephine Preston Peabody; "The Old Camp Fire," by Bret Harte; "The Voice of the Pine," by Richard Watson Gilder; "Let Me Go Where'er I Will," "Character," "The Philosopher's Camp," "The Summons," by Ralph Waldo Emerson, and "Waiting," by Mr. John Burroughs, are used by permission of and by special arrangement with Houghton Mifflin Company. "Drifting," by Thomas Buchanan Read, is included through the courtesy of J. B. Lippincott Company, and "A Valediction," from Mr. John Masefield's *Salt Water Ballads,* through the courtesy of The Macmillan Company. For permission to reprint poems mentioned below thanks are tendered: to Mr. Bliss Carman and Small, Maynard and Co., for "A Vagabond Song," "The Joys of the Road" and "Spring Song"; to Mr. Arthur Colton for verses from "The Canticle of the Road"; to Mr. Hamlin Garland for "Line up, Brave Boys"; to Miss Georgiana Goddard King and the Macmillan Co. for "Hylas" and "Peregrino's Song," from the *Way of Perfect Love;* to Miss Edith Wyatt and to Doubleday, Page and Company and Collier's respectively, for "Crystal Water" and "The August Sky"; and to Miss Ethelwyn Wetherald for "The House of the Trees." Through the courtesy of Mrs. Richard Hovey and Duffield & Company "From the Faun," "The Sea Gypsy," and "The Wanderer" are included.

August First, 1914.

THE GYPSY TRAIL

TABLE OF CONTENTS

THE CALL OF THE OPEN

SPRING

i

TABLE OF CONTENTS

TABLE OF CONTENTS

TABLE OF CONTENTS

TABLE OF CONTENTS

TABLE OF CONTENTS

THE HILLS

THE ROAD TO ELFLAND

TABLE OF CONTENTS

TABLE OF CONTENTS

TABLE OF CONTENTS

TABLE OF CONTENTS

THE CALL OF THE OPEN

Oh, the wild joys of living! the leaping from rock up to
  rock,
The strong rending of boughs from the fir-tree, the cool
  silver shock
Of the plunge in the pool's living water, the hunt of the
  bear,
And the sultriness showing the lion is couched in his lair.
And the meal, the rich dates yellowed over with gold
  dust divine,
And the locust-flesh steeped in the pitcher, the full draft
  of wine,
And the sleep in the dried river-channel where bulrushes
  tell
That the water was wont to go warbling so softly and
  well.
How good is man's life, the mere living! how fit to em-
  ploy
All the heart and the soul and the senses forever in joy!
                                        Robert Browning

Radiant health!
O kisses of sun and wind, tall fir-trees and moss-covered
        rocks! O boundless joy of Nature on the mountain-
        tops — coming back at last to you!
O joy of the liberated soul . . . daring all things!
                                        Edward Carpenter

THE CALL OF THE OPEN

GOOD-BYE

GOOD-BYE, proud world! I'm going home,
Thou'rt not my friend, and I'm not thine.
Long through thy weary crowds I roam;
A river-ark on the ocean brine,
Long I've been tossed like the driven foam;
But now, proud world, I'm going home.

Good-bye to Flattery's fawning face,
To Grandeur, with his wise grimace,
To upstart Wealth's averted eye,
To supple Office low and high,
To crowded halls, to court, and street,
To frozen hearts, and hasting feet,
To those who go, and those who come;
Good-bye, proud world! I'm going home.

I'm going to my own hearth-stone
Bosomed in yon green hills, alone,—
A secret nook in a pleasant land,
Whose groves the frolic fairies planned;
Where arches green the livelong day
Echo the blackbird's roundelay,
And vulgar feet have never trod
A spot that is sacred to thought and God.

O, when I am safe in my sylvan home,
I tread on the pride of Greece and Rome;
And when I am stretched beneath the pines
Where the evening star so holy shines,

3

THE GYPSY TRAIL

I laugh at the lore and the pride of man,
At the sophist schools, and the learned clan;
For what are they all, in their high conceit,
When man in the bush with God may meet?
Ralph Waldo Emerson

SPRING SONG

MAKE me over, mother April,
    When the sap begins to stir!
When thy flowery hand delivers
All the mountain-prisoned rivers,
And thy great heart beats and quivers
To revive the days that were,
Make me over, mother April,
When the sap begins to stir!

Take my dust and all my dreaming,
Count my heart-beats one by one,
Send them where the winters perish;
Then some golden noon re-cherish
And restore them in the sun,
Flower and scent and dust and dreaming,
With their heart-beats every one.

Set me in the urge and tide-drift
Of the streaming hosts a-wing!
Breast of scarlet, throat of yellow,
Raucous challenge, wooings mellow —
Every migrant is my fellow,
Making northward with the spring.
Loose me in the urge and tide-drift
Of the streaming hosts a-wing!

4

THE CALL OF THE OPEN

Shrilling pipe or fluting whistle,
In the valleys come again;
Fife of frog and call of tree-toad,
All my brothers, five or three-toed,
With their revel no more vetoed,
Making music in the rain;
Shrilling pipe or fluting whistle,
In the valleys come again.

Make me of thy seed to-morrow,
When the sap begins to stir!
Tawny light-foot, sleepy bruin,
Bright-eyes in the orchard ruin,
Gnarl the good life goes askew in,
Whisky-jack or tanager,—
Make me anything to-morrow,
When the sap begins to stir!

Make me even (How do I know?)
Like my friend the gargoyle there;
It may be the heart within him
Swells that doltish hands should pin him
Fixed forever in mid-air.
Make me even sport for swallows,
Like the soaring gargoyle there!

Give me the old clue to follow,
Through the labyrinth of night!
Clod of clay with heart of fire,
Things that burrow and aspire,
With the vanishing desire,
For the perishing delight,—
Only the old clue to follow,
Through the labyrinth of night!

Make me over, mother April,
When the sap begins to stir!

THE GYPSY TRAIL

Fashion me from swamp or meadow,
Garden plot or ferny shadow,
Hyacinth or humble burr!
Make me over, mother April,
When the sap begins to stir!

Let me hear the far, low summons,
When the silver winds return;
Rills that run and streams that stammer,
Goldenwing with his loud hammer,
Icy brooks that brawl and clamor,
Where the Indian willows burn;
Let me hearken to the calling,
When the silver winds return,

Till recurring and recurring,
Long since wandered and come back,
Like a whim of Grieg's or Gounod's,
This same self, bird, bud, or Bluenose,
Some day I may capture (Who knows?)
Just the one last joy I lack,
Waking to the far new summons,
When the old spring winds come back.

For I have no choice of being,
When the sap begins to climb,—
Strong insistence, sweet intrusion,
Vasts and verges of illusion,—
So I win, to time's confusion,
The one perfect pearl of time,
Joy and joy and joy forever,
Till the sap forgets to climb!

Make me over in the morning
From the rag-bag of the world!
Scraps of dream and duds of daring,
Home-brought stuff from far sea-faring,

THE CALL OF THE OPEN

Faded colors once so flaring,
Shreds of banners long since furled!
Hues of ash and glints of glory,
In the rag-bag of the world!

Let me taste the old immortal
Indolence of life once more;
Not recalling or foreseeing,
Let the great slow joys of being
Well my heart through as of yore!
Let me taste the old immortal
Indolence of life once more!

Give me the old drink for rapture,
The delirium to drain!
All my fellows drank in plenty
At the Three-Score Inns and Twenty
From the mountains to the main!
Give me the old drink for rapture,
The delirium to drain!

Only make me over, April,
When the sap begins to stir!
Make me man or make me woman,
Make me oaf or ape or human,
Cup of flower or cone of fir;
Make me anything but neuter
When the sap begins to stir!

Bliss Carman

THE LAKE ISLE OF INNISFREE

I WILL arise and go now, and go to Innisfree,
  And a small cabin build there, of clay and
    wattles made;

THE GYPSY TRAIL

Nine bean rows will I have there, a hive for the
 honey bee,
 And live alone in the bee-loud glade.

And I shall have some peace there, for peace
 comes dropping slow,
Dropping from the veils of the morning to where
 the cricket sings;
There midnight's all a glimmer, and noon a pur-
 ple glow,
 And evening full of the linnet's wings.

I will arise and go now, for always night and
 day
I hear lake-water lapping with low sounds by the
 shore;
While I stand on the roadway or on the pave-
 ments grey,
 I hear it in the deep heart's core.
       William Butler Yeats

INTO THE TWILIGHT

OUTWORN heart in a time outworn,
 Come clear of the nets of wrong and right;
Laugh, heart, again in the grey twilight,
Sigh, heart, again in the dew of the morn.

Your mother Erie is always young,
Dew ever shining and twilight grey;
Though hope fall from you and love decay,
Burning in fires of a slanderous tongue.

Come, heart, where hill is heaped upon hill:
For there the mystical brotherhood
8

THE CALL OF THE OPEN

Of sun and moon and hollow and wood
And river and stream work out their will;

And God stands winding His lonely horn,
And time and the world are ever in flight;
And love is less kind than the grey twilight,
And hope is less clear than the dew of the morn.
                                    William Butler Yeats

THE INVITATION

BEST and brightest, come away!
     Fairer far than this fair Day,
Which, like thee to those in sorrow,
Comes to bid a sweet good-morrow
To the rough Year just awake
In its cradle on the brake.
The brightest hour of unborn Spring,
Thro' the winter wandering,
Found, it seems, the halcyon Morn
To hoar February born;
Bending from Heaven, in azure mirth,
It kissed the forehead of the Earth,
And smiled upon the silent sea,
And bade the frozen streams be free,
And waked to music all their fountains,
And breathed upon the frozen mountains,
And like a prophetess of May
Strewed flowers upon the barren way,
Making the wintry world appear
Like one on whom thou smilest, dear.

Away, away, from men and towns,
To the wild wood and the downs —
To the silent wilderness

THE GYPSY TRAIL

Where the soul need not repress
Its music lest it should not find
An echo in another's mind,
While the touch of Nature's art
Harmonizes heart to heart.
I leave this notice on my door
For each accustomed visitor: —
" I am gone into the fields
To take what this sweet hour yields; —
Reflection, you may come to-morrow,
Sit by the fireside with Sorrow.—
You with the unpaid bill, Despair,—
You tiresome verse-reciter, Care,—
I will pay you in the grave,—
Death will listen to your stave.
Expectation too, be off!
To-day is for itself enough;
Hope in pity mock not Woe
With smiles, nor follow where I go;
Long having lived on thy sweet food,
At length I find one moment's good
After long pain — with all your love,
This you never told me of."
Radiant Sister of the Day,
Awake! arise! and come away!
To the wild woods and the plains,
And the pools where Winter rains
Image all their roof of leaves,
Where the pine its garland weaves
Of sapless green and ivy dun
Round stems that never kiss the sun;
Where the lawns and pastures be,
And the sandhills of the sea; —
Where the melting hoar-frost wets
The daisy-star that never sets,
And wind-flowers, and violets,

THE CALL OF THE OPEN

Which yet joined not scent to hue,
Crown the pale year weak and new;
When the night is left behind
In the deep east, dun and blind,
And the blue noon is over us,
And the multitudinous
Billows murmur at our feet,
Where the earth and ocean meet,
And all things seem only one
In the universal sun.

Percy Bysshe Shelley

SPRING

Diffugere nives, redeunt iam gramina campis
Arboribusque comae.

Horace

Now the North wind ceases,
The warm South-West awakes;
Swift fly the fleeces,
Swift the blossom-flakes.

Meredith

Wie herrlich leuchtet
Mir die Natur!
Wie glänzt die Sonne!
Wie lacht die Flur!

Es dringen Blüten
Aus jedem Zweig
Und tausend Stimmen
Aus dem Gesträuch.

Und Freud' und Wonne
Aus jeder Brust.
O Erd', O Sonne!
O Glück, O Lust!

Goethe

SPRING

FOOTPRINTS IN THE SNOW

WORN is the winter rug of white,
    And in the snow-bare spots once more
Glimpses of faint green grass in sight,—
  Spring's footprints on the floor.

Upon the sombre forest gates
  A crimson flush the mornings catch,
The token of the Spring who waits
  With finger on the latch.

Blow, bugles of the south, and win
  The warders from their dreams too long,
And bid them let the new guest in
  With her glad hosts of song.

She shall make bright the dismal ways
  With broideries of bud and bloom,
With music fill the nights and days
  And end the garden's gloom.

Her face is lovely with the sun;
  Her voice — ah, listen to it now!
The silence of the year is done:
  The bird is on the bough!

Spring here,— by what magician's touch?
  'Twas winter scarce an hour ago.
And yet I should have guessed as much,—
  Those footprints in the snow!

Frank Dempster Sherman

15

THE GYPSY TRAIL

AFTER CIVILIZATION

IN the first soft winds of spring, while snow
yet lay on the ground —
Forth from the city into the great woods wan-
dering,
Into the great silent white woods where they
waited in their beauty and majesty
For man their companion to come:
There, in vision, out of the wreck of cities and
civilizations,
I saw a new life arise.

.   .   .   .

The winter woods stretched all around so
still!
Every bough laden with snow — the faint pur-
ple waters rushing on in the hollows, with steam
on the soft still air!
Far aloft the arrowy larch reached into the
sky, the high air trembled with the music of the
loosened brooks.
O sound of waters, jubilant, pouring, pouring
— O hidden song in the hollows!
Secret of the earth, swelling, sobbing to divulge
itself!

Slowly, building, lifting itself up atom by atom,
Gathering itself together round a new centre —
or rather round the world-old centre once more
revealed —
I saw a new life, a new society, arise.
Man I saw arising once more to dwell with Na-
ture;
(The old, old story — the prodigal son return-
ing, so loved,

SPRING

The long estrangement, the long entanglement
in vain things)—
The child returning to its home, companion of
the winter woods once more,
Companion of the stars and waters, hearing
their words at first hand (more than all science
ever taught),
The near contact, the dear, dear mother so
close, the twilight sky and the young tree-tops
against it;
The huts on the mountain-side, companionable
of the sun and the winds, the lake unsullied be-
low;
The daily bath in natural running waters, or in
the parallel foam-lines of the sea, the pressure of
the naked foot to the earth;
The few needs, the exhilarated radiant life.

   •   •   •   •

Edward Carpenter

NOW FADES THE LAST LONG STREAK OF SNOW

NOW fades the last long streak of snow,
   Now burgeons every maze of quick
   About the flowering squares, and thick
By ashen roots the violets blow.

Now rings the woodland loud and long,
   The distance takes a lovelier hue,
   And drown'd in yonder living blue
The lark becomes a sightless song.

Now dance the lights on lawn and lea,
   The flocks are whiter down the vale,
   And milkier every milky sail
On winding stream or distant sea;

THE GYPSY TRAIL

Where now the seamew pipes, or dives
    In yonder greening gleam, and fly
    The happy birds, that change their sky
To build and brood; that live their lives

From land to land; and in my breast
    Spring wakens too; and my regret
    Becomes an April violet,
And buds and blossoms like the rest.
                Alfred, Lord Tennyson

FROM AN OLD RITUAL

O DWELLERS in the dust, arise,
    My little brothers of the field,
And put the sleep out of your eyes!
Your death-doom is repealed.

Lift all your golden faces now,
You dandelions in the ground!
You quince and thorn and apple bough,
Your foreheads are unbound.

O dwellers in the frost, awake,
My little brothers of the mould!
It is the time to forth and slake
Your being as of old.

You frogs and newts and creatures small
In the pervading urge of spring,
Who taught you in the dreary fall
To guess so glad a thing?

From every swale your watery notes,
Piercing the rainy cedar lands,
Proclaim your tiny silver throats
Are loosened of their bands.

18

SPRING

O dwellers in the desperate dark,
My brothers of the mortal birth,
Is there no whisper bids you mark
The Easter of the earth?

Let the great flood of spring's return
Float every fear away, and know
We all are fellows of the fern
And children of the snow.

Bliss Carman

APRIL WEATHER

SOON, ah, soon the April weather
  With the sunshine at the door,
And the mellow melting rain-wind
  Sweeping from the South once more.

Soon the rosy maples budding,
  And the willows putting forth,
Misty crimson and soft yellow
  In the valleys of the North.

Soon the hazy purple distance,
  Where the cabined heart takes wing,
Eager for the old migration
  In the magic of the spring.

Soon, ah, soon the budding windflowers
  Through the forest white and frail,
And the odorous wild cherry
  Gleaming in her ghostly veil.

Soon, about the waking uplands
  The hepaticas in blue,—
Children of the first warm sunlight
  In their sober Quaker hue,—

THE GYPSY TRAIL

All our shining little sisters
  Of the forest and the field,
Lifting up their quiet faces
  With the secret half revealed.

Soon across the folding twilight
  Of the round earth hushed to hear,
The first robin at his vespers
  Calling far, serene and clear.

Soon the waking and the summons,
  Starting sap in bole and blade,
And the bubbling marshy whisper
  Seeping up through bog and glade.

Soon the frogs in silver chorus
  Through the night, from marsh and
    swale,
Blowing in their tiny oboes
  All the joy that shall not fail,—

Passing up the old earth rapture
  By a thousand streams and rills,
From the red Virginian valleys
  To the blue Canadian hills.

Soon, ah, soon the splendid impulse,
  Nomad longing, vagrant whim,
When a man's false angels vanish
  And the truth comes back to him.

Soon the majesty, the vision,
  And the old unfaltering dream,
Faith to follow, strength to stablish,
  Will to venture and to seem;

SPRING

All the radiance, the glamour,
The expectancy and poise,
Of this ancient life renewing
Its temerities and joys.

Soon the immemorial magic
Of the young Aprilian moon,
And the wonder of thy friendship
In the twilight — soon, ah, soon!

Bliss Carman

DIFFUGERE NIVES

DIFFUGERE nives, redeunt iam gramina
campis
Arboribusque comae;
Mutat terra vices et decrescentia ripas
Flumina praetereunt;
Gratia cum Nymphis geminisque sororibus audet
Ducere nuda choros.
Immortalia ne speres, monet annus et almum
Quae rapit hora diem.
Frigora mitescunt Zephyris, ver proterit aestas,
Interitura simul
Pomifer autumnus fruges effuderit, et mox
Bruma recurrit iners.
Damna tamen celeres reparant caelestia lunae:
Nos, ubi decidimus,
Quo pius Aeneas, quo Tullus dives et Ancus,
Pulvis et umbra sumus.
Quis scit an adiciant hodiernae crastina summae
Tempora di superi?
Cuncta manus avidas fugient heredis, amico
Quae dederis animo.
Cum semel occideris et de te splendida Minos
Fecerit arbitria,

THE GYPSY TRAIL

Non, Torquate, genus, non te facundia, non te
    Restituet pietas:
Infernis neque enim tenebris Diana pudicum
    Liberat Hippolytum,
Nec Lethaea valet Theseus abrumpere caro
    Vincula Pirithoo.

                        Horace

VENUS GENETRIX

A ENEADUM genetrix, hominum divomque
    voluptas,
Alma Venus, caeli subter labentia signa
Quae mare navigerum, quae terras frugiferentis
Concelebras, per te quoniam genus omne animan
    tum
Concipitur visitque exortum lumina solis:
Te, dea, te fugiunt venti, te nubila caeli
Adventumque tuum, tibi suavis daedala tellus
Summittit flores, tibi rident aequora ponti
Placatumque nitet diffuso lumine caelum.

                        Lucretius

THE HOUNDS OF SPRING

W HEN the hounds of spring are on winter's
    traces,
    The mother of months in meadow or plain
Fills the shadows and windy places
    With lisp of leaves and ripple of rain;
And the brown bright nightingale amorous
Is half assuaged for Itylus,
For the Thracian ships and the foreign faces,
    The tongueless vigil, and all the pain.

SPRING

Come with bows bent and with emptying of
    quivers,
  Maiden most perfect, lady of light,
With a noise of winds and many rivers
  With a clamor of waters, and with might;
Bind on thy sandals, O thou most fleet,
Over the splendor and speed of thy feet;
For the faint east quickens, the wan west shivers,
  Round the feet of the day and the feet of the
    night.

Where shall we find her, how shall we sing to her,
  Fold our hands round her knees, and cling?
O that man's heart were as fire and could spring
    to her,
  Fire, or the strength of the streams that
    spring!
For the stars and the winds are unto her
As raiment, as songs of the harp-player;
For the risen stars and the fallen cling to her,
  And the southwest-wind and the west-wind
    sing.

For winter's rains and ruins are over,
  And all the season of snows and sins;
The days dividing lover and lover,
  The light that loses, the night that wins;
And time remembered is grief forgotten,
And frosts are slain and flowers begotten,
And in green underwood and cover
  Blossom by blossom the spring begins.

The full streams feed on flower of rushes,
  Ripe grasses trammel a travelling foot,
The maiden flame of the young year flushes
  From leaf to flower and flower to fruit;

THE GYPSY TRAIL

And fruit and leaf are as gold and fire,
And the oat is heard above the lyre,
And the hoofèd heel of a satyr crushes
    The chestnut-husk at the chestnut-root.

And Pan by noon and Bacchus by night,
    Fleeter of foot than the fleet-foot kid,
Follows with dancing and fills with delight
    The Maenad and the Bassarid;
And soft as lips that laugh and hide
The laughing leaves of the trees divide,
And screen from seeing and leave in sight
    The god pursuing, the maiden hid.

The ivy falls with the Bacchanal's hair,
    Over her eyebrows hiding her eyes;
The wild vine slipping down leaves bare
    Her bright breast shortening into sighs;
The wild vine slips with the weight of its leaves,
But the berried ivy catches and cleaves
To the limbs that glitter, the feet that scare
    The wolf that follows, the fawn that flies.
                    Algernon Charles Swinburne

HIRTENLIED

FRAU HOLDA kam aus dem Berg hervor,
    Zu ziehen durch Fluren und Auen.
Gar süssen Klang vernahm da mein Ohr,
Mein Auge begehrte zu schauen: —
Da träumt' ich manchen holden Traum,
Und als mein Aug' erschlossen kaum,
Da strahlten warm die Sonnen:
Der Mai, der Mai war kommen.
Nun spiel' ich lustig die Schalmei: —
Der Mai ist da, der liebe Mai!
                    Richard Wagner

SPRING

FRÜHLINGSGRUSS

ES steht ein Berg im Feuer,
   In feurigem Morgenbrand,
Und auf des Berges Spitze
Ein Tannbaum überm Land.

Und auf dem höchsten Wipfel
Steh' ich und schau' vom Baum;
O Welt, du schöne Welt du,
Man sieht dich vor Blüten kaum!
Joseph von Eichendorff

SPRING

SPRING, the sweet Spring, is the year's pleas-
   ant king;
Then blooms each thing, then maids dance in a
   ring,
Cold doth not sting, the pretty birds do sing —
   Cuckoo, jug-jug, pu-we, to-witta-woo!

The palm and may make country houses gay,
Lambs frisk and play, the shepherds pipe all day,
And we hear aye birds tune this merry lay —
   Cuckoo, jug-jug, pu-we, to-witta-woo!

The fields breathe sweet, the daisies kiss our feet,
Young lovers meet, old wives a-sunning sit,
In every street these tunes our ears do greet —
   Cuckoo, jug-jug, pu-we, to-witta-woo!
     Spring, the sweet Spring!
Thomas Nash

THE GYPSY TRAIL

THE BELLS OF YOUTH

THE Bells of Youth are ringing in the gate-
ways of the South:
The bannerets of green are now unfurled:
Spring has risen with a laugh, a wild-rose in her
mouth,
And is singing, singing, singing thro' the
world.

The Bells of Youth are ringing in all the silent
places,
The primrose and the celandine are out:
Children run a-laughing with joy upon their
faces,
The west wind follows after with a shout.

The Bells of Youth are ringing from the forests
to the mountains,
From the meadows to the moorlands, hark their
ringing!
Ten thousand thousand splashing rills and fern-
dappled fountains
Are flinging wide the Song of Youth and on-
ward flowing, singing!

The Bells of Youth are ringing in the gate-ways
of the South:
The bannerets of green are now unfurled:
Spring has risen with a laugh, a wild-rose in her
mouth,
And is singing, singing, singing thro' the
world.

Fiona Macleod

SPRING

LINES WRITTEN IN EARLY SPRING

I HEARD a thousand blended notes,
  While in a grove I sate reclined,
In that sweet mood when pleasant thoughts
  Bring sad thoughts to the mind.

To her fair works did Nature link
  The human soul that through me ran;
And much it grieved my heart to think
  What man has made of man.

Through primrose tufts, in that green bower,
  The periwinkle trailed its wreaths;
And 'tis my faith that every flower
  Enjoys the air it breathes.

The birds around me hopped and played,
  Their thoughts I cannot measure:—
But the least motion which they made
  It seemed a thrill of pleasure.

The budding twigs spread out their fan,
  To catch the breezy air;
And I must think, do all I can,
  That there was pleasure there.

If this belief from heaven be sent,
  If such be Nature's holy plan,
Have I not reason to lament
  What man has made of man?

William Wordsworth

THE GYPSY TRAIL

THE TABLES TURNED

UP! up! my Friend, and quit your books;
  Or surely you'll grow double:
Up! up! my Friend, and clear your looks;
  Why all this toil and trouble?

The sun, above the mountain's head,
  A freshening lustre mellow
Through all the long green fields has spread,
  His first sweet evening yellow.

Books! 't is a dull and endless strife:
  Come, hear the woodland linnet,
How sweet his music! on my life,
  There's more of wisdom in it.

And hark! how blithe the throstle sings!
  He, too, is no mean preacher:
Come forth into the light of things,
  Let Nature be your teacher.

She has a mind of ready wealth,
  Our minds and hearts to bless —
Spontaneous wisdom breathed by health,
  Truth breathed by cheerfulness.

One impulse from a vernal wood
  May teach you more of man,
Of moral evil and of good,
  Than all the sages can.

Sweet is the lore which Nature brings;
  Our meddling intellect
Mis-shapes the beauteous forms of things: —
  We murder to dissect.

SPRING

Enough of Science and of Art;
  Close up those barren leaves;
Come forth, and bring with you a heart
  That watches and receives.
                        William Wordsworth

TO THE CUCKOO

O BLITHE New-comer! I have heard,
    I hear thee and rejoice.
O Cuckoo! shall I call thee Bird,
  Or but a wandering Voice?

While I am lying on the grass
  Thy twofold shout I hear,
From hill to hill it seems to pass,
  At once far off, and near.

Though babbling only to the Vale
  Of sunshine and of flowers,
Thou bringest unto me a tale
  Of visionary hours.

Thrice welcome, darling of the Spring!
  Even yet thou art to me
No bird, but an invisible thing,
  A voice, a mystery;

The same whom in my school-boy days
  I listened to; that Cry
Which made me look a thousand ways
  In bush, and tree, and sky.

To seek thee did I often rove
  Through woods and on the green;
And thou wert still a hope, a love;
  Still longed for, never seen.

29

THE GYPSY TRAIL

And I can listen to thee yet;
 Can lie upon the plain
And listen, till I do beget
 That golden time again.

O blessed Bird! the earth we pace
 Again appears to be
An unsubstantial, faery place,
 That is fit home for Thee!
     William Wordsworth

I WANDERED LONELY AS A CLOUD

I WANDERED lonely as a cloud
 That floats on high o'er vales and
  hills,
When all at once I saw a crowd
 A host, of golden daffodils;
Beside the lake, beneath the trees,
Fluttering and dancing in the breeze.

Continuous as the stars that shine
 And twinkle on the milky way,
They stretched in never-ending line
 Along the margin of a bay:
Ten thousand saw I at a glance
Tossing their heads in sprightly dance.

The waves beside them danced; but they
 Outdid the sparkling waves in glee:
A poet could not but be gay,
 In such a jocund company:
I gazed — and gazed — but little thought
What wealth the show to me had brought:

SPRING

For oft, when on my couch I lie
 In vacant or in pensive mood,
They flash upon that inward eye
 Which is the bliss of solitude;
And then my heart with pleasure fills,
And dances with the daffodils.

William Wordsworth

WARBLE FOR LILAC-TIME

WARBLE me now for joy of Lilac-time,
 Sort me, O tongue and lips, for Nature's
  sake, and sweet life's sake — and
  death's the same as life's,
Souvenirs of earliest summer — birds' eggs, and
 the first berries;
Gather the welcome signs, (as children, with peb-
 bles, or stringing shells;)
Put in April and May — the hylas croaking in the
 ponds — the elastic air,
Bees, butterflies, the sparrow with its simple
 notes,
Blue-bird, and darting swallow — nor forget the
 high-hole flashing his golden wings,
The tranquil sunny haze, the clinging smoke, the
 vapor,
Spiritual, airy insects, humming on gossamer
 wings,
Shimmer of waters, with fish in them — the ceru-
 lean above;
All that is jocund and sparkling — the brooks
 running,
The maple woods, the crisp February days, and
 the sugar-making;
The robin where he hops, bright-eyed, brown-
 breasted,

THE GYPSY TRAIL

With musical clear call at sunrise, and again at
  sunset,
Or flitting among the trees of the apple-orchard,
  building the nest of his mate;
The melted snow of March — the willow sending
  forth its yellow-green sprouts;
— For spring-time is here! the summer is here!
  and what is this in it and from it?
Thou, Soul, unloosen'd — the restlessness after I
  know not what;
Come! let us lag here no longer — let us be up
  and away!
O for another world! O if one could fly like a
  bird!
O to escape — to sail forth as in a ship!
To glide with thee, O Soul, o'er all, in all, as a
  ship o'er the waters!
— Gathering these hints, these preludes — the
  blue sky, the grass, the morning drops of
  dew;
(With additional songs — every spring will I
  now strike up additional songs,
Nor ever again forget, these tender days, the
  chants of Death as well as Life;)
The lilac-scent, the bushes, and the dark green,
  heart-shaped leaves,
Wood violets, the little delicate pale blossoms
  called innocence,
Samples and sorts not for themselves, but for
  their atmosphere,
To tally, drench'd with them, tested by them,
Cities and artificial life, and all their sights and
  scenes,
My mind henceforth, and all its meditations —
  my recitatives,

SPRING

My land, my age, my race, for once to serve in
    songs,
(Sprouts, tokens ever of death indeed the same
    as life,)
To grace the bush I love — to sing with the birds,
A warble for joy of Lilac-time.

Walt Whitman

SIR LAUNCELOT AND QUEEN GUINEVERE

L IKE souls that balance joy and pain,
    With tears and smiles from heaven
    again
The maiden Spring upon the plain
Came in a sun-lit fall of rain.
    In crystal vapor everywhere
Blue isles of heaven laugh'd between,
And, far in forest-deeps unseen,
The topmost elm-tree gather'd green
    From draughts of balmy air.

Sometimes the linnet piped his song:
Sometimes the throstle whistled strong:
Sometimes the sparhawk, wheel'd along,
Hush'd all the groves from fear of wrong:
    By grassy capes with fuller sound
In curves the yellowing river ran,
And drooping chestnut-buds began
To spread into the perfect fan,
    Above the teeming ground.

Then, in the boyhood of the year,
Sir Launcelot and Queen Guinevere
Rode thro' the coverts of the deer,
With blissful treble ringing clear.
    She seem'd a part of joyous Spring:

33

THE GYPSY TRAIL

A gown of grass-green silk she wore,
Buckled with golden clasps before;
A light green tuft of plumes she bore
    Closed in a golden ring.

Now on some twisted ivy-net,
Now by some tinkling rivulet,
In mosses mixt with violet
Her cream-white mule his pastern set:
    And fleeter now she skimm'd the plains
Than she whose elfin prancer springs
By night to eery warblings,
When all the glimmering moorland rings
    With jingling bridle-reins.

As she fled fast thro' sun and shade,
The happy winds upon her play'd,
Blowing the ringlet from the braid:
She look'd so lovely, as she sway'd
    The rein with dainty finger-tips,
A man had given all other bliss,
And all his worldly worth for this,
To waste his whole heart in one kiss
    Upon her perfect lips.
                Alfred, Lord Tennyson

SURSUM CORDA

To see a world in a grain of sand,
  And a heaven in a wild flower;
Hold infinity in the palm of your hand,
  And eternity in an hour.

William Blake

Die Geisterwelt ist nicht verschlossen;
Dein Sinn ist zu, dein Herz ist tot!
Auf, bade, Schüler, unverdrossen
Die ird'sche Brust im Morgenrot!

Goethe

SURSUM CORDA

O MOST high, almighty, good Lord God, to thee belong praise, glory honor, and all blessing!

Praised be my Lord with all his creatures; and specially our brother the sun, who brings us the day, and who brings us the light; fair is he, and shining with a very great splendor: O Lord, he signifies to us thee!

Praised be my Lord for our sister the moon, and for the stars, the which he has set clear and lovely in heaven.

Praised be my Lord for our brother the wind, and for air and cloud, calms and all weather, by the which thou upholdest in life all creatures.

Praised be my Lord for our sister water, who is very serviceable unto us, and humble, and precious, and clean.

Praised be my Lord for our brother fire, through whom thou givest us light in the darkness; and he is bright and pleasant, and very mighty and strong.

Praised be my Lord for our mother the earth, the which doth sustain us and keep us, and bringeth forth divers fruits, and flowers of many colours, and grass.

Praised be my Lord for all those who pardon one another for his love's sake, and who endure weakness and tribulation; blessed are they who peaceably shall endure, for thou, O most Highest, shalt give them a crown!

Praised be my Lord for our sister, the death of the body, from whom no man escapeth. Woe to him who dieth in mortal sin! Blessed are they who are found walking by thy most holy will, for the second death shall have no power to do them harm.

Praise ye, and bless ye the Lord, and give thanks unto him, and serve him with great humility.

Saint Francis of Assisi

LORD OF MY HEART'S ELATION

LORD of my heart's elation,
  Spirit of things unseen,
Be thou my aspiration
Consuming and serene!

Bear up, bear out, bear onward
This mortal soul alone,
To selfhood or oblivion,
Incredibly thine own,—

As the foamheads are loosened
And blown along the sea,
Or sink and merge forever
In that which bids them be.

I, too, must climb in wonder,
Uplift at thy command,—
Be one with my frail fellows
Beneath the wind's strong hand,

SURSUM CORDA

A fleet and shadowy column
Of dust or mountain rain,
To walk the earth a moment
And be dissolved again.

Be thou my exaltation
Or fortitude of mien,
Lord of the world's elation
Thou breath of things unseen!

Bliss Carman

BRAHMA

IF the red slayer think he slays,
  Or if the slain think he is slain,
They know not well the subtle ways
  I keep, and pass, and turn again.

Far or forgot to me is near;
  Shadow and sunlight are the same;
The vanished gods to me appear;
  And one to me are shame and fame.

They reckon ill who leave me out;
  When me they fly, I am the wings;
I am the doubter and the doubt,
  And I the hymn the Brahmin sings.

The strong gods pine for my abode,
  And pine in vain the sacred Seven;
But thou, meek lover of the good!
  Find me, and turn thy back on heaven.

Ralph Waldo Emerson

THE GYPSY TRAIL

HEROISM

RUBY wine is drunk by knaves,
  Sugar spends to fatten slaves,
Rose and vine-leaf deck buffoons;
Thunder-clouds are Jove's festoons,
Drooping oft in wreaths of dread,
Lightning-knotted round his head;
The hero is not fed on sweets,
Daily his own heart he eats;
Chambers of the great are jails,
And head-winds right for royal sails.
                    Ralph Waldo Emerson

CHARACTER

THE sun set, but set not his hope:
  Stars rose; his faith was earlier up:
Fixed on the enormous galaxy,
Deeper and older seemed his eye;
And matched his sufferance sublime
The taciturnity of time.
He spoke, and words more soft than rain
Brought the Age of Gold again:
His action won such reverence sweet
As hid all measure of the feat.
                    Ralph Waldo Emerson

WORSHIP

THIS is he, who, felled by foes,
  Sprung harmless up, refreshed by
    blows:
He to captivity was sold,
But him no prison-bars would hold:

SURSUM CORDA

Though they sealed him in a rock,
Mountain chains he can unlock:
Thrown to lions for their meat,
The crouching lions kissed his feet;
Bound to the stake, no flames appalled,
But arched o'er him an honoring vault.
This is he men miscall Fate,
Threading dark ways, arriving late,
But ever coming in time to crown
The truth, and hurl wrong-doers down.
He is the oldest and best-known,
More near than aught thou call'st thy own,
Yet, greeted in another's eyes,
Disconcerts with glad surprise.
This is Jove, who deaf to prayers,
Floods with blessings unawares.
Draw, if thou canst, the mystic line
Severing rightly his from thine,
Which is human, which divine.

Ralph Waldo Emerson

THE FORERUNNERS

LONG I followed happy guides,
   I could never reach their sides.
Their step is forth, and, ere the day,
Breaks up their leaguer, and away.
Keen my sense, my heart was young,
Right good-will my sinews strung,
But no speed of mine avails
To hunt upon their shining trails.
On and away, their hasting feet
Make the morning proud and sweet.
Flowers they strew, I catch the scent;
Or tone of silver instrument

THE GYPSY TRAIL

Leaves on the wind melodious trace,
Yet I could never see their face.
On eastern hills I see their smokes
Mixed with mist by distant lochs.
I met many travellers
Who the road had surely kept;
They saw not my fine revellers,—
These had crossed them while they slept.
Some had heard their fair report
In the country or the court.
Fleetest couriers alive
Never yet could once arrive,
As they went or they returned,
At the house where these sojourned.
Sometimes their strong speed they slacken
Though they are not overtaken;
In sleep their jubilant troop is near,—
I tuneful voices overhear,
It may be in wood or waste,—
At unawares 'tis come and passed.
Their near camp my spirit knows
By signs gracious as rainbows.
I thenceforward and long after
Listen for their harp-like laughter,
And carry in my heart for days
Peace that hallows rudest ways.

Ralph Waldo Emerson

LET ME GO WHERE'ER I WILL

LET me go where'er I will,
    I hear a sky-born music still:
It sounds from all things old,
It sounds from all things young,
From all that's fair, from all that's foul,

SURSUM CORDA

Peals out a cheerful song.
It is not only in the rose,
It is not only in the bird,
Not only where the rainbow glows,
Nor in the song of woman heard,
But in the darkest, meanest things
There alway, alway something sings.
'T is not in the high stars alone,
Nor in the cups of budding flowers,
Nor in the red-breast's mellow tone,
Nor in the bow that smiles in showers,
But in the mud and scum of things
There alway, alway something sings.

Ralph Waldo Emerson

MY HEART LEAPS UP WHEN I BEHOLD

MY heart leaps up when I behold
    A rainbow in the sky:
So was it when my life began;
So is it now I am a man:
So be it when I shall grow old,
    Or let me die!
The Child is father of the Man
And I could wish my days to be
Bound each to each by natural piety.

William Wordsworth

PASSAGE TO INDIA

.   .   .   .

O VAST Rondure, swimming in space!
    Cover'd all over with visible power and
        beauty!
Alternate light and day, and the teeming spiritual
    darkness;

43

THE GYPSY TRAIL

Unspeakable, high processions of sun and moon,
and countless stars, above;
Below, the manifold grass and waters, animals,
mountains, trees;
With inscrutable purpose — some hidden, pro-
phetic intention;
Now, first, it seems, my thought begins to span
thee.

. . . .

O we can wait no longer!
We too take ship, O soul!
Joyous, we too launch out on trackless seas!
Fearless, for unknown shores, on waves of ecstasy
to sail,
Amid the wafting winds (thou pressing me to
thee, I thee to me, O soul),
Caroling free — singing our song of God,
Chanting our chant of pleasant exploration.

With laugh, and many a kiss,
(Let others deprecate — let others weep for sin,
remorse, humiliation;)
O soul, thou pleasest me — I thee.

Ah, more than any priest, O soul, we too believe
in God;
But with the mystery of God we dare not dally.

O soul, thou pleasest me — I thee;
Sailing these seas, or on the hills, or waking in
the night,
Thoughts, silent thoughts, of Time, and Space,
and Death, like waters flowing,
Bear me, indeed, as through the regions infinite,
Whose air I breathe, whose ripples hear — lave
me all over;

SURSUM CORDA

Bathe me, O God, in thee — mounting to thee,
I and my soul to range in range of thee.

O Thou transcendent!
Nameless — the fibre and the breath!
Light of the light — shedding forth universes —
thou centre of them!
Thou mightier centre of the true, the good, the
loving!
Thou moral, spiritual fountain! affection's
source! thou reservoir!
(O pensive soul of me! O thirst unsatisfied!
waitest not there?
Waitest not haply for us, somewhere there, the
Comrade perfect?)
Thou pulse! thou motive of the stars, suns, sys-
tems,
That, circling, move in order, safe, harmonious,
Athwart the shapeless vastnesses of space!
How should I think — how breathe a single
breath — how speak — if, out of myself,
I could not launch, to those, superior universes?

Swiftly I shrivel at the thought of God,
At Nature and its wonders, Time and Space and
Death,
But that I, turning, call to thee, O soul, thou ac-
tual Me,
And lo! thou gently masterest the orbs,
Thou matest Time, smilest content at Death,
And fillest, swellest full, the vastnesses of Space.

Greater than stars or suns,
Bounding, O soul, thou journeyest forth;
— What love, than thine and ours could wider
amplify?

THE GYPSY TRAIL

What aspirations, wishes, outvie thine and ours,
  O soul?
What dreams of the ideal? what plans of purity,
  perfection, strength?
What cheerful willingness, for others' sake, to
  give up all?
For others' sake to suffer all?

Reckoning ahead, O soul, when thou, the time
  achiev'd,
(The seas all cross'd, weather'd the capes, the
  voyage done,)
Surrounded, copest, frontest God, yieldest, the
  aim attain'd,
As, fill'd with friendship, love complete, the Elder
  Brother found,
The `Younger melts in fondness in his arms.

Passage to more than India!
Are thy wings plumed indeed for such far flights?
O Soul, voyagest thou indeed on voyages like
  these?
Disportest thou on waters such as these?
Soundest below the Sanscrit and the Vedas?
Then have thy bent unleash'd.

Passage to you, your shores, ye aged fierce enig-
  mas!
Passage to you, to mastership of you, ye stran-
  gling problems!
You, strew'd with the wrecks of skeletons, that,
  living, never reach'd you.

Passage to more than India!
O secret of the earth and sky!
Of you, O waters of the sea! O winding creeks
  and rivers!

SURSUM CORDA

Of you, O woods and fields! Of you, strong
    mountains of my land!
Of you, O prairies! Of you, gray rocks!
O morning red! O clouds! O rain and snows!
O day and night, passage to you!

O sun and moon, and all you stars! Sirius and
    Jupiter!
Passage to you!

Passage — immediate passage! the blood burns in
    my veins!
Away, O soul! hoist instantly the anchor!
Cut the hawsers — haul out — shake out every
    sail!
Have we not stood here like trees in the ground
    long enough?
Have we not grovell'd here long enough, eating
    and drinking like mere brutes?
Have we not darken'd and dazed ourselves with
    books long enough?

Sail forth! steer for the deep waters only!
Reckless, O soul, exploring, I with thee, and
    thou with me;
For we are bound where mariner has not yet
    dared to go,
And we will risk the ship, ourselves and all.

O my brave soul!
O farther, farther sail!
O daring joy, but safe! Are they not all the
    seas of God?
O farther, farther, farther sail!

                    Walt Whitman

THE BOOK OF JOB
Ch. xxxviii

THEN the Lord answered Job out of the
    whirlwind, and said:
Who is this that darkeneth counsel by words
    without knowledge?
Gird up now thy loins like a man;
For I will demand of thee and answer thou me.

Where wast thou when I laid the foundations of
    the earth?
    Declare, if thou hast understanding.
Who hath laid the measures thereof, if thou
    knowest?
Or who hath stretched the line upon it?
Whereupon are the foundations thereof fastened?
Or who laid the corner stone thereof;
  When the morning stars sang together,
  And all the sons of God shouted for joy?
Or who shut up the sea with doors,
When it brake forth, as if it had issued out of
    the womb;
  When I made the cloud the garment thereof,
  And thick darkness a swaddling band for it,
  And brake up for it my decreed place,
  And set bars and doors,
  And said, "Hitherto shalt thou come, but no
    further;
  And here shall thy proud waves be stayed?"
Hast thou commanded the morning since thy
    days;
And caused the day-spring to know his place;
  That it might take hold of the ends of the
    earth,
  That the wicked might be shaken out of it?
  It is turned as clay to the seal;

And they stand as a garment:
And from the wicked their light is withholden,
And the high arm shall be broken.
Hast thou entered into the springs of the sea?
Or hast thou walked in the search of the depth?
Have the gates of death been opened unto thee?
Or hast thou seen the doors of the shadow of
   death?
Hast thou perceived the breadth of the earth?
  — Declare, if thou knowest it all —
Where is the way where light dwelleth?
And as for darkness, where is the place thereof,
That thou shouldest take it to the bound thereof,
And that thou shouldest know the paths to the
   house thereof?
  — Knowest thou it because thou wast then
   born?
  Or because the number of thy days is
   great? —
Hast thou entered into the treasures of the snow,
Or hast thou seen the treasures of the hail,
Which I have reserved against the time of trou-
  ble,
 Against the day of battle and war?
By what way is the light parted,
Which scattereth the east wind upon the earth?
Who hath divided a watercourse for the over-
   flowing of waters,
Or a way for the lightning of thunder;
 To cause it to rain on the earth where no man
  is;
 On the wilderness wherein there is no man;
 To satisfy the desolate and waste ground;
 And to cause the bud of the tender herb **to**
  spring forth?
Hath the rain a father?
Or who hath begotten the drops of dew?

THE GYPSY TRAIL

Out of whose womb came the ice?
And the hoary frost of heaven, who hath gen-
    dered it?
  The waters are hid as with a stone,
  And the face of the deep is frozen.
Canst thou bind the sweet influences of Pleiades,
Or loose the bands of Orion?
Canst thou bring forth Mazzaroth in his season?
Or canst thou guide Arcturus with his sons?
Knowest thou the ordinances of heaven?
Canst thou set the dominion thereof in the earth?
Canst thou lift up thy voice to the clouds,
That abundance of waters may cover thee?
Canst thou send lightnings, that they may go,
And say unto thee, Here we are?
Who hath put wisdom in the inward parts?
Or who hath given understanding to the heart?
Who can number the clouds in wisdom?
Or who can stay the bottles of heaven,
  When the dust groweth into hardness,
  And the clods cleave fast together?
Wilt thou hunt the prey for the lion?
Or fill the appetite of the young lions,
  When they couch in their dens,
  And abide in the covert to lie in wait?
Who provideth for the raven his food,
  When his young ones cry unto God,
  And wander for lack of meat?

THE APOCRYPHA

Ecclesiasticus, ch. xlii, xliii

I WILL make mention now of the works of
  the Lord,
And will declare the things that I have seen:
In the words of the Lord are his works.

SURSUM CORDA

The sun that giveth light looketh upon all
    things;
And the work of the Lord is full of his glory.
      .   .   .   .

The pride of the height is the firmament in its
    clearness,
The appearance of heaven in the spectacle of its
    glory.
The sun when he appeareth, bringing tidings as
    he goeth forth,
Is a marvellous instrument, the work of the
    Most High:
At his noon he drieth up the country,
And who shall stand against his burning heat?
A man blowing a furnace is in works of heat,
But the sun three times more, burning up the
    mountains:
Breathing out fiery vapors,
And sending forth bright beams, he dimmeth the
    eyes.
Great is the Lord that made him;
And at his word, he hasteneth his course.

The moon also is in all things for her season,
For a declaration of times, and a sign of the
    world.
From the moon is the sign of the feast day;
A light that waneth when she is come to the
    full.
The month is called after her name.
Increasing wonderfully in her changing;
An instrument of the hosts on high,
Shining forth in the firmament of heaven;
The beauty of heaven, the glory of the stars,
An ornament giving light in the highest places of
    the Lord.

At the word of the Holy One they will stand in
    due order,
And they will not faint in their watches.
Look upon the rainbow, and praise him that
    made it;
Exceeding beautiful in the brightness thereof.
It compasseth the heaven round about with a
    circle of glory;
The hands of the Most High have stretched it.

By his commandment he maketh the snow to fall
    apace,
And sendeth swiftly the lightnings of his judg-
    ment.
By reason thereof the treasure-houses are
    opened;
And clouds fly forth as fowls.
By his mighty power he maketh strong the
    clouds,
And the hailstones are broken small:
And at his appearing the mountains will be
    shaken,
And at his will the south wind will blow.
The voice of his thunder maketh the wind to
    travail;
So doth the northern storm and the whirlwind:
As birds flying down he sprinkleth the snow;
And as the lighting of the locust is the falling
    down thereof:
The eye will marvel at the beauty of its white-
    ness,
And the heart will be astonished at the raining
    of it.
The hoar frost also he poureth on the earth as
    salt;
And when it is concealed it is as points of
    thorns.

SURSUM CORDA

The cold north wind shall blow,
And the ice shall be congealed on the water:
It shall lodge upon every gathering together of
    water,
And the water shall put on as it were a breast-
    plate.
It shall devour the mountains and burn up the
    wilderness,
And consume the green herb as fire.
A mist coming speedily is the healing of all
    things;
A dew coming after heat shall bring cheerful-
    ness.
By his counsel he hath stilled the deep,
And planted islands therein.
They that sail on the sea tell of the danger
    thereof;
And when we hear it with our ears, we marvel.
Therein be also those strange and wondrous
    works,
Variety of all that hath life, the race of sea-
    monsters.
By reason of him his end hath success,
And by his word all things consist.

PSALM CXLVIII

PRAISE ye the Lord. Praise ye the Lord
from the heavens: praise him in the heights.
  Praise ye him, all his angels: praise ye him, all
his hosts.
  Praise ye him, sun and moon: praise him all
ye stars of light.
  Praise him ye heavens of heavens, and ye
waters that be above the heavens.

THE GYPSY TRAIL

Let them praise the name of the Lord: for he commanded and they were created.

He hath also stablished them forever and ever: he hath made a decree which shall not pass.

Praise the Lord from the earth, ye dragons and all deeps:

Fire, and hail; snow, and vapors; stormy wind fulfilling his word:

Mountains, and all hills; fruitful trees, and all cedars:

Beasts, and all cattle; creeping things, and flying fowl:

Kings of the earth, and all people; princes, and all judges of the earth:

Both young men, and maidens; old men, and children:

Let them praise the name of the Lord; for his name alone is excellent; his glory is above the earth and heaven.

He also exalteth the horn of his people, the praise of all his saints; even of the children of Israel, a people near unto him. Praise ye the **Lord.**

THE JOY OF THE ROAD

My father was a piper's son,
He used to play when day was done,
But all the tune that he could play
Was " Over the hills and far away."

The birds that wing their way through
    the blue
Direct my feet to the strange and new;
And the open road lies straight and free,
It calls and calls till it tortures me.

G. G. King

I follow the silver spears flung from the hands of dawn.
Through silence, through singing of stars, I journey on
    and on.

Ethna Carbery

I love and understand
One joy: with staff and scrip
To walk a wild west land,
The winds my fellowship.

Lionel Johnson

THE JOY OF THE ROAD

VERSES

FROM *The Canticle of the Road*

I

ON the open road, with the wind at heel
    Who is keen of scent and yelping loud,
Stout heart and bounding blood we feel,
Who follow fancy till day has bowed
Her forehead pure to her evening prayer
And drawn the veil on her wind-blown hair.
Free with the hawk and the wind we stride
The open road, and the world is wide
From rim to rim, and the skies hung high,
And room between for a hawk to fly
With tingling wing and lust of the eye.

II

Broad morning, blue morning, oh, jubilant wind!
Lord, Thou hast made our souls to be
Fluent and yearning long, as the sea
Yearns after the moon, and follows her,
With boom of waves and sibilant purr,
Round this world and past and o'er
All waste sea-bottoms and curving shore,
Only once more and again to find
The same sea-bottoms and beaten beach,
The same sweet moon beyond his reach
And drawing him onward as before.

    .   .   .   .

Arthur Colton

57

THE GYPSY TRAIL

SONG OF THE OPEN ROAD

I

A FOOT and light-hearted, I take to the open
road,
Healthy, free, the world before me,
The long brown path before me, leading wher-
ever I choose.

Henceforth I ask not good-fortune — I myself
am good-fortune;
Henceforth I whimper no more, postpone no
more, need nothing,
Strong and content I travel the open road.

The earth — that is sufficient;
I do not want the constellations any nearer;
I know they are very well where they are;
I know they suffice for those who belong to them.

(Still here I carry my old delicious burdens;
I carry them, men and women — I carry them
with me wherever I go;
I swear it is impossible for me to get rid of
them;
I am fill'd with them, and I will fill them in re-
turn.)

II

You road I enter upon and look around! I be-
lieve you are not all that is here;
I believe that much unseen is also here.

THE JOY OF THE ROAD

Here the profound lesson of reception, neither
preference or denial;
The black with his woolly head, the felon, the
diseas'd, the illiterate person, are not de-
nied;
The birth, the hasting after the physician, the
beggar's tramp, the drunkard's stagger, the
laughing party of mechanics,
The escaped youth, the rich person's carriage,
the fop, the eloping couple,
The early market-man, the hearse, the moving
of furniture into the town, the return back
from the town,
They pass — I also pass — anything passes —
none can be interdicted;
None but are accepted — none but are dear to
me.

III

You air that serves me with breath to speak!
You objects that call from diffusion my mean-
ings, and give them shape!
You light that wraps me and all things in deli-
cate equable showers!
You paths worn in the irregular hollows by the
roadsides!
I think you are latent with unseen existences —
you are so dear to me.

You flagg'd walks of the cities! you strong curbs
at the edges!
You ferries! you planks and posts of wharves!
you timber-lined sides! you distant ships!
You rows of houses! you window-pierced
façades! you roofs!

59

THE GYPSY TRAIL

You porches and entrances! you copings and
 iron guards!
You windows whose transparent shells might ex-
 pose so much!
You doors and ascending steps! you arches!
You gray stones of interminable pavements! you
 trodden crossings!
From all that has been near you I believe you
 have imparted to yourselves, and now would
 impart the same secretly to me;
From the living and the dead I think you have
 peopled your impassive surfaces and the spir-
 its thereof would be evident and amicable
 with me.

IV

The earth expanding right hand and left hand,
The picture alive, every part in its best light,
The music falling in where it is wanted, and
 stopping where it is not wanted,
The cheerful voice of the public road — the gay
 fresh sentiment of the road.

O highway I travel! O public road! do you say
 to me, *Do not leave me?*
Do you say, *Venture not? If you leave me, you
 are lost?*
Do you say, *I am already prepared — I am well-
 beaten and undenied — adhere to me?*

O public road! I say back, I am not afraid to
 leave you — yet I love you;
You express me better than I can express my-
 self;
You shall be more to me than my poem.

THE JOY OF THE ROAD

I think heroic deeds were all conceiv'd in the
  open air, and all great poems also;
I think I could stop here myself, and do mira-
  cles;
(My judgments, thoughts, I henceforth try by
  the open air, the road;)
I think whatever I shall meet on the road I shall
  like, and whoever beholds me shall like me;
I think whoever I see must be happy.

v

From this hour, freedom!
From this hour I ordain myself loos'd of limits
  and imaginary lines,
Going where I list, my own master, total and
  absolute,
Listening to others, and considering well what
  they say,
Pausing, searching, receiving, contemplating,
Gently, but with undeniable will, divesting my-
  self of the holds that would hold me.

I inhale great draughts of space;
The east and the west are mine, and the north
  and the south are mine.

I am larger, better than I thought;
I did not know I held so much goodness.
All seems beautiful to me;
I can repeat over and over to men and women,
    You have done such good to me, I would
    do the same to you.

I will recruit for myself and you as I go;
I will scatter myself among men and women as
  I go;

I will toss the new gladness and roughness
  among them;
Whoever denies me, it shall not trouble me;
Whoever accepts me, he or she shall be blessed,
  and shall bless me.

VI

Now if a thousand perfect men were to appear,
  it would not amaze me;
Now if a thousand beautiful forms of women
  appear'd, it would not astonish me.

Now I see the secret of the making of the best
  persons,
It is to grow in the open air, and to eat and
  sleep with the earth.

Here a great personal deed has room;
A great deed seizes upon the hearts of the whole
  race of men,
Its effusion of strength and will overwhelms law,
  and mocks all authority and all argument
  against it.

Here is the test of wisdom;
Wisdom is not finally tested in schools;
Wisdom cannot be pass'd from one having it, to
  another not having it;
Wisdom is of the soul, is not susceptible of
  proof, is its own proof,
Applies to all stages and objects and qualities,
  and is content,
Is the certainty of the reality and immortality of
  things, and the excellence of things;
Something there is in the float of the sight of
  things that provokes it out of the Soul.

THE JOY OF THE ROAD

Now I reëxamine philosophies and religions,
They may prove well in lecture-rooms, yet not
    prove at all under the spacious clouds, and
    along the landscape and flowing currents.
Here is realization;
Here is a man tallied — he realizes here what
    he has in him;
The past, the future, majesty, love — if they are
    vacant of you, you are vacant of them.

Only the kernel of every object nourishes;
Where is he who tears off the husks for you and
    me?
Where is he that undoes stratagems and en-
    velopes for you and me?

Here is adhesiveness — it is not previously fash-
    ion'd — it is àpropos;
Do you know what it is, as you pass, to be loved
    by strangers?
Do you know the talk of those turning eyeballs?

VII

Here is the efflux of the Soul.
The efflux of the Soul comes from within,
    through embower'd gates, ever provoking
    questions:
These yearnings, why are they? These thoughts
    in the darkness, why are they?
Why are there men and women that while they
    are nigh me the sun-light expands my blood?
Why, when they leave me, do my pennants of joy
    sink flat and lank?
Why are there trees I never walk under, but
    large and melodious thoughts descend upon
    me?

63

(I think they hang there winter and summer on
those trees, and always drop fruit as I pass;)
What is it I interchange so suddenly with
strangers?
What with some driver, as I ride on the seat
by his side?
What with some fisherman, drawing his seine by
the shore, as I walk by and pause?
What gives me to be free to a woman's or man's
goodwill? What gives them to be free to
mine?

VIII

The efflux of the Soul is happiness — here is
happiness;
I think it pervades the open air, waiting at all
times;
Now it flows unto us — we are rightly charged.
Here rises the fluid and attaching character;
The fluid and attaching character is the fresh-
ness and sweetness of man and woman;
(The herbs of the morning sprout no fresher
and sweeter every day out of the roots of
themselves, than it sprouts fresh and sweet
continually out of itself.)

Toward the fluid and attaching character exudes
the sweat of the love of young and old;
From it falls distill'd the charm that mocks
beauty and attainments;
Toward it heaves the shuddering longing ache of
contact.

IX

Allons! whoever you are, come travel with me!
Travelling with me, you find what never tires.

THE JOY OF THE ROAD

The earth never tires;
The earth is rude, silent, incomprehensible at
  first — Nature is rude and incomprehensible
  at first;
Be not discouraged — keep on — there are di-
  vine things, well envelop'd;
I swear to you there are divine things more
  beautiful than words can tell.

Allons! we must not stop here!
However sweet these laid-up stores — however
  convenient this dwelling, we cannot remain
  here;
However shelter'd this port, and however calm
  these waters, we must not anchor here;
However welcome the hospitality that surrounds
  us, we are permitted to receive it but a little
  while.

x

Allons! the inducements shall be greater;
We will sail pathless and wild seas;
We will go where winds blow, waves dash, and
  the Yankee clipper speeds by under full sail.

Allons! with power, liberty, the earth, the ele-
  ments!
Health, defiance, gayety, self-esteem, curiosity;
Allons! from all formules!
From your formules, O bat-eyed and material-
  istic priests!
The stale cadaver blocks up the passage — the
  burial waits no longer.

65

THE GYPSY TRAIL

Allons! yet take warning!
He travelling with me needs the best blood,
thews, endurance;
None may come to the trial, till he or she bring
courage and health.

Come not here if you have already spent the best
of yourself;
Only those may come who come in sweet and
determin'd bodies;
No diseas'd person — no rum-drinker or venereal
taint is permitted here.

I and mine do not convince by arguments,
similes, rhymes;
We convince by our presence.

XI

Listen! I will be honest with you;
I do not offer the old smooth prizes, but offer
rough new prizes;
These are the days that must happen to you:

You shall not heap up what is call'd riches,
You shall scatter with lavish hand all that you
earn or achieve,
You but arrive at the city to which you were
destin'd — you hardly settle yourself to satis-
faction, before you are call'd by an irresisti-
ble call to depart,
You shall be treated to the ironical smiles and
mockings of those who remain behind you;
What beckonings of love you receive, you shall
only answer with passionate kisses of part-
ing,
You shall not allow the hold of those who
spread their reach'd hands toward you.

THE JOY OF THE ROAD

Allons! after the GREAT COMPANIONS! and to be-
long to them!

They too are on the road! they are the swift
and majestic men! they are the greatest
women.

Over that which hinder'd them — over that
which retarded — passing impediments large
or small,

Committers of crimes, committers of many beau-
tiful virtues,

Enjoyers of calms of seas and storms of seas,

Sailors of many a ship, walkers of many a mile
of land,

Habitués of many distant countries, habitués of
far-distant dwellings,

Trusters of men and women, observers of cities,
solitary toilers,

Pausers and contemplators of tufts, blossoms,
shells of the shore,

Dancers at wedding dances, kissers of brides, ten-
der helpers of children, bearers of children,

Soldiers of revolts, standers by gaping graves,
lowerers down of coffins,

Journeyers over consecutive seasons, over the
years — the curious years, each emerging
from that which preceded it,

Journeyers as with companions, namely, their
own diverse phases,

Forth-steppers from the latent unrealized baby-
days,

Journeyers gayly with their own youth — Jour-
neyers with their bearded and well-grain'd
manhood,

Journeyers with their womanhood, ample, unsur-
pass'd, content.

THE GYPSY TRAIL

Journeyers with their own sublime old age of
   manhood or womanhood,
Old age, calm, expanded, broad with the haughty
   breath of the universe,
Old age, flowing free with the delicious near-by
   freedom of death. .

XIII

Allons! to that which is endless as it was be-
   ginningless,
To undergo much, tramps of days, rests of
   nights,
To merge all in the travel they tend to, and the
   days and nights they tend to,
Again to merge them in the start of superior
   journeys;
To see nothing anywhere but what you may
   reach it and pass it,
To conceive no time, however distant, but what
   you may reach it and pass it,
To look up or down no road but it stretches and
   waits for you — however long, but it stretches
   and waits for you;
To see no being, not God's or any, but you also
   go thither,
To see no possession but you may possess it —
   enjoying all without labor or purchase — ab-
   stracting the feast, yet not abstracting one
   particle of it;
To take the best of the farmer's farm and the
   rich man's elegant villa, and the chaste bless-
   ings of the well-married couple, and the
   fruits of orchards and flowers of gardens,
To take to your use out of the compact cities
   as you pass through,

THE JOY OF THE ROAD

To carry buildings and streets with you afterwards wherever you go,

To gather the minds of man out of their brains as you encounter them — to gather the love out of their hearts,

To take your lovers on the road with you, for all that you leave them behind you,

To know the universe itself as a road — as many roads — as roads for travelling souls.

XIV

The Soul travels;

The body does not travel as much as the soul;

The body has just as great a work as the soul; and parts away at last for the journeys of the soul.

All parts away for the progress of souls;

All religion, all solid things, arts, governments,— all that was or is apparent upon this globe or any globe, falls into niches and corners before the procession of Souls along the grand roads of the universe.

Of the progress of the souls of men and women along the grand roads of the universe, all other progress is the needed emblem and sustenance.

Forever alive, forever forward,

Stately, solemn, sad, withdrawn, baffled, mad, turbulent, feeble, dissatisfied,

Desperate, proud, fond, sick, accepted by men, rejected by men,

THE GYPSY TRAIL

They go! they go! I know that they go, but I
    know not where they go;
But I know that they go toward the best — to-
    ward something great.

xv

Allons! whoever you are! come forth!
You must not stay sleeping and dallying there in
    the house, though you built it, or though it
    has been built for you.
Allons! out of the dark confinement!
It it useless to protest — I know all, and expose
    it.

Behold, through you as bad as the rest,
Through the laughter, dancing, dining, supping,
    of people,
Inside of dresses and ornaments, inside of those
    wash'd and trimm'd faces,
Behold a secret silent loathing and despair.

No husband, no wife, no friend, trusted to hear
    the confession;
Another self, a duplicate of everyone, skulking
    and hiding it goes,
Formless and wordless through the streets of the
    cities, polite and bland in the parlors,
In the cars of railroads, in steamboats, in the
    public assembly,
Home to the houses of men and women, at the
    table, in the bedroom, everywhere,
Smartly attired, countenance smiling, form up-
    right, death under the breast-bones, hell un-
    der the skull-bones,
Under the broadcloth and gloves, under the rib-
    bons and artificial flowers,

THE JOY OF THE ROAD

Keeping fair with the customs, speaking not a
   syllable of itself,
Speaking of anything else, but never of itself.

XVI

Allons! through struggles and wars!
The goal that was named cannot be counter-
   manded.

Have the past struggles succeeded?
What has succeeded? yourself? your nation? na-
   ture?
Now understand me well — It is provided in the
   essence of things, that from any fruition of
   success, no matter what, shall come forth
   something to make a greater struggle neces-
   sary.

My call is the call of battle — I nourish active
   rebellion;
He going with me must go well arm'd;
He going with me goes often with spare diet,
   poverty, angry enemies, desertions.

XVII

Allons! the road is before us!
It is safe — I have tried it — my own feet have
   tried it well.

Allons! be not detain'd!
Let the paper remain on the desk unwritten, and
   the book on the shelf unopen'd!
Let the tools remain in the workshop! let the
   money remain unearn'd!
Let the school stand! mind not the cry of the
   teacher!

THE GYPSY TRAIL

Let the preacher preach in his pulpit! let the
    lawyer plead in the court, and the judge ex-
    pound the law.

Camerado! I give you my hand!
I give you my love, more precious than money,
I give you myself, before preaching or law;
Will you give me yourself? will you come travel
    with me?
Shall we stick by each other as long as we live?
                        Walt Whitman

PEREGRINO'S SONG

FROM *The Way of Perfect Love*

SOMETHING calls and whispers, along the
    city street,
Through shrill cries of children and soft stir of
    feet,
And makes my blood to quicken and makes my
    flesh to pine.
The mountains are calling; the winds wake the
    pine.

Past the quivering poplars that tell of water near
The long road is sleeping, the white road is
    clear.
Yet scent and touch can summon, afar from
    brook and tree,
The deep boom of surges, the grey waste of
    sea.

THE JOY OF THE ROAD

Sweet to dream and linger, in windless orchard
    close,
On bright brows of ladies to garland the rose;
But all the time are glowing, beyond this little
    world,
The still light of planets and the star-swarms
    whirled.

Georgiana Goddard King

THE MERRY BEGGARS

COME, come; away! the Spring,
    By every bird that can but sing,
Or chirp a note, doth now invite
Us forth to taste of his delight,
In field, in grove, on hill, in dale;
But above all the nightingale,
Who in her sweetness strives t' outdo
The loudness of the hoarse cuckoo.
    "Cuckoo," cries he; "jug, jug, jug,"
        sings she;
    From bush to bush, from tree to tree:
    Why in one place then tarry we?

Come away! why do we stay?
We have no debt or rent to pay;
No bargains or accounts to make,
Nor land or lease to let or take:
Or if we had, should that remore us
When all the world's our own before us,
And where we pass and make resort,
It is our kingdom and our court.

73

THE GYPSY TRAIL

"Cuckoo," cries he; "jug, jug, jug,"
    sings she;
From bush to bush, from tree to tree:
Why in one place then tarry we?
Alexander Brome

WANDERSCHAFT

VOM Grund bis zu den Gipfeln,
    So weit man sehen kann,
Jetzt blüht's in allen Wipfeln,
Nun geht das Wandern an:

Die Quellen von den Klüften,
Die Ström' auf grünem Plan,
Die Lerchen hoch in Lüften,
Der Dichter frisch voran.

Und die im Thal verderben
In trüber Sorgen Haft,
Er möcht' sie alle werben
Zu dieser Wanderschaft.

Und von den Bergen nieder
Erschallt sein Lied ins Thal,
Und die zerstreuten Brüder
Fasst Heimweh allzumal.

Da wird die Welt so munter
Und nimmt die Reiseschuh,
Sein Liebchen mitten drunter,
Die nickt ihm heimlich zu.

Und über Felsenwände
Und auf dem grünen Plan
Das wirrt und jauchzt ohn' Ende—
Nun geht das Wandern an!
Joseph von Eichendorff

THE JOY OF THE ROAD

DER MAI IST GEKOMMEN

DER Mai ist gekommen, die Bäume schlagen
aus,
Da bleibe, wer Lust hat, mit Sorgen zu Haus!
Wie die Wolken wandern am himmlischen Zelt,
So steht auch mir der Sinn in die weite, weite
Welt.

Herr Vater, Frau Mutter, dass Gott euch behüt'!
Wer weiss, wo in der Ferne mein Glück mir noch
blüht!
Es giebt so manche Strasse, die nimmer ich
marschiert,
Es giebt so manchen Wein, den ich nimmer noch
probiert.

Frisch auf drum, frisch auf, im hellen Sonnen-
strahl!
Wohl über die Berge, wohl durch das tiefe Thal!
Die Quellen erklingen, die Bäume rauschen all,
Mein Herz ist wie'ne Lerche und stimmt ein mit
Schall.

Und abends im Städtlein, da kehr' ich durstig
ein:
"Herr Wirt, Herr Wirt, eine Kanne blanken
Wein!
Ergreife die Fiedel, du lust'ger Spielmann du,
Von meinem Schatz das Liedel das sing' ich
dazu."

Und find' ich keine Herberg', so lieg ich zu
Nacht
Wohl unter blauem Himmel, die Sterne halten
Wacht:

THE GYPSY TRAIL

Im Winde die Linde, die rauscht mich ein
  gemach,
Es küsset in der Früh' das Morgenrot mich wach.

O Wandern, O Wandern, du freie Burschenlust!
Da wehet Gottes Odem so frisch in die Brust;
Da singet und jauchzet das Herz zum Himmels-
  zelt:
Wie bist du doch so schön, O du weite weite
  Welt!

Emanuel von Geibel

DER FROHE WANDERSMANN

WEM Gott will rechte Gunst erweisen,
    Den schickt er in die weite Welt;
Dem will er seine Wunder weisen
In Berg und Wald, und Strom und Feld.

Die Trägen die zu Hause liegen,
Erquicket nicht das Morgenrot;
Sie wissen nur von Kinderwiegen,
Von Sorgen, Last und Not um Brot.

Die Bächlein von den Bergen springen,
Die Lerchen schwirren hoch vor Lust,
Was sollt' ich nicht mit ihnen singen
Aus voller Kehl' und frischer Brust?

Den lieben Gott lass ich nur walten;
Der Bächlein, Lerchen, Wald und Feld
Und Erd' und Himmel will erhalten,
Hat auch mein' Sach' aufs best' bestellt!

Joseph von Eichendorff

76

THE JOY OF THE ROAD

THE SEA GYPSY

I AM fevered with the sunset,
    I am fretful with the bay,
For the wander-thirst is on me
And my soul is in Cathay.

There's a schooner in the offing,
With her top-sails shot with fire,
And my heart has gone aboard her
For the Islands of Desire.

I must forth again to-morrow!
With the sunset I must be
Hull down on the trail of rapture
In the wonder of the Sea.

Richard Hovey

THE VOYAGE

I

WE left behind the painted buoy
    That tosses at the harbor mouth;
And madly danced our hearts with joy,
    As fast we fleeted to the South:
How fresh was every sight and sound
    On open main or winding shore!
We knew the merry world was round,
    And we might sail for evermore.

II

Warm broke the breeze against the brow,
    Dry sang the tackle, sang the sail:
The Lady's-head upon the prow
    Caught the shrill salt, and sheer'd the gale.

77

THE GYPSY TRAIL

The broad seas swell'd to meet the keel,
 And swept behind; so quick the run,
We felt the good ship shake and reel,
 We seem'd to sail into the Sun!

III

How oft we saw the Sun retire,
 And burn the threshold of the night,
Fall from his Ocean-lane of fire,
 And sleep beneath his pillar'd light!
How oft the purple-skirted robe
 Of twilight slowly downward drawn,
As thro' the slumber of the globe
 Again we dash'd into the dawn!

IV

New stars all night above the brim
 Of waters lighten'd into view;
They climb'd as quickly, for the rim
 Changed every moment as we flew.
Far ran the naked moon across
 The houseless ocean's heaving field
Or flying shone, the silver boss
 Of her own halo's dusky shield;

V

The peaky islet shifted shapes,
 High towns on hills were dimly seen,
We passed long lines of Northern capes
 And dewy Northern meadows green.
We came to warmer waves, and deep
 Across the boundless east we drove,
Where those long swells of breaker sweep
 The nutmeg rocks and isles of clove.

THE JOY OF THE ROAD

VI

By peaks that flamed, or, all in shade,
  Gloom'd the low coast and quivering brine
With ashy rains that spreading made
  Fantastic plume or sable pine;
By sands and steaming flats, and floods
  Of mighty mouth, we scudded fast,
And hills and scarlet-mingled woods
  Glow'd for a moment as we past.

VII

O hundred shores of happy climes,
  How swiftly stream'd ye by the bark!
At times the whole sea burn'd, at times
  With wakes of fire we tore the dark;
At times a carven craft would shoot
  From havens hid in fairy bowers,
With naked limbs and flowers and fruit,
  But we nor paused for fruit nor flowers.

VIII

For one fair Vision ever fled
  Down the waste waters day and night,
And still we follow'd where she led,
  In hope to gain upon her flight.
Her face was evermore unseen,
  And fixt upon the far sea-line;
But each man murmur'd, "O my Queen,
  I follow till I make thee mine."

IX

And now we lost her, now she gleam'd
  Like Fancy made of golden air,
Now nearer to the prow she seem'd
  Like Virtue firm, like Knowledge fair,

THE GYPSY TRAIL

Now high on waves that idly burst
  Like Heavenly Hope she crown'd the sea,
And now, the bloodless point reversed,
  She bore the blade of Liberty.

x

And only one among us — him
  We pleased not — he was seldom pleased:
He saw not far: his eyes were dim:
  But ours he swore were all diseased.
"A ship of fools," he shriek'd in spite,
  "A ship of fools," he sneer'd and wept.
And overboard one stormy night
  He cast his body, and on we swept.

xi

And never sail of ours was furl'd,
  Nor anchor dropt at eve or morn;
We lov'd the glories of the world,
  But laws of Nature were our scorn.
For blasts would rise and rave and cease,
  But whence were those that drove the sail
Across the whirlwind's heart of peace,
  And to and thro' the counter gale?

xii

Again to colder climes we came,
  For still we follow'd where she led:
Now mate is blind and captain lame,
  And half the crew are sick or dead;
But, blind or lame or sick or sound,
  We follow that which flies before:
We know the merry world is round,
  And we may sail for evermore.
Alfred, Lord Tennyson

THE JOY OF THE ROAD

ULYSSES

IT little profits that an idle king,
By this still hearth, among these barren
crags,
Match'd with an aged wife, I mete and dole
Unequal laws unto a savage race,
That hoard, and sleep, and feed, and know not
me.
I cannot rest from travel: I will drink
Life to the lees: all times I have enjoy'd
Greatly, have suffer'd greatly, both with those
That loved me, and alone; on shore, and when
Thro' scudding drifts the rainy Hyades
Vext the dim sea: I am become a name;
For always roaming with a hungry heart
Much have I seen and known; cities of men
And manners, climates, councils, governments,
Myself not least, but honor'd of them all;
And drunk delight of battle with my peers,
Far on the ringing plains of windy Troy.
I am a part of all that I have met;
Yet all experience is an arch where thro'
Gleams that untravell'd world, whose margin
fades
For ever and for ever when I move.
How dull it is to pause, to make an end,
To rust unburnish'd, not to shine in use!
As tho' to breathe were life. Life piled on life
Were all too little, and of one to me
Little remains: but every hour is saved
From that eternal silence, something more,
A bringer of new things; and vile it were
For some three suns to store and hoard myself,
And this gray spirit yearning in desire
To follow knowledge, like a sinking star,
Beyond the utmost bound of human thought.

THE GYPSY TRAIL

This is my son, mine own Telemachus,
To whom I leave the sceptre and the isle —
Well-loved of me, discerning to fulfil
This labour, by slow prudence to make mild
A rugged people, and thro' soft degrees
Subdue them to the useful and the good.
Most blameless is he, centred in the sphere
Of common duties, decent not to fail
In offices of tenderness, and pay
Meet adoration to my household gods,
When I am gone. He works his work, I mine.
  There lies the port: the vessel puffs her sail:
There gloom the dark broad seas. My mariners,
Souls that have toil'd, and wrought, and thought
        with me —
That ever with a frolic welcome took
The thunder and the sunshine, and opposed
Free hearts, free foreheads — you and I are old;
Old age hath yet his honor and his toil;
Death closes all: but something ere the end,
Some work of noble note, may yet be done,
Not unbecoming men that strove with Gods.
The lights begin to twinkle from the rocks:
The long day wanes: the slow moon climbs: the
        deep
Moans round with many voices. Come, my
        friends,
'Tis not too late to seek a newer world.
Push off, and sitting well in order smite
The sounding furrows; for my purpose holds
To sail beyond the sunset, and the baths
Of all the western stars, until I die.
It may be that the gulfs will wash us down:
It may be we shall touch the Happy Isles,
And see the great Achilles, whom we knew.
Tho' much is taken, much abides; and tho'
We are not now that strength which in old days

THE JOY OF THE ROAD

Moved earth and heaven; that which we are, we'
    are;
One equal temper of heroic hearts,
Made weak by time and fate, but strong in will
To strive, to seek, to find, and not to yield.
                Alfred, Lord Tennyson

THE GOLDEN SHOES

T HE winds are lashing on the sea;
    The roads are blind with storm.
And it's far and far away with me;
    So bide you there, stay warm.
It's forth I must, and forth today;
    And I have no path to choose.
The highway hill, it is my way still.
    Give me my golden shoes.

God gave them me on that first day
    I knew that I was young.
And I looked forth, from west to north;
    And I heard the Songs unsung.

This cloak is worn too threadbare thin,
    But ah, how weatherwise!
This girdle serves to bind it in;
    What heed of wondering eyes? —
And yet beside, I wear one pride
    — Too bright, think you, to use? —
That I must wear, and still keep fair.—
    Give here my golden shoes.

God gave them me, on that first day
    I heard the Stars all chime.
And I looked forth far, from road to star;
    And I knew it was far to climb.

THE GYPSY TRAIL

,They would buy me house and hearth, no doubt,
  And the mirth to spend and share;
Could I sell that gift, and go without,
  Or wear — what neighbors wear.
But take my staff, my purse, my scrip;
  For I have one thing to choose.
For you,— Godspeed! May you soothe your
    need.
  For me, my golden shoes!

He gave them me, that far, first day
  When I heard all songs unsung.
And I looked far forth, from west to north.
  God saw that I was young!
Josephine Preston Peabody

THE MERRY GUIDE

ONCE in the wind of morning
  I ranged the thymy wold;
The world-wide air was azure
  And all the brooks ran gold.

There through the dews beside me
  Behold a youth that trod,
With feathered cap on forehead,
  And poised a golden rod.

With mien to match the morning
  And gay delightful guise
And friendly brows and laughter
  He looked me in the eyes.

Oh whence, I asked, and whither?
  He smiled and would not say,

THE JOY OF THE ROAD

And looked at me and beckoned
  And laughed and led the way.

And with kind looks and laughter
  And nought to say beside
We two went on together,
  I and my happy guide.

Across the glittering pastures
  And empty upland still
And solitude of shepherds
  High in the folded hill,

By hanging woods and hamlets
  That gaze through orchards down
On many a windmill turning
  And far-discovered town,

With gay regards of promise
  And sure unslackened stride
And smiles and nothing spoken
  Led on my merry guide.

By blowing realms of woodland
  With sunstruck vanes afield
And cloud-led shadows sailing
  About the windy weald,

By valley-guarded granges
  And silver waters wide,
Content at heart I followed
  With my delightful guide.

And like the cloudy shadows
  Across the country blown
We two fare on forever,
  But not we two alone.

THE GYPSY TRAIL

With the great gale we journey
   That breathes from gardens thinned,
Borne in the drift of blossoms
   Whose petals throng the wind;

Buoyed on the heaven-heard whisper
   Of dancing leaflets whirled
From all the woods that autumn
   Bereaves in all the world.

And midst the fluttering legion
   Of all that ever died
I follow, and before us
   Goes the delightful guide,

With lips that brim with laughter
   But never once respond,
And feet that fly on feathers,
   And serpent-circled wand.
                              A. E. Housman

THE WANDERER

WHOSE farthest footstep never strayed
      Beyond the village of his birth
Is but a lodger for the night
In this old wayside inn of earth.

To-morrow he shall take his pack
And set out for the ways beyond
On the old trail from star to star,
An alien and a vagabond.
                              Richard Hovey

THE CAMP

Who hath smelt wood-smoke at twilight? Who hath heard
the birch-log burning?

Kipling

Im kühlen Tannenwalde
Da steht mein freies Haus.

Adolf Stöber

For thou shalt be in league with the stones of the field:
and the beasts of the field shall be at peace with thee.
And thou shalt know that thy tabernacle shall be in
peace.

Book of Job, V. 23-4

THE CAMP

A NIGHT AMONG THE PINES

NIGHT is a dead monotonous period under a roof; but in the open world it passes lightly, with its stars and dews and perfumes, and the hours are marked by changes in the face of Nature. What seems a kind of temporal death to people choked between walls and curtains, is only a light and living slumber to the man who sleeps afield. All night long he can hear Nature breathing deeply and freely; even as she takes her rest, she turns and smiles; and there is one stirring hour unknown to those who dwell in houses, when a wakeful influence goes abroad over the sleeping hemisphere, and all the outdoor world are on their feet. It is then that the cock first crows, not this time to announce the dawn, but like a cheerful watchman speeding the course of night. Cattle awake on the meadows; sheep break their fast on dewy hillsides, and change to a new lair among the ferns; and houseless men, who have lain down with the fowls, open their dim eyes and behold the beauty of the night.

· · · ·

We are disturbed in our slumber only, like the luxurious Montaigne, " that we may the better and more sensibly relish it." We have a moment to look upon the stars. And there is a special pleasure for some minds in the reflection that we share the impulse with all out-door creatures in our neighborhood, that we have escaped out of the Bastille of civilization, and are become, for the time being, a mere kindly animal and a sheep of Nature's flock.

Robert Louis Stevenson

UNDER THE GREENWOOD TREE

UNDER the green wood tree,
　　Who loves to lie with me,
And tune his merry note
Unto the sweet bird's throat,
Come hither, come hither, come hither:
　　Here shall he see
　　No enemy
But winter and rough weather.

　　Who doth ambition shun,
　　And loves to live i' the sun,
　　Seeking the food he eats,
　　And pleased with what he gets,
Come hither, come hither, come hither:
　　Here shall he see
　　No enemy
But winter and rough weather.

Shakespeare

FAIRY BREAD

COME up here, O dusty feet!
　　Here is fairy bread to eat.
Here in my retiring room,
Children, you may dine
On the golden smell of broom
And the shade of pine;
And when you have eaten well,
Fairy stories hear and tell.

Robert Louis Stevenson

THE CAMP

A CAMP

THE bed was made, the room was fit,
    By punctual eve the stars were lit;
The air was still, the water ran,
No need was there for maid or man,
When we put up, my ass and I,
At God's green caravanserai.

Robert Louis Stevenson

THE FAIRIES

IF ye will with Mab find grace,
    Set each platter in his place;
Rake the fire up, and get
Water in, ere sun be set.
Wash your pails and cleanse your dairies,
Sluts are loathsome to the fairies;
Sweep your house; Who doth not so,
Mab will pinch her by the toe.

Robert Herrick

TO PHILLIS, TO LOVE AND LIVE WITH HIM

LIVE, live with me, and thou shalt see
    The pleasures I'll prepare for thee:
What sweets the country can afford
Shall bless thy bed, and bless thy board.
The soft sweet moss shall be thy bed,
With crawling woodbine over-spread:
By which the silver-shedding streams
Shall gently melt thee into dreams.

.   .   .   .

THE GYPSY TRAIL

Thy feasting-table shall be hills
With daisies spread, and daffodils;
Where thou shalt sit, and Red-breast by,
For meat, shall give thee melody.

. . . .

Robert Herrick

THE HOUSE OF THE TREES

OPE your doors and take me in,
    Spirit of the wood,
Wash me clean of dust and din,
    Clothe me in your mood.

Take me from the noisy light
    To the sunless peace,
Where at mid-day standeth **Night**
    Signing Toil's release.

All your dusky twilight stores
    To my senses give;
Take me in and lock the doors,
    Show me how to live.

Lift your leafy roof for me,
    Part your yielding walls:
Let me wander lingeringly
    Through your scented halls.

Ope your doors and take me in,
    Spirit of the wood;
Take me — make me next of kin
    To your leafy brood.

Ethelwyn Wetherald

THE CAMP

CRYSTAL WATER

CRYSTAL water every day
I may drink upon my way,
Fresh as dews of star-eyed Spring,
Cool as airs the light winds bring —
Child of Dust though I may be,
Here is joy, is meant for me.

Every night the arms of sleep
Take me to a refuge deep,
Some far off and silent place
In the utmost caves of space —
Child of Dust though I may be,
Here is joy, is meant for me.

Edith Wyatt

" SOME UNSUSPECTED ISLE "

FROM *The Euganean Hills*

FOR me, and those I love,
May a windless bower be built,
Far from passion, pain, and guilt,
In a dell, 'mid lawny hills,
Which the wild sea-murmur fills,
And soft sunshine, and the sound
Of old forests echoing round,
And the light and smell divine
Of all flowers that breathe and shine:
We may live so happy there,
That the spirits of the air,
Envying us, may even entice
To our healing paradise
The polluting multitude;

93

But their rage would be subdued
By that clime divine and calm,
And the wind whose wings rain balm
On the uplifted soul, and leaves
Under which the bright sea heaves;
While each breathless interval
In their whisperings musical
The inspired soul supplies
With its own deep melodies,
And the love which heals all strife
Circling, like the breath of life,
All things in that sweet abode
With its own mild brotherhood:
They, not it, would change; and soon
Every sprite beneath the moon
Would repent its envy vain,
And the earth grow young again.

Percy Bysshe Shelley

EINKEHR

BEI einem Wirthe wundermild
    Da war ich jüngst zu Gaste;
Ein goldner Apfel war sein Schild
An einem langen Aste.

Es war der gute Apfelbaum,
Bei dem ich eingekehret;
Mit süsser Kost und frischem Schaum
Hat er mich wohlgenähret.

Es kamen in sein grünes Haus
Viel leicht beschwingte Gäste;
Sie sprangen frei und hielten Schmaus
Und sangen auf das Beste.

THE CAMP

Ich fand ein Bett zu süsser Ruh
Auf weichen grünen Matten;
Der Wirth, der deckte selbst mich zu
Mit seinem kühlen Schatten.

Nun fragt' ich nach der Schuldigkeit,
Da schüttelt' er den Wipfel.
Gesegnet sei er alle Zeit
Von der Wurzel bis zum Gipfel.

Ludwig Uhland

DIE NACHT

WIE schön, hier zu verträumen
    Die Nacht im stillen Wald,
Wenn in den dunklen Bäumen
    Das alte Märchen hallt.

Die Berg' im Mondesschimmer
    Wie in Gedanken stehn,
Und durch verworrne Trümmer
    Die Quellen klagend gehn.

Denn müd' ging auf den Matten
    Die Schönheit nun zur Ruh',
Es deckt mit kühlen Schatten
    Die Nacht das Liebchen zu.

Das ist das irre Klagen
    In stiller Waldespracht,
Die Nachtigallen schlagen
    Von ihr die ganze Nacht.

THE GYPSY TRAIL

Die Stern' gehn auf und nieder —
Wann kommst du, Morgenwind,
Und hebst die Schatten wieder
Von dem verträumten Kind?

Schon rührt sich's in den Bäumen,
Die Lerche weckt sie bald—
So will ich treu verträumen
Die Nacht im stillen Wald.

Joseph von Eichendorff

THE CAMP

WÄR'S DUNKEL, ICH LÄG' IM WALDE

WÄR'S dunkel, ich läg' im Walde,
  Im Walde rauscht's so sacht,
Mit ihrem Sternenmantel
Bedecket mich da die Nacht;
Da kommen die Bächlein gegangen:
Ob ich schon schlafen thu'?
Ich schlaf' nicht, ich hör' noch lange
Den Nachtigallen zu,
Wenn die Wipfel über mich schwanken,
Es klinget die ganze Nacht,
Das sind im Herzen die Gedanken,
Die singen, wenn niemand wacht.

Joseph von Eichendorff

LAY ME TO SLEEP IN SHELTERING FLAME

LAY me to sleep in sheltering flame,
  O Master of the Hidden Fire!
Wash pure my heart, and cleanse for me
  My soul's desire.

96

THE CAMP

In flame of sunrise bathe my mind,
  O Master of the Hidden Fire,
That, when I wake, clear-eyed may be
  My soul's desire.

                        Fiona Macleod

THE PHILOSOPHERS' CAMP

FROM *The Adirondacs*

"WELCOME!" the wood-god murmured
    through the leaves,—
"Welcome, though late, unknowing, yet known
  to me."

Evening drew on; stars peeped through maple-
    boughs,
Which o'erhung like a cloud, our camping fire.
Decayed millenial trunks, like moonlight flecks,
Lit with phosphoric crumbs the forest floor.

Ten scholars, wonted to lie warm and soft
In well-hung chambers daintily bestowed,
Lie here on hemlock-boughs, like Sacs and Sioux,
And greet unanimous the joyful change.
So fast will Nature acclimate her sons,
Though late returning to her pristine ways.
Off soundings, seamen do not suffer cold;
And, in the forest, delicate clerks unbrowned,
Sleep on the fragrant brush, as on down-beds.
Up with the dawn, they fancied the light air
That circled freshly in their forest dress
Made them to boys again. Happier that they
Slipped off their pack of duties, leagues behind,
At the first mounting of the giant stairs.
            .   .   .   .

97

THE GYPSY TRAIL

                         Lords of this realm,
Bounded by dawn and sunset, and the day
Rounded by hours where each outdid the last
In miracles of pomp, we must be proud,
As if associates of the sylvan gods.
We seemed the dwellers of the zodiac,
So pure the Alpine element we breathed,
So light, so lofty pictures came and went.

  . . . .

The holidays were fruitful, but must end; . . .
We struck our camp and left the happy hills.
The fortunate star that rose on us sank not;
The prodigal sunshine rested on the land,
The rivers gambolled onward to the sea,
And Nature, the inscrutable and mute,
Permitted on her infinite repose
Almost a smile to steal to cheer her sons,
As if one riddle of the Sphinx were guessed.
       Ralph Waldo Emerson

NIGHT IN CAMP

FIERCE burns our fire of driftwood; over-
 head
Gaunt maples lift long arms against the night.
Black shadows backward reel when tall and
 bright
The broad flames stand and fling a golden light
On mats of soft green moss around us spread.

  . . . .

A sudden breeze comes in from off the sea,
The vast, old forest draws a troubled breath,
A leaf awakens; up the shore of sand
The slow tide, silver-lipped, creeps noiselessly;
The camp-fire dies; then silence deep as death;
The darkness pushing down upon the land.
       Herbert Bashford

THE CAMP

THE VOICE OF THE PINE

'TIS night upon the lake. Our bed of
   boughs
Is built where, high above, the pine-tree soughs.
'Tis still — and yet what woody noises loom
Against the background of the silent gloom!
One well might hear the opening of a flower
If day were hushed as this. A mimic shower
Just shaken from a branch, how large it sounded,
As 'gainst our canvas roof its three drops
   bounded!
Across the rumpling waves the hoot-owl's bark
Tolls forth the midnight hour upon the dark.
What mellow booming from the hills doth
   come? —
The mountain quarry strikes its mighty drum.

Long had we lain beside our pine-wood fire.
From things of sport our talk had risen higher.
How frank and intimate the words of men
When tented lonely in some forest glen!
No dallying now with masks, from whence
   emerges
Scarce one true feature forth. The night-wind
   urges
To straight and simple speech. So we had
   thought
Aloud; no secrets but to light were brought.
The hid and spiritual hopes, the wild
Unreasoned longings that, from child to child,
Mortals still cherish (though with modern
   shame) —
To these, and things like these, we gave a name;
And as we talked, the intense and resinous fire

99

Lit up the towering boles, till nigh and nigher
They gather round, a ghostly company,
Like beasts who seek to know what men may
   be.

   Then to our hemlock beds, but not to sleep —
For listening to the stealthy steps that creep
About the tent, or falling branch, but most
A noise was like the rustling of a host,
Or like the sea that breaks upon the shore —
It was the pine-tree's murmur. More and more
It took a human sound. These words I felt
Into the skyey darkness float and melt: —
"Heardst thou these wanderers reasoning of a
   time
When men more near the Eternal One shall
   climb?
How like the new-born child who cannot tell
A mother's arm that wraps it warm and well!
Leaves of His rose; drops in His sea that flow,—
Are they, alas, so blind they may not know
Here in this breathing world of joy and fear,
They can no nearer get to God than here?"
                         Richard Watson Gilder

NIGHT ON THE PRAIRIES

NIGHT on the prairies;
      The supper is over — the fire on the
      ground burns low;
The wearied emigrants sleep, wrapt in their
   blankets:
I walk by myself — I stand and look at the stars,
   which I think now I never realized before.

Now I absorb immortality and peace,
I admire death, and test propositions.

THE CAMP

How plenteous! How spiritual! How resumé!
The same Old Man and Soul — the same old
    aspirations, and the same content.

I was thinking the day most splendid, till I saw
    what the not-day exhibited,
I was thinking this globe enough, till there
    sprang out so noiseless around me myriads
    of other globes.

Now, while the great thoughts of space and eter-
    nity fill me, I will measure myself by them;
And now, touch'd with the lives of other globes,
    arrived as far along as those of the earth,
Or waiting to arrive, or pass'd on farther than
    those of the earth,
I henceforth no more ignore them, than I ignore
    my own life,
Or the lives of the earth arrived as far as mine,
    or waiting to arrive.

O I see now that life cannot exhibit all to me —
    as the day cannot;
I see that I am to wait for what will be exhibited
    by death.

Walt Whitman

BY THE BIVOUAC'S FITFUL FLAME

BY the bivouac's fitful flame,
    A procession winding around me, solemn
    and sweet and slow;— but first I note,
The tents of the sleeping army, the fields' and
    woods' dim outline,
The darkness, lit by spots of kindled fire — the
    silence;

THE GYPSY TRAIL

Like a phantom far or near an occasional figure
    moving;
The shrubs and trees, (as I lift my eyes they
    seem to be stealthily watching me;)
While wind in procession thoughts, O tender and
    wondrous thoughts,
Of life and death — of home and the past and
    loved, and of those that are far away;
A solemn and slow procession there as I sit on
    the ground,
By the bivouac's fitful flame.

Walt Whitman

BIVOUAC ON A MOUNTAIN SIDE

I SEE before me now a travelling army halt-
    ing;
Below, a fertile valley spread, with barns, and
    the orchards of summer;
Behind, the terraced sides of a mountain, abrupt
    in places, rising high;
Broken, with rocks, with clinging cedars, with
    tall shapes, dingily seen;
The numerous camp-fires scatter'd near and far,
    some away up on the mountains;
The shadowy forms of men and horses, looming,
    large-sized, flickering;
And over all, the sky — the sky! far, far out of
    reach, studded, breaking out, the eternal stars.

Walt Whitman

THE CAMP

THE OLD CAMP-FIRE

NOW shift your blanket pad before your sad-
  dle back you fling,
And draw your cinch up tighter till the sweat
  drops from the ring:
We've a dozen miles to cover ere we reach the
  next divide.
Our limbs are stiffer now than when we first set
  out to ride,
And worse, the horses know it, and feel the
  leg-grip tire,
Since in the days when, long ago, we sought
  the old camp-fire.

Yes, twenty years! Lord! how we'd scent its
  incense down the trail,
Through balm of bay and spice of spruce, and
  eye and ear would fail,
And worn and faint from useless quest we crept
  like this to rest,
Or, flushed with luck and youthful hope, we
  rode, like this, abreast.
Ay! straighten up, old friend and let the mus-
  tang think he's nigher,
Through looser rein and stirrup strain, the wel-
  come old camp-fire.

You know the shout that would ring out be-
  fore us down the glade,
And start the blue jays like a flight of arrows
  through the shade,
And sift the thin pine needles down like slant-
  ing, shining rain,
And send the squirrels scampering back to their
  holes again,

THE GYPSY TRAIL

Until we saw, blue-veiled and dim, or leaping
    like desire,
That flame of twenty years ago, which lit the
    old camp-fire.

And then the rest on Nature's breast, when talk
    had dropped, and slow
The night wind went from tree to tree with
    challenge soft and low!
We lay on lazy elbows propped, or stood to stir
    the flame,
Till up the soaring redwood's shaft our shad-
    ows danced and came,
As if to draw us with the sparks, high o'er its
    unseen spire,
To the five stars that kept their ward above
    the old camp-fire,—

Those picket stars whose tranquil watch half
    soothed, half shamed our sleep.
What recked we then what beasts or men around
    might lurk or creep?
We lay and heard with listless ears the far-off
    panther's cry,
The near coyote's snarling snap, the grizzly's
    deep-drawn sigh,
The brown bear's blundering human tread, the
    gray wolves' yelping choir
Beyond the magic circle drawn round the old
    camp-fire.

And then that morn! Was ever morn so filled
    with all things new?

THE CAMP

The light that fell through long brown aisles
    from out the kindling blue,
The creak and yawn of stretching boughs, the
    jay-bird's early call.
The rat-tat-tat of woodpecker that waked the
    woodland hall,
The fainter stir of lower life in fern and brake
    and brier,
Till flashing leaped the torch of Day from last
    night's old camp-fire!

      .   .   .   .

                    Bret Harte

LINE UP, BRAVE BOYS!

THE packs are on, the cinches tight,
    The patient horses wait,
Upon the grass the frost lies white,
The dawn is gray and late.
The leader's cry rings sharp and clear,
The camp-fires smoulder low;
Before us lies a shallow mere,
Beyond, the mountain snow.
    "Line up, Billy, line up, boys,
      The east is gray with coming day,
      We must away, we cannot stay.
      Hy-o, hy-ak, brave boys!"

Five hundred miles behind us lie,
As many more ahead,
Through mud and mire on mountains **high**
Our weary feet must tread.
So one by one, with loyal mind,
The horses swing to place,

THE GYPSY TRAIL

The strong in lead, the weak behind,
In patient plodding grace.
    "Hy-o, Buckskin, brave boy, Joe!
    The sun is high,
    The hid loons cry:
    Hy-ak away! Hy-o!"

Hamlin Garland

SUNRISE AND MORNING

Morn in the white wake of the morning star
Came furrowing all the Orient into gold.

Tennyson

Wake! For the Sun who scattered into flight
The Stars before him from the field of Night,
Drives Night along with them from Heav'n —

Omar Khayyám

All things that love the sun are out of doors;
The sky rejoices in the morning's birth;
The air is bright with rain-drops.

Wordsworth

SUNRISE AND MORNING

SONG

HARK, hark! the lark at heaven's gate
    sings
  And Phœbus 'gins arise,
His steeds to water at those springs
  On chaliced flowers that lies:
And winking Mary-buds begin
  To ope their golden eyes:
With everything that pretty bin,
  My lady sweet, arise,
    Arise, arise!

Shakespeare

REVEILLE

WAKE: the silver dusk returning
    Up the beach of darkness brims,
And the ship of sunrise burning
  Strands upon the eastern rims.

Wake: the vaulted shadow shatters,
  Trampled to the floor it spanned,
And the tent of night in tatters
  Straws the sky-pavilioned land.

Up, lad, up, 'tis late for lying:
  Hear the drums of morning play;
Hark, the empty highways crying
  "Who'll beyond the hills away?"

THE GYPSY TRAIL

Towns and countries woo together,
  Forelands beacon, belfries call;
Never lad that trod on leather
  Lived to feast his heart with all.

Up, lad: thews that lie and cumber
  Sunlit pallets never thrive;
Morns abed and daylight slumber
  Were not meant for man alive.

Clay lies still, but blood's a rover;
  Breath's a ware that will not keep.
Up, lad: when the journey's over
  There'll be time enough to sleep.
               A. E. Housman

MORGENGEBET

O WUNDERBARES, tiefes Schweigen,
  Wie einsam ist's noch auf der Welt!
Die Wälder nur sich leise neigen,
Als ging der Herr durchs stille Feld.

    .   .   .   .

Ich fühl' mich recht wie neu geschaffen,
Wo ist die Sorge nun und Not?
Was mich noch gestern wollt' erschlaffen,
Ich schäm' mich des im Morgenrot.
               Joseph von Eichendorff.

PACK CLOUDS AWAY

PACK, clouds, away, and welcome day,
  With nigl.t we banish sorrow;
Sweet air, blow soft; mount, lark, aloft,
  To give my Love good-morrow!

SUNRISE AND MORNING

Wings from the wind to please her mind,
  Notes from the lark I'll borrow:
Bird, prune thy wing; nightingale, sing,
    To give my Love good-morrow,
      To give my Love good-morrow!
      Notes from them all I'll borrow.

Wake from thy nest, robin red-breast,
  Sing, birds, in every furrow;
And from each hill let music shrill
  Give my fair Love good-morrow!
Blackbird and thrush in every bush,
  Stare, linnet, and cock-sparrow:
You pretty elves, amongst yourselves,
  Sing my fair Love good-morrow!
    To give my Love good-morrow,
    Sing, birds, in every furrow!
                    Thomas Heywood

SUNRISE

From *Pippa Passes*

D AY!
    Faster and more fast,
O'er night's brim, day boils at last:
Boils, pure gold, o'er the cloud-cup's brim
Where spurting and suppressed it lay,
For not a froth-flake touched the rim
Of yonder gap in the solid gray
Of the eastern cloud, an hour away;
But forth one wavelet, then another, curled,
Till the whole sunrise, not to be suppressed,
Rose, reddened, and its seething breast
Flickered in bounds, grew gold, then overflowed
    the world.
                    Robert Browning

THE GYPSY TRAIL

PIPPA'S SONG

THE year's at the spring,
    And day's at the morn;
Morning's at seven;
The hill-side's dew-pearled.
The lark's on the wing;
The snail's on the thorn;
God's in his heaven —
All's right with the world!
                  Robert Browning

TO MORNING

O HOLY virgin, clad in purest white,
    Unlock heaven's golden gates and issue
        forth;
Awake the dawn that sleeps in heaven; let light
Rise from the chambers of the east, and bring
The honeyed dew that cometh on waking day.
O radiant Morning, salute the Sun,
Roused like a huntsman to the chase, and with
Thy buskined feet appear upon our hills.
                  William Blake

ON THE BRINK OF THE NIGHT AND THE MORNING

FROM *Prometheus Unbound*

MY coursers are fed with the lightning,
    They drink of the whirlwind's stream,
And when the red morning is bright'ning
    They bathe in the fresh sunbeam;
    They have strength for their swiftness I deem.

SUNRISE AND MORNING

I desire: and their speed makes night kindle;
I fear: they outstrip the Typhoon;
Ere the cloud piled on Atlas can dwindle
  We encircle the earth and the moon:
  We shall rest from long labors at noon.

On the brink of the night and the morning
  My coursers are wont to respire;
But the Earth has just whispered a warning
  That their flight must be swifter than fire:
  They shall drink the hot speed of desire!
             Percy Bysshe Shelley

HYMN TO THE SUN

ONCE again thou flamest heavenward, once
  again we see thee rise.
Every morning is thy birthday gladdening hu-
  man hearts and eyes.
    Every morning here we greet it, bowing lowly
    down before thee,
Thee the Godlike, thee the changeless in thine
  ever-changing skies.

Shadow-maker, shadow-slayer, arrowing light
  from clime to clime,
Hear thy myriad laureates hail thee monarch in
  their woodland rhyme.
    Warble bird, and open flower, and, men, be-
    low the dome of azure
Kneel adoring Him the Timeless in the flame
  that measures Time!
             Alfred, Lord Tennyson

HYMN OF APOLLO

I

THE sleepless Hours who watch me as I lie,
   Curtained with star-inwoven tapestries,
From the broad moonlight of the sky,
   Fanning the busy dreams from my dim eyes,—
Waken me when their Mother, the gray Dawn,
Tells them that dreams and that the moon is
     gone.

II

Then I arise, and climbing Heaven's blue dome,
   I walk over the mountains and the waves,
Leaving my robe upon the ocean foam;
   My footsteps pave the clouds with fire; the
     caves
Are filled with my bright presence, and the air
Leaves the green earth to my embraces bare.

III

The sunbeams are my shafts, with which I kill
   Deceit, that loves the night and fears the day;
All men who do or even imagine ill
   Fly me, and from the glory of my ray
Good minds and open actions take new might,
Until diminished by the reign of night.

IV

I feed the clouds, the rainbows and the flowers
   With their ethereal colors; the Moon's globe
And the pure stars in their eternal bowers
   Are cinctured with my power as with a robe;
Whatever lamps on Earth or Heaven may shine,
Are portions of one power, which is mine.

SUNRISE AND MORNING

V

I stand at noon upon the peak of Heaven,
  Then with unwilling steps I wander down
Into the clouds of the Atlantic even;
  For grief that I depart they weep and frown:
What look is more delightful than the smile
With which I soothe them from the western isle?

VI

I am the eye with which the Universe
  Beholds itself and knows itself divine;
All harmony of instrument or verse,
  All prophecy, all medicine are mine,
All light of Art or Nature; — to my song
Victory and praise in their own right belong.
                              Percy Bysshe Shelley

A MORNING

THE glad, mad wind went singing by,
    The white clouds drove athwart the blue,
Bold beauty of the morning sky
    And all the world was sun and dew,
And sweet cold air with sudden glints of gold
Like spilled stars glowing in the cedars' hold.

I laughed for very joy of life,
  Oh, thrilling veins, oh, happy heart,
Of this glad world with beauty rife,
  Exult that we too are a part;
Rejoice! Rejoice! that miracle of birth
Gave us this golden heritage of earth.

THE GYPSY TRAIL

Oh, bold, blue sky, oh, keen, glad wind,
   I wonder me if this may be,
That some day, leaving life behind,
   Our eyes shall view new land, new sea
So exquisite that, lo! with thrilling breath,
We shall laugh loud for very joy of death.
                        Theodosia Garrison

THE WILD WOOD

I have come from the spring woods,
From the fragrant solitudes;
Listen what the poplar tree,
And murmuring waters counselled me.

Emerson

" Welcome! " the wood-god murmured through the
leaves —

Emerson

Es ist hier schön. Es rauscht so fremd und voll.
Der Tannen dunkle Arme regen sich
So rätselhaft. Sie wiegen ihre Häupter
So feierlich. Das Märchen! ja, das Märchen
Weht durch den Wald.

Hauptman

THE WILD WOOD

HIE AWAY, HIE AWAY

HIE away, hie away,
  Over bank and over brae,
Where the copsewood is the greenest,
Where the fountains glisten sheenest,
Where the lady-fern grows strongest,
Where the morning dew lies longest,
Where the black-cock sweetest sips it,
Where the fairy latest trips it:
  Hie to haunts right seldom seen,
  Lovely, lonesome, cool, and green,
  Over bank and over brae,
  Hie away, hie away.
                          Sir Walter Scott

THRICE HAPPY HE WHO BY SOME SHADY GROVE

THRICE happy he who by some shady grove,
  Far from the clamorous world doth live
    his own;
Though solitary, who is not alone,
But doth converse with that eternal love.
O how more sweet is bird's harmonious moan,
Or the hoarse sobbings of the widowed dove,
Than those smooth whisperings near a prince's
    throne,
Which good make doubtful, do the evil approve!

119

THE GYPSY TRAIL

Or how more sweet is Zephyr's wholesome
    breath,
And sighs enbalmed which new-born flowers un-
    fold,
Than that applause vain honor doth bequeath!
How sweet are streams to poison drunk in gold!
The world is full of horrors, troubles, slights;
Woods' harmless shades have only true delights.
William Drummond

THE SYLVAN LIFE

WHEN in the woods I wander all alone,
    The woods that are my solace and de-
      light,
Which I more covet than a prince's throne,
My toil by day and canopy by night;
(Light heart, light foot, light food, and slumber
    light,
These lights shall light me to old age's gate,
While monarchs, whom rebellious dreams af-
    fright,
Heavy with fear, death's fearful summons wait;)
Whilst here I wander, pleased to be alone,
Weighing in thought the world's no-happiness,
I cannot choose but wonder at its moan,
Since so plain joys the woody life can bless:
Then live who may where honied words prevail,
I with the deer, and with the nightingale!
Edward, Lord Thurlow

THE OUTLAW

O, BRIGNALL banks are wild and fair,
    And Greta woods are green,
And you may gather garlands there
    Would grace a summer queen.

THE WILD WOOD

And as I rode by Dalton Hall,
  Beneath the turrets high,
A Maiden on the castle wall
  Was singing merrily:

"O, Brignall banks are fresh and fair,
  And Greta woods are green;
I'd rather rove with Edmund there
  Than reign our English queen."

"If, Maiden, thou wouldst wend with me,
  To leave both tower and town,
Thou first must guess what life lead we
  That dwell by dale and down.
And if thou canst that riddle read,
  As read full well you may,
Then to the greenwood shalt thou speed,
  As blythe as Queen of May."

Yet sang she, "Brignall banks are fair,
  And Greta woods are green;
I'd rather rove with Edmund there
  Than reign our English queen.

"I read you, by your bugle-horn
  And by your palfrey good,
I read you for a Ranger sworn
  To keep the king's greenwood."
"A Ranger, lady, winds his horn,
  And 'tis at peep of light;
His blast is heard at merry morn,
  And mine at dead of night."

Yet sang she, "Brignall banks are fair,
  And Greta woods are gay;
I would I were with Edmund there,
  To reign his Queen of May.

THE GYPSY TRAIL

"With burnished brand and musketoon
  So gallantly you come,
I read you for a bold Dragoon
  That lists the tuck of drum."
"I list no more the tuck of drum,
  No more the trumpet hear;
But when the beetle sounds his hum,
  My comrades take the spear.

"And O! though Brignall banks be fair,
  And Greta woods be gay,
Yet mickle must the maiden dare
  Would reign my Queen of May!

"Maiden! a nameless life I lead,
  A nameless death I'll die!
The fiend, whose lantern lights the mead,
  Were better mate than I!
And when I'm with my comrades met,
  Beneath the Greenwood bough,
What once we were we all forget,
  Nor think what we are now.

"Yet Brignall banks are fresh and fair,
  And Greta woods are green,
And you may gather garlands there
  Would grace a summer queen."
                              Sir Walter Scott

ENTER THESE ENCHANTED WOODS

FROM *The Woods of Westermain*

ENTER these enchanted woods,
  You who dare.
Nothing harms beneath the leaves
More than waves a swimmer cleaves.
Toss your heart up with the lark,

THE WILD WOOD

Foot at peace with mouse and worm,
   Fair you fare.
Only at a dread of dark
Quaver, and they quit their form:
Thousand eyeballs under hoods
   Have you by the hair.
Enter these enchanted woods,
   You who dare.
Here the snake across your path
Stretches in his golden bath:
Mossy-footed squirrels leap
Soft as winnowing plumes of Sleep:
Yaffles on a chuckle skin
Low to laugh from branches dim:
Up the pine, where sits the star,
Rattles deep the moth-winged jar.
Each has business of his own;
But should you distrust a tone,
   Then beware.
Shudder all the haunted roods,
All the eyeballs under hoods
   Shroud you in their glare.
Enter these enchanted woods,
   You who dare.

.   .   .   .

George Meredith

THE TIGER

TIGER, Tiger, burning bright
   In the forest of the night,
What immortal hand or eye
Framed thy fearful symmetry?

In what distant deeps or skies
Burned that fire within thine eyes?

THE GYPSY TRAIL

On what wings dared he aspire?
What the hand dared seize the fire?

And what shoulder and what art
Could twist the sinews of thy heart?
When thy heart began to beat,
What dread hand formed thy dread feet?

What the hammer, what the chain,
Knit thy strength and forged thy brain?
What the anvil? What dread grasp
Dared thy deadly terrors clasp?

When the stars threw down their spears,
And watered heaven with their tears,
Did he smile his work to see?
Did he who made the lamb make thee?

William Blake

LINES

From *The Faun*

HIST! there's a stir in the brush.
      Was it a face through the leaves?
Back of the laurels a skurry and rush
Hillward, then silence except for the thrush
That throws one song from the dark of the bush
And is gone; and I plunge in the wood, and the
      swift soul cleaves
Through the swirl and the flow of the leaves,
As a swimmer stands with his white limbs bare
      to the sun
For the space that a breath is held, and drops in
      the sea;
And the undulant woodland folds round me, in-
      timate, fluctant, free

THE WILD WOOD

Like the clasp and the cling of waters, and the
    reach and the effort is done,—
There is only the glory of living, exultant to be.

O goodly damp smell of the ground!
O rough sweet bark of the trees!
O clear sharp cracklings of sound!
O life that's athrill and a-bound
With the vigor of boyhood and morning, and the
    noon-tide's rapture of ease!
Was there ever a weary heart in the world?
A lag in the body's urge or a flag of the spirit's
    wings?
Did a man's heart ever break
For a lost hope's sake?
For here there is lilt in the quiet and calm in the
    quiver of things.   *Richard Hovey*

LOCKUNG

HÖRST du nicht die Bäume rauschen
    Draussen durch die stille Rund'?
Lockt's dich nicht, hinabzulauschen
Von dem Söller in den Grund,
Wo die vielen Bäche gehen
Wunderbar im Mondenschein,
Und die stillen Schlösser sehen
In den Fluss vom hohen Stein?

Kennst du noch die irren Lieder
Aus der alten, schönen Zeit?
Sie erwachen alle wieder
Nachts in Waldeseinsamkeit,
Wenn die Bäume traümend lauschen
Und der Flieder duftet schwül
Und im Fluss die Nixen rauschen —
Komm herab, hier ist's so kühl.
    Joseph von Eichendorff

THE GYPSY TRAIL

ABSCHIED

O THÄLER weit, O Höhen,
  O schöner, grüner Wald,
Du meiner Lust und Wehen
Andächt'ger Aufenthalt!
Da draussen, stets betrogen,
Saust die geschäft'ge Welt,
Schlag noch einmal die Bogen
Um mich, du grünes Zelt!

Wenn es beginnt zu tagen,
Die Erde stampft und blinkt,
Die Vögel lustig schlagen,
Dass dir dein Herz erklingt:
Da mag vergehn, verwehen
Das trübe Erdenleid,
Da sollst du auferstehen
In jünger Herrlichkeit!

   .   .   .

Bald werd' ich dich verlassen,
Fremd in die Fremde gehn,
Auf buntbewegten Gassen
Des Lebens Schauspiel sehen;
Und mitten in dem Leben
Wird deines Ernsts Gewalt
Mich Einsamen erheben,
So wird mein Herz nicht alt.

Joseph von Eichendorff

THE RECOLLECTION

   .   .   .

WE wandered to the Pine Forest
  That skirts the Ocean's foam,
The lightest breeze was in its nest,
  The tempest in its home.

126

THE WILD WOOD

The whispering waves were half asleep,
  The clouds were gone to play,
And on the bosom of the deep,
  The smile of Heaven lay;
It seemed as if the hour were one
  Sent from beyond the skies,
Which scattered from above the sun
  A light of Paradise.

We paused amid the pines that stood
  The giants of the waste,
Tortured by storms to shapes as rude
  As serpents interlaced,
And soothed by every azure breath,
  That under heaven is blown,
To harmonies and hues beneath,
  As tender as its own:
Now all the tree-tops lay asleep,
  Like green waves on the sea,
As still as in the silent deep
  The ocean woods may be.

How calm it was! — the silence there
  By such a chain was bound
That even the busy woodpecker
  Made stiller by her sound
The inviolable quietness;
  The breath of peace we drew
With its soft motion made not less
  The calm that round us grew.
There seemed from the remotest seat
  Of the white mountain waste,
To the soft flower beneath our feet,
  A magic circle traced,—
A spirit interfused around
  A thrilling silent life,
To momentary peace it bound

THE GYPSY TRAIL

Our mortal nature's strife; —
And still I felt the centre of
  The magic circle there,
Was one fair form that filled with love
  The lifeless atmosphere.

We paused beneath the pools that lie
  Under the forest bough,
Each seemed as 'twere a little sky
  Gulft in a world below;
A firmament of purple light
  Which in the dark earth lay,
More boundless than the depth of night,
  And purer than the day —
In which the lovely forests grew
  As in the upper air,
More perfect both in shape and hue
  Than any spreading there,
There lay the glade and neighboring lawn,
  And thro' the dark green wood
The white sun twinkling like the dawn
  Out of a speckled cloud.
Sweet views that in our world above
  Can never well be seen,
Were imaged by the water's love
  Of that fair forest green.
And all was interfused beneath
  With an elysian glow,
An atmosphere without a breath,
  A softer day below.
Like one beloved the scene had lent
  To the dark water's breast,
Its every leaf and lineament
  With more than truth exprest;
Until an envious wind crept by,
  Like an unwelcome thought,
Which from the mind's too faithful eye

THE WILD WOOD

Blots one dear image out.
Tho' thou art ever fair and kind,
    The forest ever green,
Less oft is peace in Shelley's mind,
    Than calm in waters seen.

Percy Bysshe Shelley

WALDEINSAMKEIT

I DO not count the hours I spend
    In wandering by the sea;
The forest is my loyal friend,
Like God it useth me.

In plains that room for shadows make
Of skirting hills to lie,
Bound in by streams which gave and take
Their colors from the sky;

Or on the mountain-crest sublime,
Or down the oaken glade,
O what have I to do with time?
For this the day was made.

Cities of mortals woe-begone
Fantastic care derides,
But in the serious landscape lone
Stern benefit abides.

Sheen will tarnish, honey cloy,
And merry is only a mask of sad,
But, sober on a fund of joy,
The woods at heart are glad.

There the great Planter plants
Of fruitful worlds the grain,
And with a million spells enchants
The souls that walk in pain.

THE GYPSY TRAIL

Still on the seeds of all he made
The rose of beauty burns;
Through times that wear and forms that
    fade,
Immortal youth returns.

The black ducks mounting from the lake,
The pigeon in the pines,
The bittern's boom, a desert make
Which no false art refines.

Down in yon watery nook,
Where bearded mists divide,
The gray old gods whom Chaos knew,
The sires of Nature hide.

Aloft in secret veins of air,
Blows the sweet breath of song,
O few to scale those uplands dare,
Though they to all belong!

See thou bring not to field or stone
The fancies found in books;
Leave authors' eyes, and fetch your own
To brave the landscape's looks.

Oblivion here thy wisdom is,
Thy thrift, the sleep of cares;
For a proud idleness like this
Crowns all thy mean affairs.

Ralph Waldo Emerson

THE WILD WOOD

WOOD NOTES

I

WHEN the pine tosses its cones
       To the song of its waterfall tones,
Who speeds to the woodland walks?
To birds and trees who talks?
Caesar of his leafy Rome,
There the poet is at home.
He goes to the riverside,—
Not hook nor line hath he:
He stands in the meadows wide,—
Nor gun nor scythe to see.
Sure some god his eye enchants,
What he knows, nobody wants.
In the wood he travels glad
Without better fortune had,
Melancholy without bad.
Knowledge this man prizes best
Seems fantastic to the rest,
Pondering shadows, colors, clouds,
Grass buds, and caterpillar-shrouds,
Boughs on which the wild bees settle,
Tints that spot the violet's petal,
Why Nature loves the number five,
And why the star-form she repeats:
Lover of all things alive,
Wonderer at all he meets,
Wonderer chiefly at himself,
Who can tell him what he is,
Or how meet in human elf
Coming and past eternities?

And such I knew, a forest seer,
A minstrel of the natural year,
Foreteller of the vernal ides,

THE GYPSY TRAIL

Wise harbinger of spheres and tides,
A lover true who knew by heart
Each joy the mountain dales impart;
It seemed that nature could not raise
A plant in any secret place,
In quaking bog, on snowy hill,
Beneath the grass that shades the rill,
Under the snow, between the rocks,
In damp fields known to bird and fox,
But he would come in the very hour
It opened in its virgin bower,
As if a sunbeam showed the place,
And tell its long-descended race.
It seemed as if the breezes brought him,
It seemed as if the sparrows taught him,
As if by secret sight he knew
Where in far fields the orchis grew.
Many haps fall in the field
Seldom seen by wishful eyes,
But all her shows did Nature yield
To please and win this pilgrim wise.
He saw the partridge drum in the woods,
He heard the woodcock's evening hymn,
He found the tawny thrush's broods,
And the shy hawk did wait for him.
What others did at distance hear,
And guessed within the thicket's gloom,
Was shown to this philosopher,
And at his bidding seemed to come.

In unploughed Maine, he sought the lumberer's
    gang,
Where from a hundred lakes young rivers
    sprang;
He trod the unplanted forest-floor, whereon
The all-seeing sun for ages hath not shone,

THE WILD WOOD

Where feeds the moose, and walks the surly
    bear,
And up the tall mast runs the woodpecker.
He saw, beneath dim aisles, in odorous beds,
The slight Linnæa hang its twin-born heads,
And blessed the monument of the man of flow-
    ers,
Which breathes his sweet fame through the
    Northern bowers.
He heard when in the grove, at intervals,
With sudden roar the aged pine tree falls,—
One crash, the death-hymn of the perfect tree,
Declares the close of its green century.
Low lies the plant to whose creation went
Sweet influence from every element;
Whose living towers the years conspired to
    build,
Whose giddy top the morning loved to gild.
Through these green tents, by eldest nature drest,
He roamed, content alike with man and beast.
Where darkness found him, he lay glad at night;
There the red morning touched him with its
    light.
Three moons his great heart him a hermit made,
So long he roved at will the boundless shade.
The timid it concerns to ask their way,
And fear what foe in caves and swamps can
    stray,
To make no step until the event is known,
And ills to come as evils past bemoan:
Not so the wise; no coward watch he keeps,
To spy what danger on his pathway creeps;
Go where he will, the wise man is at home,
His hearth the earth; — his hall the azure dome;
Where his clear spirit leads him, there's his road,
By God's own light illumined and foreshowed.

THE GYPSY TRAIL

'Twas one of the charmed days
When the genius of God doth flow,
The wind may alter twenty ways,
A tempest cannot blow:
It may blow north, it still is warm;
Or south, it still is clear;
Or east, it smells like a clover farm;
Or west, no thunder fear.
The musing peasant lowly great
Beside the forest water sate:
The rope-like pine-roots crosswise grown
Composed the network of his throne;
The wide lake edged with sand and grass
Was burnished to a floor of glass,
Painted with shadows green and proud
Of the tree and of the cloud.
He was the heart of all the scene,
On him the sun looked more serene,
To hill and cloud his face was known,
It seemed the likeness of their own.
They knew by secret sympathy
The public child of earth and sky.
"You ask," he said, "what guide
Me through trackless thickets led,
Through thick-stemmed woodlands rough
    and wide?
I found the waters' bed.
The watercourses were my guide;
I travelled grateful by their side,
Or through their channel dry;
They led me through the thicket damp,
Through brake and fern, the beavers' camp,
Through beds of granite cut my road,
And their resistless friendship showed.
The falling waters led me,
The foodful waters fed me,
And brought me to the lowest land,

THE WILD WOOD

Unerring to the ocean sand.
The moss upon the forest bark
Was pole-star when the night was dark;
The purple berries in the wood
Supplied me necessary food.
For Nature ever faithful is
To such as trust her faithfulness.
When the forest shall mislead me,
When the night and morning lie,
When sea and land refuse to feed me,
'Twill be time enough to die;
Then will yet my mother yield
A pillow in her greenest field,
Nor the June flowers scorn to cover
The clay of their departed lover."

II

As sunbeams stream through liberal space,
And nothing jostle or displace,
So waved the pine-tree through my
*   thought,*
And fanned the dreams it never brought.

"Whether is better, the gift or the donor?
Come to me,"
Quoth the pine-tree,
"I am the giver of honor.
My garden is the cloven rock,
And my manure the snow,
And drifting sand-heaps feed my stock,
In summer's scorching glow.
He is great who can live by me;
The rough and bearded forester
Is better than the lord;
God fills the scrip and canister,
Sin piles the loaded board.

THE GYPSY TRAIL

The lord is the peasant that was,
The peasant the lord that shall be;
The lord is hay, the peasant grass,
One dry and one the living tree.
Who liveth by the ragged pine,
Foundeth a heroic line;
Who liveth in the palace hall,
Waneth fast and spendeth all:
He goes to my savage haunts,
With his chariot and his care,
My twilight realm he disenchants,
And finds his prison there.
What prizes the town and the tower?
Only what the pine-tree yields,
Sinew that subdued the fields,
The wild-eyed boy who in the woods
Chants his hymn to hills and floods,
Whom the city's poisoning spleen
Made not pale, or fat, or lean,
Whom the rain and the wind purgeth,
Whom the dawn and the day-star urgeth,
In whose cheek the rose-leaf blusheth,
In whose feet the lion rusheth,
Iron arms and iron mould,
That know not fear, fatigue, or cold.
I give my rafters to his boat,
My billets to his boiler's throat,
And I will swim the ancient sea
To float my child to victory,
And grant to dwellers with the pine
Dominion o'er the palm and vine.
Who leaves the pine-tree, leaves his friend,
Unnerves his strength, invites his end.
Cut a bough from my parent stem,
And dip it in thy porcelain vase;
A little while each russet gem

THE WILD WOOD

Will swell and rise with wonted grace,
But when it seeks enlarged supplies,
The orphan of the forest dies.

"Whoso walketh in solitude,
And inhabiteth the wood,
Choosing light, wave, rock, and bird,
Before the money-loving herd,
Into that forester shall pass
From these companions power and grace;
Clean shall he be, without, within,
From the old adhering sin;
All ill dissolving in the light
Of his triumphant piercing sight.
Not vain, sour, nor frivolous,
Not mad, athirst, nor garrulous,
Grave, chaste, contented, though retired,
And of all other men desired.
On him the light of star and moon
Shall fall with purer radiance down;
All constellations of the sky
Shed their virtue through his eye.
Him Nature giveth for defence
His formidable innocence,
The mounting sap, the shells, the sea,
All spheres, all stones, his helpers be;
He shall meet the speeding year,
Without wailing, without fear;
He shall be happy in his love,
Like to like shall joyful prove.
He shall be happy whilst he wooes,
Muse-born, a daughter of the Muse;
But if with gold she bind her hair,
And deck her breast with diamond,
Take off thine eyes, thy heart forbear,
Though thou lie alone on the ground.

THE GYPSY TRAIL

"Heed the old oracles,
Ponder my spells,
Song wakes in my pinnacles,
When the wind swells.
Soundeth the prophetic wind,
The shadows shake on the rock behind,
And the countless leaves of the pine are
     strings
Tuned to the lay the wood-god sings.
Hearken! hearken!
If thou wouldst know the mystic song
Chanted when the sphere was young.
Aloft, abroad, the paean swells,
O wise man, hear'st thou half it tells?
O wise man, hear'st thou the least part?
'Tis the chronicle of art.
To the open ear it sings
Sweet the genesis of things;
Of tendency through endless ages,
Of star-dust, and star-pilgrimages,
Of rounded worlds, of space, and time,
Of the old flood's subsiding slime,
Of chemic matter, force, and form,
Of poles and powers, cold, wet, and warm:
The rushing metamorphosis
Dissolving all that fixture is,
Melts things that be to things that seem,
And solid nature to a dream.
O, listen to the under song,
The ever old, the ever young,
And far within those cadent pauses,
The chorus of the ancient Causes.
Delights the dreadful Destiny
To fling his voice into the tree,
And shock thy weak ear with a note
Breathed from the everlasting throat.
In music he repeats the pang

THE WILD WOOD

Whence the fair flock of Nature sprang.
O mortal! thy ears are stones;
These echoes are laden with tones
Which only the pure can hear,
Thou canst not catch what they recite
Of Fate, and Will, of Want, and Right,
Of man to come, of human life,
Of Death, and Fortune, Growth, and
    Strife."

Once again the pine-tree sung; —
" Speak not thy speech my boughs among,
Put off thy years, wash in the breeze,
My hours are peaceful centuries.
Talk no more with feeble tongue;
No more the fool of space and time,
Come weave with mine a nobler rhyme.
Only thy Americans
Can read thy line, can meet thy glance,
But the runes that I rehearse
Understands the universe.
The least breath my boughs which tossed
Brings again the Pentecost;
        .   .   .   .

Come learn with me the fatal song
Which knits the world in music strong,
Come lift thine eyes to lofty rhymes
Of things with things, of times with times,
Primal chimes of sun and shade,
Of sound and echo, man and maid;
The land reflected in the flood;
Body with shadow still pursued.
For Nature beats in perfect tune,
And rounds with rhyme her every rune,
Whether she work in land or sea,
Or hide underground her alchemy.
Thou canst not wave thy staff in air,

THE GYPSY TRAIL

Or dip thy paddle in the lake,
But it carves the bow of beauty there,
And the ripples in rhymes the oar forsake.
The wood is wiser far than thou:
The wood and wave each other know.
Not unrelated, unaffied,
But to each thought and thing allied,
Is perfect Nature's every part,
Rooted in the mighty heart.
But thou, poor child! unbound, un-
    rhymed,
Whence camest thou, misplaced, mistimed?
Who thee divorced, deceived, and left;
Thee of thy faith who hath bereft,
And torn the ensigns from thy brow,
And sunk the immortal eye so low?
Thy cheek too white, thy form too
    slender,
Thy gait too slow, thy habits tender,
For royal man; they thee confess
An exile from the wilderness,—
The hills where health with health
    agrees,
And the wise soul expels disease.
Hark! in thy ear I will tell the sign
By which thy hurt thou mayst divine.
When thou shalt climb the mountain
    cliff,
Or see the wide shore from thy skiff.
To thee the horizon shall express
But emptiness on emptiness;
There is no man of Nature's worth
In the circle of the earth,
And to thine eye the vast skies fall
Dire and satirical
On clucking hens, and prating fools,
On thieves, on drudges and on dolls.

THE WILD WOOD

And thou shalt say to the Most High,
' Godhead! all this astronomy,
And Fate, and practice, and invention,
Strong art, and beautiful pretension,
This radiant pomp of sun and star,
Throes that were, and worlds that are,
Behold! were in vain and in vain; —
It cannot be,— I will look again.—
Surely now will the curtain rise,
And earth's fit tenant me surprise;
But the curtain doth *not* rise,
And Nature has miscarried wholly
Into failure, into ' folly.'

" Alas! thine is the bankruptcy,
Blessed Nature so to see.
Come lay thee in my soothing shade,
And heal the hurts which sin has
     made.
I see thee in the crowd alone;
I will be thy companion.
Quit thy friends as the dead in doom,
And build to them a final tomb;
Let the starred shade that nightly falls
Still celebrate their funerals,
And the bell of beetle and of bee
Knell their melodious memory.
Behind thee leave thy merchandise,
Thy churches, and thy charities,
And leave thy peacock wit behind;
Enough for thee the primal mind
That flows in streams, that breathes
     in wind;
Leave all thy pedant lore apart;
God hid the whole world in thy heart.
Love shuns the sage, the child it
     crowns,

THE GYPSY TRAIL

Gives all to them who all renounce.
The rain comes when the wind calls,
The river knows the way to the sea,
Without a pilot it runs and falls,
Blessing all lands with its charity.
The sea tosses and foams to find
Its way up to the cloud and wind,
The shadow sits close to the flying
    ball,
The date fails not on the palm-tree
    tall,
And thou,— go burn thy wormy pages,—
Shalt outsee the seer, and outwit sages.
Oft didst thou thread the woods in
    vain
To find what bird had piped the
    strain,—
Seek not, and the little eremite
Flies gaily forth and sings in sight.

"Hearken once more!
I will tell the mundane lore.
Older am I than thy numbers wot,
Change I may, but I pass not.
    •   •   •   •

All the forms are fugitive,
But the substances survive.
Ever fresh the broad creation,
A divine improvisation,
From the heart of God proceeds,
A single will, a million deeds.
Once slept the world an egg of stone,
And pulse, and sound, and light was
    none;
And God said, 'Throb!' and there
    was motion,
And the vast mass became vast ocean.

THE WILD WOOD

Onward and on, the eternal Pan
Who layeth the world's incessant plan,
Halteth never in one shape,
But forever doth escape,
Like wave or flame, into new forms
Of gem, and air, of plants and worms.
                    .   .   .   .

As the bee through the garden ranges,
From world to world the godhead
        changes;
As the sheep go feeding in the waste,
From form to form He maketh haste.
This vault which glows immense with
        light
Is the inn where he lodges for a
        night.
What recks such Traveller if the
        bowers
Which bloom and fade like meadow
        flowers,
A bunch of fragrant lilies be,
Or the stars of eternity?
Alike to him the better, the worse,
The glowing angel, the outcast corse.
Thou metest him by centuries,
And lo! he passes like the breeze;
Thou seek'st in globe and galaxy,
He hides in pure transparency;
Thou askest in fountains and in fires,
He is the essence that inquires.
He is the axis of the star;
He is the sparkle of the spar;
He is the heart of every creature;
He is the meaning of each feature;
And his mind is the sky
Than all it holds more deep, more
        high."
                    Ralph Waldo Emerson
143

THE GYPSY TRAIL

AMONG THE FERNS

I LAY among the ferns,
    Where they lifted their fronds innumerable,
        in the greenwood wilderness, like wings
        winnowing the air;
And their voices went past me continually.

And I listened, and lo! softly inaudibly raining
    I heard not the voices of the ferns only,
    but of all living creatures:
Voices of mountain and star,
Of cloud and forest and ocean,
And of the little rills tumbling amid the rocks,
And of the high tops where the moss-beds are
    and the springs arise.
As the wind at mid-day rains whitening over
    the grass,
As the night-bird glimmers a moment, fleeting
    between the lonely watcher and the moon,
So softly inaudibly they rained,
Where I sat silent.

And in the silence of the greenwood I knew the
    secret of the growth of the ferns;
I saw their delicate leaflets tremble breathing
    an undescribed and unuttered life;
And, below, the ocean lay sleeping;
And round them the mountains and the stars
    dawned in glad companionship for ever.
And a voice came to me, saying:
In every creature, in forest and ocean, in leaf
    and tree and bird and beast and man, there
    moves a spirit other than its mortal own,
Pure, fluid, as air — intense as fire,
Which looks abroad and passes along the spirits

of all other creatures, drawing them close
    to itself,
Nor dreams of other law than that of perfect
    equality;
And this is the spirit of immortality and peace.

And whatsoever creature has this spirit, to it no
    harm may befall:
No harm can befall, for wherever it goes it has
    its nested home,
And to it every loss comes charged with an
    equal gain;
It gives — but to receive a thousand-fold;
It yields its life — but at the hands of love;
And death is the law of its eternal growth.

And I saw that was the law of every creature
    — that this spirit should enter in and take
    possession of it,
That it might have no more fear or doubt or
    be at war within itself any longer.
And lo! in the greenwood all around me it
    moved,
Where the sunlight floated fragrant under the
    boughs, and the fern-fronds winnowed the
    air;
In the oak-leaves dead of last year, and in the
    small shy things that rustled among them;
In the songs of the birds and the broad shadow-
    ing leaves overhead;
In the fields sleeping below, and in the river
    and the high dreaming air;
Gleaming ecstatic it moved — with joy incarnate.
And it seemed to me, as I looked, that it pene-
    trated all these things, suffusing them;
And wherever it penetrated, behold! there was

nothing left down to the smallest atom which
was not a winged spirit instinct with life.

Who shall understand the words of the ferns
    lifting their fronds innumerable?
What man shall go forth into the world, hold-
    ing his life in his open palm —
With high adventurous joy from sunrise to sun-
    set —
Fearless, in his sleeve laughing, having out-
    flanked his enemies?
His heart like Nature's garden — that all men
    abide in —
Free, where the great winds blow, rains fall,
    and the sun shines,
And manifold growths come forth and scatter
    their fragrance?
Who shall be like a grave, where men may bury
Sin and sorrow and shame, to rise in the new
    day
Glorious out of their grave? who, deeply listen-
    ing,
Shall hear through his soul the voices of all
    creation,
Voices of mountain and star, voices of all men,
Softly, audibly raining? — shall seize and fix
    them,
Rivet them fast with love, no more to lose
    them?
Who shall *be* that spirit of deep fulfilment,
Himself, self-centred? yet evermore from that
    centre
Over the world expanding, along all creatures
Loyally passing — with love, in perfect equality?

Him immortality crowns. In him all sorrow

THE WILD WOOD

And mortal passion of death shall pass from
    creation.
They who sit by the road and are weary shall
    rise up
As he passes. They who despair shall arise.

Who shall understand the words of the ferns
    winnowing the air?
*Death shall change as the light in the morning
    changes;*
*Death shall change as the light 'twixt moon-
    set and dawn.*

                    Edward Carpenter

I HEARD THE VOICE OF THE WOODS

I HEARD the voice of the woods and of the
    grass growing silently and of the delicate
    bending ferns,
And it said:
For the dumb and for the generations of them
    that have no voice my speech is —
For them too help comes.

I am the spirit of the Earth.
Round me the woods and mountains roll, rising
    and falling to the far sea;
In the hollow below me roars the great river to
    its doom;
The clouds draw onward; and the voices of the
    generations of men are woven like thin
    gossamer through the air about me.
Yet here where I am there is peace — such as
    mortal yet on earth hath hardly known,
But which shall be known, and even now is
    known.

THE GYPSY TRAIL

Where the stems stand dividing the winnowed
    sunlight,
Where the green floor is dappled with soft warm
    moss, and the swift hum of the bee is heard,
And the air glides through like a gracious spirit
    inbreathing beauty,
I walk — meditating the voiceless children, draw-
    ing them to myself with deep unearthly love.

Come unto me, O yearning and inarticulate (for
    whom so many ages I have waited),
Breathing your lives out like a long unuttered
    prayer,
Come unto me: and I will give you rest.
For I am not the woods nor the grass nor the
    bending ferns;
Nor any pale moonlight spirit of these;
And I am not the air;
Nor the light multitudinous life therein;
Nor the sun and its radiant warmth;
But I am one who include — and am greater —
One (out of thousands) who hold all these, em-
    bosomed,
Safe in my heart: fear not.

In your eyes deep-looking I will touch you so as
    to be free from all pain;
Where the last interpretations are, in the utter-
    most recesses, I will reach you;
Utterance at length shall your pent-up spirit have,
To pour out all that is in you — to speak and be
    not afraid.

Dear brother, listen!
I am no shadow, no fickle verse-maker's fiction,
Many are the words which are not spoken, but
    here there is speech;

THE WILD WOOD

Many are the words which are not spoken, but
  in due time all shall be spoken:
There is neither haste nor delay, but all shall be
  spoken.

Come up into the fragrant woods and walk with
  me.
The voices of the trees and the silent-growing
  grass and waving ferns ascend;
Beyond the birth-and-death veil of the seasons
  they ascend and are born again;
The voices of the trees and the silent-growing
  cry of the heart — they too ascend into new
  perpetual birth.
All is interpreted anew:
In man the cataracts descend, and the winds
  blow, and autumn reddens and ripens;
And in the woods a spirit walks which is not
  wholly of the woods,
But which looks out over the wide Earth and
  draws to itself all men with deep unearthly
  love.

Come, walk with me:
On the soft moss — though you guess not my
  arm is about you —
By the white stems where the gracious air is
  breathing,
On the green floor, through the pale green win-
  nowed sunlight,
Walk: and leave all to me.

Edward Carpenter

THE GYPSY TRAIL

O DREAMY, GLOOMY, FRIENDLY TREES!

O DREAMY, gloomy, friendly trees,
  I came along your narrow track
To bring my gifts unto your knees
  And gifts did you give back;
For when I brought this heart that burns —
  These thoughts that bitterly repine —
And laid them here among the ferns
  And the hum of boughs divine,
Ye, vastest breathers of the air,
  Shook down with slow and mighty poise
Your coolness on the human care,
  Your wonder on its toys,
Your greenness on the heart's despair,
  Your darkness on its noise.

Herbert Trench

CHORUS

From *The Bacchae*

WILL they ever come to me, ever again,
  The long long dances,
On through the dark till the dim stars wane?
Shall I feel the dew on my throat, and the
    stream
Of wind in my hair? Shall our white feet
    gleam
  In the dim expanses?
Oh, feet of a fawn to the greenwood fled,
  Alone in the grass and the loveliness;
Leap of the hunted, no more in dread,
  Beyond the snares and the deadly press:
Yet a voice still in the distance sounds,
A voice and a fear and a haste of hounds;

150

THE WILD WOOD

O wildly laboring, fiercely fleet,
   Onward yet by river and glen. . . .
Is it joy or terror, ye storm-swift feet? . . .
   To the dear lone lands, untroubled of men,
Where no voice sounds, and amid the shadowy
      green
The little things of the woodland live unseen.

What else is Wisdom? What of man's endeavor
   Or God's high grace, so lovely and so great?
   To stand from fear set free, to breathe and
      wait;
   To hold a hand uplifted over Hate;
And shall not Loveliness be loved forever?

   O Strength of God, slow art thou and still,
      Yet failest never!
On them that worship the Ruthless Will,
On them that dream, doth His judgment wait.
Dreams of the proud man, making great
     And greater ever,
Things which are not of God. In wide
   And devious coverts, hunter-wise,
He coucheth Time's unhasting stride,
   Following, following, him whose eyes
Look not to Heaven. For all is vain,
The pulse of the heart, the plot of the brain,
That striveth beyond the laws that live.
   And is thy Faith so much to give,
Is it so hard a thing to see,
   That the Spirit of God, whate'er it be,
The Law that abides and changes not, ages long,
The Eternal and Nature-born — these things be
     strong?

What else is Wisdom? What of man's endeavor

Or God's high grace so lovely and so great?
To stand from fear set free, to breathe and
wait;
To hold a hand uplifted over Hate;
And shall not Loveliness be loved forever?

Happy he, on the weary sea
Who hath fled the tempest and won the haven.
Happy whoso hath risen, free,
Above his striving. For strangely graven
  Is the orb of life, that one and another
  In gold and power may outpass his brother.
And men in their millions float and flow
And seethe with a million hopes as leaven;
  And they win their Will, or they miss their
  Will,
  And the hopes are dead or are pined for still;
    But whoe'er can know,
    As the long days go,
That To Live is happy, has found his Heaven!
                    Euripides
        Translation by Gilbert Murray

FORTUNATUS ET ILLE

From *The Georgics*

ME vero primum dulces ante omnia Musae,
    Quarum sacra fero ingenti percussus
    amore,
Accipiant, caelique vias et sidera monstrent,
Defectus solis varios, lunaeque labores;
Unde tremor terris, qua vi maria alta tumescant
Obiicibus ruptis rursusque in se ipsa residant,
Quid tantum Oceano properent se tinguere soles
Hiberni, vel quae tardis mora noctibus obstet.

THE WILD WOOD

Sin, has ne possim naturae accedere partis,
Frigidus obstiterit circum praecordia sanguis,
Rura mihi et rigui placeant in vallibus amnes,
Flumina amem silvasque inglorius. O, ubi campi
Spercheusque, et virginibus bacchata Lacaenis
Taygeta! O, qui me gelidis convallibus Haemi
Sistat, et ingenti ramorum protegat umbra!
Felix, qui potuit rerum cognoscere causas,
Atque metus omnis et inexorabile fatum
Subiecit pedibus strepitumque Acherontis avari!
Fortunatus et ille, deos qui novit agrestis,
Panaque Silvanumque senem Nymphasque soro-
    res!

Vergil

INLAND WATERS

A noise like of a hidden brook
In the leafy month of June,
That to¹ the sleeping woods all night
    Singeth a quiet tune.

Coleridge

I will arise and go now, for always night and day
I hear lake-water lapping with low sounds by the shore.

Yeats

"Nice? It's the *only* thing," said the Water Rat
solemnly, as he leant forward for his stroke. "Believe
me, my young friend, there is *nothing* — absolute nothing
— half so much worth doing as simply messing about in
boats. Simply messing," he went on dreamily: "mess-
ing — about — in — boats. . . . Nothing seems really to
matter, that's the charm of it. Whether you get away,
or whether you don't; whether you arrive at your destina-
tion or whether you reach somewhere else, or whether
you never get anywhere at all, you're always busy, and
you never do anything in particular; and when you've
done it there's always something else to do, and you can
do it if you like, but you'd much better not. Look here!
If you've really nothing else on hand this morning, sup-
posing we drop down the river together and have a long
day of it?"

Kenneth Grahame

INLAND WATERS

THE BIRCH CANOE

FROM *Hiawatha*

GIVE me of your bark, O Birch-Tree!
Of your yellow bark, O Birch-Tree!
Growing by the rushing river,
Tall and stately in the valley!
I a light canoe will build me,
Build a swift Cheemaun for sailing,
That shall float upon the river,
Like a yellow leaf in Autumn,
Like a yellow water-lily!
  "Lay aside your cloak, O Birch-Tree!
Lay aside your white-skin wrapper,
For the Summer-time is coming,
And the sun is warm in heaven,
And you need no white-skin wrapper!"
  Thus aloud cried Hiawatha
In the solitary forest,
By the rushing Taquamenaw,
When the birds were singing gaily,
In the Moon of Leaves were singing,
And the sun, from sleep awaking,
Started up and said, "Behold me!
Geezis, the great Sun, behold me!"
  And the tree with all its branches
Rustled in the breeze of morning,
Saying, with a sigh of patience,
"Take my cloak, O Hiawatha!"
  With his knife the tree he girdled;

Just beneath its lowest branches,
Just above the roots, he cut it,
Till the sap came oozing outward;
Down the trunk, from top to bottom,
Sheer he cleft the bark asunder,
With a wooden wedge he raised it,
Stripped it from the trunk unbroken.
　"Give me of your boughs, O Cedar!
Of your strong and pliant branches,
My canoe to make more steady,
Make more strong and firm beneath me!"
　Through the summit of the Cedar
Went a sound, a cry of horror,
Went a murmur of resistance;
But it whispered, bending downward,
"Take my boughs, O Hiawatha!"
　Down he hewed the boughs of cedar,
Shaped them straightway to a frame-work,
Like two bows he formed and shaped them,
Like two bended bows together.
　"Give me of your roots, O Tamarack!
Of your fibrous roots, O Larch-Tree!
My canoe to bind together,
So to bind the ends together
That the water may not enter,
That the river may not wet me!"
　And the Larch, with all its fibres,
Shivered in the air of morning,
Touched his forehead with its tassels,
Said, with one long sigh of sorrow,
"Take them all, O Hiawatha!"
　From the earth he tore the fibres,
Tore the tough roots of the Larch-Tree,
Closely sewed the bark together,
Bound it closely to the framework.
　"Give me of your balm, O Fir-Tree!

Of your balsam and your resin,
So to close the seams together
That the water may not enter,
That the river may not wet me!"
    And the Fir-Tree, tall and sombre,
Sobbed through all its robes of darkness,
Rattled like a shore with pebbles,
Answered wailing, answered weeping,
"Take my balm, O Hiawatha!"
    And he took the tears of balsam,
Took the resin of the Fir-Tree.
Smeared therewith each seam and fissure,
Made each crevice safe from water,
    "Give me of your quills, O Hedgehog!
All your quills, O Kagh, the Hedgehog!
I will make a necklace of them,
Make a girdle for my beauty,
And two stars to deck her bosom!"
    From a hollow tree the Hedgehog
With his sleepy eyes looked at him,
Shot his shining quills like arrows,
Saying, with a drowsy murmur,
Through the tangle of his whiskers,
"Take my quills, O Hiawatha!"
    From the ground the quills he gathered,
All the little shining arrows,
Stained them red and blue and yellow,
With the juice of roots and berries;
Into his canoe he wrought them,
Round its waist a shining girdle,
Round its bows a gleaming necklace,
On its breast two stars resplendent.
    Thus the Birch Canoe was builded
In the valley, by the river,
In the bosom of the forest;
And the forest's life was in it,

THE GYPSY TRAIL

All its mystery and its magic,
All the lightness of the birch-tree,
All the toughness of the cedar,
All the larch's supple sinews;
And it floated on the river
Like a yellow leaf in Autumn,
Like a yellow water-lily.

Henry W. Longfellow

WHERE GO THE BOATS?

DARK brown is the river,
Golden is the sand.
It flows along forever,
With trees on either hand.

Green leaves a-floating,
Castles of the foam,
Boats of mine a-boating —
Where will all come home?

On goes the river
And out past the mill,
Away down the valley,
Away down the hill.

Away down the river,
A hundred miles or more,
Other little children
Shall bring my boats ashore.

Robert Louis Stevenson

160

INLAND WATERS

THE RIVER

CLEAR, and cool, clear and cool,
  By   laughing   shallow,   and   dreaming
      pool;
    Cool and clear, cool and clear,
  By shining shingle, and foaming weir;
Under the crag where the ouzel sings,
And the ivied wall where the church-bell rings,
    Undefiled for the undefiled;
  Play by me, bathe in me, mother and child.

    Dank and foul, dank and foul,
  By the smoky town in its murky cowl;
    Foul and dank, foul and dank,
  By wharf and sewer and slimy bank;
Darker and darker the further I go,
Baser and baser the richer I grow;
    Who dare sport with the sin defiled?
  Shrink from me, turn from me, mother and
      child.

    Strong and free, strong and free;
  The floodgates are open, away to the sea.
    Free and strong, free and strong,
  Cleansing my streams as I hurry along
To the golden sands, and the leaping bar,
And the taintless tide that awaits me afar,
As I lose myself in the infinite main,
Like a soul that has sinned and is pardoned
      again.
    Undefiled for the undefiled;
  Play by me, bathe in me, mother and child.
                              Charles Kingsley

THE GYPSY TRAIL

THUS THE MAYNE GLIDETH

THUS the Mayne glideth
   Where my love abideth.
Sleep's no softer: it proceeds
On through lawns, on through meads,
On and on, whate'er befall,
Meandering and musical,
Though the niggard pasturage
Bears not on its shaven ledge
Aught but weeds and waving grasses
To view the river as it passes,
Save here and there a scanty patch
Of primroses too faint to catch
A weary bee. And scarce it pushes
Its gentle way through strangling rushes
Where the glossy kingfisher
Flutters when noon-heats are near,
Glad the shelving banks to shun,
Red and steaming in the sun,
Where the shrew-mouse with pale throat
Burrows, and the speckled stoat;
Where the quick sandpipers flit
In and out the marl and grit
That seems to breed them, brown as they:
Naught disturbs its quiet way,
Save some lazy stork that springs,
Trailing it with legs and wings,
Whom the shy fox from the hill
Rouses, creep he ne'er so still.
              Robert Browning

INLAND WATERS

LITTLE LAC GRENIER

L EETLE Lac Grenier, she's all alone,
  Right on de mountain top,
But cloud sweepin' by, will fin' tam to stop
No matter how quickly he want to go,
So he'll kiss leetle Grenier down below.

Leetle Lac Grenier, she's all alone,
Up on de mountain high
But she never feel lonesome, 'cos for w'y?
So soon as de winter was gone away
De bird come an' sing to her ev'ry day.

Leetle Lac Grenier, she's all alone,
Back on de mountain dere,
But de pine tree an' spruce stan' ev'rywhere
Along by de shore, an' mak' her warm
For dey kip off de win' an' de winter storm.

Leetle Lac Grenier, she's all alone,
No broder, no sister near,
But de swallow will fly, an' de beeg moose deer
An' caribou too, will go long way
To drink de sweet water of Lac Grenier.

Leetle Lac Grenier, I see you now,
Onder de roof of spring,
Ma canoe's afloat, an' de robin sing,
De lily's beginnin' her summer dress,
An' trout's wakin' up from hees long long res'.

Leetle Lac Grenier, I'm happy now,
Out on de ole canoe,
For I'm all alone, ma chere, wit' you,

THE GYPSY TRAIL

An' if only a nice light rod I had
I'd try dat fish near de lily pad!

Leetle Lac Grenier, O! let me go,
Don't spik no more,
For your voice is strong lak de rapid's roar,
An' you know youse'f I'm too far away,
For visit you now — Leetle Lac Grenier!
William Henry Drummond

CANADIAN BOAT SONG

FAINTLY as tolls the evening chime,
   Our voices keep tune, and our oars keep
     time,
Soon as the woods on shore look dim
We'll sing at St. Anne's our parting hymn.
  Row, brothers, row! the stream runs fast,
  The rapids are near, and the daylight's past!

Why should we yet our sail unfurl?
There is not a breath the blue wave to curl.
But when the wind blows off the shore
O, sweetly we'll rest our weary oar!
  Blow, breezes, blow! the stream runs fast,
  The rapids are near, and the daylight's past!

Utawa's tide! this trembling moon
Shall see us float over thy surges soon.
Saint of this green isle, hear our prayers —
O, grant us cool heavens and favoring airs!
  Blow, breezes, blow! the stream runs fast,
  The rapids are near, and the daylight's past!
Thomas Moore

INLAND WATERS

THE RIVULET

FROM *Alastor*

THE rivulet
 Wanton and wild, through many a green
  ravine
Beneath the forest flowed. Sometimes it fell
Among the moss with hollow harmony
Dark and profound. Now on the polished stones
It danced, like childhood laughing as it went:
Then through the plain in tranquil wanderings
  crept,
Reflecting every herb and drooping bud
That overhung its quietness.—" O stream!
Whose source is inaccessibly profound,
Whither do thy mysterious waters tend? "

  · · · ·

He must descend. With rapid steps he went
Beneath the shade of trees, beside the flow
Of the wild babbling rivulet; and now
The forest's solemn canopies were changed
For the uniform and lightsome evening sky.
Gray rocks did peep from the spare moss, and
  stemmed
The struggling brook: tall spires of windlestrae
Threw their thin shadows down the rugged slope,
And naught but gnarlèd roots of ancient pines
Branchless and blasted, clenched with grasping
  roots
The unwilling soil. A gradual change was here,
Yet ghastly. For, as fast years flow away,
The smooth brow gathers, and the hair grows
  thin
And white, and where irradiate dewy eyes

165

Had shone, gleam stony orbs: — so from his
    steps
Bright flowers departed, and the beautiful shade
Of the green groves, with all their odorous
    winds
And musical motions. Calm, he still pursued
The stream, that with a larger volume now
Rolled through the labyrinthine dell, and there
Fretted a path through its descending curves,
With its wintry speed. On every side now rose
Rocks, which, in unimaginable forms,
Lifted their black and barren pinnacles
In the light of evening, and, its precipice
Obscuring the ravine, disclosed above,
Mid toppling stones, black gulfs and yawning
    caves,
Whose windings gave ten thousand various
    tongues
To the loud stream. Lo! where the pass expands
Its stony jaws, the abrupt mountain breaks,
And seems, with its accumulated crags,
To overhang the world: for wide expand
Beneath the wan stars and descending moon
Islanded seas, blue mountains, mighty streams.
Dim tracts and vast, robed in the lustrous gloom
Of leaden-colored even, and fiery hills
Mingling their flames with twilight, on the verge
Of the remote horizon. The near scene,
In naked and severe simplicity,
Made contrast with the universe. A pine,
Rock-rooted, stretched athwart the vacancy
Its swinging boughs, to each inconstant blast
Yielding one only response, at each pause
In most familiar cadence, with the howl,
The thunder and the hiss of homeless streams
Mingling its solemn song, whilst the broad river,

INLAND WATERS

Foaming and hurrying o'er its rugged path,
Fell into that immeasurable void
Scattering its waters to the passing winds.

. . . .

The dim and hornèd moon hung low and
    poured
A sea of lustre on the horizon's verge
That overflowed its mountains. Yellow mist
Filled the unbounded atmosphere, and drank
Wan moonlight even to fulness: not a star
Shone, not a sound was heard; the very winds,
Danger's grim playmates, on that precipice
Slept, clasped in his embrace.

                Percy Bysshe Shelley

ASIA'S SONG

FROM *Prometheus Unbound*

MY soul is an enchanted boat,
   Which, like a sleeping swan, doth float
Upon the silver waves of thy sweet singing;
  And thine doth like an angel sit
  Beside a helm conducting it,
Whilst all the winds with melody are ringing.
  It seems to float ever, forever,
  Upon that many-winding river,
  Between mountains, woods, abysses,
  A paradise of wildernesses!
Till, like one in slumber bound,
Borne to the ocean, I float down, around,
Into a sea profound, of ever-spreading sound.

  Meanwhile thy spirit lifts its pinions
  In music's most serene dominions;
Catching the winds that fan that happy heaven.

THE GYPSY TRAIL

And we sail on, away, afar,
  Without a course, without a star,
But by the instinct of sweet music driven;
  Till through Elysian garden islets
  By thee, most beautiful of pilots,
  Where never mortal pinnace glided,
  The boat of my desire is guided:
Realms where the air we breathe is love,
Which in the winds and'on the waves doth move,
Harmonizing this earth with what we feel above.

We have passed Age's icy caves,
  And Manhood's dark and tossing waves,
And Youth's smooth ocean, smiling to betray:
  Beyond the glassy gulfs we flee
  Of shadow-peopled Infancy,
Through Death and Birth, to a diviner day;
  A paradise of vaulted bowers
  Lit by downward-gazing flowers,
  And watery paths that wind between
  Wildernesses calm and green,
Peopled by shapes too bright to see,
And rest, having beheld; somewhat like thee;
Which walk upon the sea, and chant melodi-
      ously!
                        Percy Bysshe Shelley

BUT THE MAJESTIC RIVER FLOATED ON

From *Sohrab and Rustum*

BUT the majestic river floated on,
      Out of the mist and hum of that low
      land,
Into the frosty starlight, and there moved,
Rejoicing, through the hushed Chorasmian waste.

INLAND WATERS

Under the solitary moon; he flowed
Right for the polar star, past Orgunjè,
Brimming, and bright, and large; then sands be-
    gin
To hem his watery march, and dam his streams,
And split his currents; that for many a league
The shorn and parcelled Oxus strains along
Through beds of sand and matted rushy isles,—
Oxus, forgetting the bright speed he had
In his high mountain cradle in Pamere,
A foiled circuitous wanderer,— till at last
The longed-for dash of waves is heard, and wide
His luminous home of waters opens, bright
And tranquil, from whose floor the new-bathed
    stars
Emerge, and shine upon the Aral Sea.
                                    Matthew Arnold

THE SEA

—Murmurs and scents of the infinite sea.

Arnold

The whole world's heart is uplifted and knows not wrong;
The whole world's life is a chant to the seatide's chorus;
Are we not as waves of the water, as notes of the song?

Swinburne

Where the great winds every morning
Sweep the sea-floor clean and white,
And upon the steel-blue arches
Burnish the great stars of night.

Carman

THE SEA

MEERGRUSS

THALATTA! Thalatta!
    Sei mir gegrüsst, du ewiges Meer!
Sei mir gegrüsst zehntausendmal
Aus jauchzendem Herzen,
Wie einst dich begrüssten
Zehntausend Griechenherzen,
Uuglückbekämpfende, heimatverlangende,
Weltberühmte Griechenherzen.

    Es wogten die Fluten,
Sie wogten und brausten,
Die Sonne goss eilig herunter
Die spielenden Rosenlichter,
Die aufgescheuchten Möwenzüge
Flatterten fort, laut schreiend,
Es stampften die Rosse, es klirrten die Schilde,
Und weithin erscholl es wie Siegesruf:
"Thalatta! Thalatta!"

    Sei mir gegrüsst, du ewiges Meer,
Wie Sprache der Heimat rauscht mir dein Was-
    ser,
Wie Träume der Kindheit seh' ich es flimmern
Auf deinem wogenden Wellengebiet,
Und alte Erinn'rung erzählt mir aufs Neue
Von all' dem lieben, herrlichen Spielzeug,
Von all' den blinkenden Weihnachtsgaben,

THE GYPSY TRAIL

Von all' den roten Korallenbäumen,
Goldfischchen, Perlen und bunten Muscheln,
Die du geheimnisvoll bewahrst,
Dort unten im klaren Krystallhaus.

O, wie hab' ich geschmachtet in öder Fremde!
Gleich einer welken Blume
In des Botanikers blecherner Kapsel
Lag mir das Herz in der Brust.
Mir ist als sass ich winterlange,
Ein kranker, in dunkler Krankenstube,
Und nun verlass' ich sie plötzlich,
Und blendend strahlt mir entgegen
Der smaragdene Frühling, der sonnengeweckte,
Und es rauschen die weissen Blüthenbäume,
Und die jungen Blumen schauen mich an
Mit bunten, duftenden Augen,
Und es duftet und summt und atmet und lacht,
Und in blauen Himmel singen die Vöglein —
Thalatta! Thalatta!

    ·   ·   ·   ·

Heinrich Heine

THE SEA

I CALL thee from the changing land
   To the unchanging sea;
I bring a bride-gift in my hand
Of immortality.
The land is fair, but fairer far
The pastures of the sea.
Canst thou reach down the lowest star?
My sea-fires gleam for thee.
All rivers run unto one end
And perish in the sea;
Turn thou from lover and from friend,

THE SEA

And give thy heart to me.
Thy love shall suffer change and dearth,
Thy friend the years estrange;
There is no faithfulness on earth —
The sea will never change.

Nora Chesson

THE RETURN

From *The Triumph of Time*

I WILL go back to the great sweet mother,
  Mother and lover of men, the sea.
I will go down to her, I and none other,
  Close with her, kiss her, and mix her with me;
Cling to her, strive with her, hold her fast;
O fair white mother, in days long past
Born without sister, born without brother,
  Set free my soul as thy soul is free.

O fair green-girdled mother of mine,
  Sea, that art clothed with the sun and the
    rain,
Thy sweet hard kisses are strong like wine,
  Thy large embraces are keen like pain.
Save me and hide me with all thy waves,
Find me one grave of thy thousand graves,
Those pure cold populous graves of thine,
  Wrought without hand in a world without
    stain.

I shall sleep, and move with the moving ships,
  Change as the winds change, veer in the tide;
My lips will feast on the foam of thy lips,
  I shall rise with thy rising, with thee sub-
    side;

THE GYPSY TRAIL

Sleep, and not know if she be, if she were,
Filled full with life to the eyes and hair,
As a rose is fulfilled to the roseleaf tips
　With splendid summer and perfume and
　　pride.

This woven raiment of nights and days,
　Were it once cast off and unwound from me,
Naked and glad would I walk in thy ways,
　Alive and aware of thy ways and thee;
Clear of the whole world, hidden at home,
Clothed with the green and crowned with the
　　foam,
A pulse of the life of thy straits and bays,
　A vein in the heart of the streams of the sea.

Fair mother, fed with the lives of men,
　Thou art subtle and cruel of heart, men say
Thou hast taken, and shalt not render again;
　Thou art full of thy dead, and cold as they.
But death is the worst that comes of thee;
Thou art fed with our dead, O mother, O sea,
But when hast thou fed on our hearts? or when,
　Having given us love, hast thou taken away?

O tender-hearted, O perfect lover,
　Thy lips are bitter, and sweet thine heart.
The hopes that hurt and the dreams that hover,
　Shall they not vanish away and apart?
But thou, thou art sure, thou art older than
　　earth;
Thou art strong for death and fruitful of birth;
Thy depths conceal and thy gulfs discover;
　From the first thou wert, from the end thou
　　art.

Algernon Charles Swinburne

176

THE SEA

VERS LA MER

COMME des objets frêles
    Les vaisseaux blancs semblent posés,
Sur la mer éternelle.

Le vent futile et pur n'est que baisers;
Et les écumes
Qui, doucement, échouent
Contre les proues,
Ne sont que plumes:
Il fait dimanche sur la mer!

Telles des dames
Passent, au ciel ou vers les plages,
Voilures et nuages:
Il fait dimanche sur la mer;
Et l'on voit luire, au loin, des rames,
Barres de prismes sur la mer.

Fier de soi-même et de cette heure,
Qui scintillait, en grappes de joyaux
Translucides sur l'eau,
J'ai crié, vers l'espace et sa splendeur:
"O mer de luxe frais et de moires fleuries,
Où l' immobile et vaste été
Marie
Sa force à la douceur et la limpidité;
Mer de fierté et de conquête
Où voyagent, de crête en crête,
Sur les vagues qu'elles irisent,
Les brises;
Mer de ferveurs, où des musiques de lumière
Chantent dans l'or
Immobile du fulgurant décor;
Mer de beauté sereine et de frêle merveille

177

Dont la rumeur résonne en mes oreilles
Depuis qu' enfant j'imaginais les grèves bleues
Où l'Ourse et le Centaure et le Lion des cieux
Venaient boire, le soir,
Là-bas, très loin, à l'autre bout du monde ;
O mer, qui fus ma joie étonnée et féconde,
O mer, qui fus ma jeunesse cabrée
Ainsi que tes marées
Vers l'aventure et les conquêtes,
Accueille-moi, ce jour, où tes eaux sont en fête !

J'aurai vécu, l'âme élargie.
Sous les visages clairs, profonds, certains,
Qui regardent, du haut des horizons lointains,
Surgir, vers leur splendeur, mon énergie.
J'aurai senti les flux
Unanimes de choses
Me charrier en leur métamorphoses
Et m'emporter, dans leur reflux.
J'aurai vécu le mont, le bois, la terre ;
J'aurai versé le sang des dieux dans mes artères ;
J'aurai brandi, comme un glaive exalté,
Vers l'infini, ma volonté ;
Et maintenant c'est sur tes bords, ô mer suprême,
Où tout se renouvelle, où tout se reproduit,
Après s'être disjoint, après s'être détruit,
Que je reviens pour qu'on y sème
Cet univers qui fut moi-même.

L'ombre se fait en moi ; l'âge s'étend
Comme une ornière, autour du champ,
Qui fut ma force en fleure et ma vaillance.
Plus n'est ferme toujours ni hautaine ma lance ;
L' arbre de mon orgueil reverdit moins souvent
Et son feuillage boit moins largement le vent
Qui passe en ouragan, sur les forêts humaines ;
O mer, je sens tarir les sources, dans mes plaines,

THE SEA

Mais j'ai recours à toi pour l'exalter,
Une fois encor,
Et le grandir et le transfigurer
Mon corps,
En attendant qu'on t'apporte sa mort,
Pour à jamais la dissoudre, en ta vie.
Alors,
O mer, tu te perdras en tes furies
De renaissance et de fécondité.
Tu rouleras, en tes vagues et tes crinières,
Ma pourriture et ma poussière;
Tu mêleras à ta beauté
Toute mon ombre et tout mon deuil.
J'aurai l' immensité des forces pour cerceuil
Et leur travail obscur et leur ardeur occulte;
Mon être entier sera perdu, sera fondu
Dans le brassin géant de leurs tumultes,
Mais renaîtra, après milles et milles ans,
Vierge et divin, sauvage et clair et frissonnant,

Amas subtil de matière qui pense;
Moment nouveau de conscience;
Flamme nouvelle de clarté,
Dans les yeux d'or de l'immobile éternité!"

Comme de lumineux tombeaux,
Les vaisseaux blancs semblent posés,
De loin en loin, sur les plaines des eaux.

Le vent subtil n'est que baisers;
Et les écumes
Qui doucement, échouent
Contre les proues,
Ne sont que plumes:
Il fait dimanche sur la mer!

Emile Verhaeren

170

THE GYPSY TRAIL

A VALEDICTION

W E'RE bound for blue water where the
 great winds blow,
It's time to get the tacks aboard, time for us to
 go;
The crowd's at the capstan and the tune's in the
 shout,
" A long pull, a strong pull, *and warp the hooker
 out.*"

The bow-wash is eddying, spreading from the
 bows,
Aloft and loose the topsails and someone give a
 rouse;
A salt Atlantic chanty shall be music to the dead,
" A long pull, a strong pull, *and the yard to the
 mast-head.*"

Green and merry run the seas, the wind comes
 cold,
Salt and strong and pleasant, and worth a mint
 of gold;
And she's staggering, swooping, as she feels her
 feet,
" A long pull, a strong pull, *and aft the main-
 sheet.*"

Shrilly squeal the running sheaves, the weather-
 gear strains,
Such a clatter of chain-sheets, the devil's in the
 chains;
Over us the bright stars, under us the drowned,
" A long pull, a strong pull, *and we're outward
 bound.*"

THE SEA

Yonder, round and ruddy, is the mellow old
    moon,
The red-funneled tug has gone, and now, sonny,
    soon
We'll be clear of the Channel, so watch how you
    steer,
" Ease her when she pitches, *and so-long, my
    dear.*"

John Masefield

A WET SHEET AND A FLOWING SEA

A WET sheet and a flowing sea,—
    A wind that follows fast,
That fills the white and rustling sail,
    And bends the gallant mast,—
And bends the gallant mast, my boys,
    While, like the eagle free,
Away the good ship flies, and leaves
    Old England on the lee.

O for a soft and gentle wind!
    I heard a fair one cry;
But give to me the snoring breeze,
    And white waves heaving high,—
And white waves heaving high, my boys,
    The good ship tight and free;
The world of waters is our home,
    And merry men are we.

There's tempest in yon hornèd moon,
    And lightning in yon cloud;
And hark the music, mariners!
    The wind is piping loud,—

THE GYPSY TRAIL

The wind is piping loud, my boys,
　The lightning flashing free;
While the hollow oak our palace is,
　Our heritage the sea.
Allan Cunningham

OVER THE SEA OUR GALLEYS WENT

OVER the sea our galleys went,
　　With cleaving prows in order brave
To a speeding wind and a bounding wave,
　A gallant armament:
Each bark built out of a forest-tree
　Left leafy and rough as first it grew,
And nailed all over the gaping sides,
Within and without, with black bull-hides,
Seethed in fat and suppled in flame,
To bear the playful billows' game:
So, each good ship was rude to see,
Rude and bare to the outward view,
　But each upbore a stately tent
Where cedar pales in scented row
Kept out the flakes of the dancing brine,
And an awning drooped the mast below,
In fold on fold of the purple fine,
That neither noontide nor starshine
Nor moonlight cold which maketh mad,
　Might pierce the regal tenement.
When the sun dawned, oh, gay and glad
We set the sail and plied the oar;
But when the night-wind blew like breath,
For joy of one day's voyage more,
We sang together on the wide sea,
Like men at peace on a peaceful shore;
Each sail was loosed to the wind so free,

THE SEA

Each helm made sure by the twilight star,
And in a sleep as calm as death,
We, the voyagers from afar,
    Lay stretched along, each weary crew
In a circle round its wondrous tent
Whence gleamed soft light and curled rich scent,
    And with light and perfume, music too:
So the stars wheeled round and the darkness
        past,
And at morn we started beside the mast,
And still each ship was sailing fast.

Now, one morn, land appeared — a speck
Dim trembling betwixt sea and sky:
"Avoid it," cried our pilot, "check
    The shout, restrain the eager eye!"
But the heaving sea was black behind
For many a night and many a day,
And land, though but a rock, drew nigh;
So, we broke the cedar pales away,
Let the purple awning flap in the wind,
    And a statue bright was on every deck!
We shouted, every man of us,
And steered right into the harbour thus,
With pomp and paean glorious.

A hundred shapes of lucid stone!
    All day we built its shrine for each,
A shrine of rock for every one,
Nor paused till in the westering sun
    We sat together on the beach
To sing because our task was done.
When lo! what shouts and merry songs!
What laughter all the distance stirs!
A loaded raft with happy throngs
Of gentle islanders!
"Our isles are just at hand," they cried,
    "Like cloudlets faint in even sleeping.
183

THE GYPSY TRAIL

Our temple-gates are opened wide,
    Our olive-groves thick shade are keeping
For these majestic forms"— they cried.
O, then we awoke with sudden start
From our deep dream, and knew, too late,
How bare the rock, how desolate,
Which had received our precious freight:
    Yet we called out—" Depart!
Our gifts, once given, must here abide.
    Our work is done; we have no heart
To mar our work,"— we cried.

Robert Browning

SONG

THE boat is chafing at our long delay,
    And we must leave too soon
The spicy sea-pinks and the inborne spray,
    The tawny sands, the moon.

Keep us, O Thetis, in our western flight!
    Watch from thy pearly throne
Our vessel, plunging deeper into night
    To reach a land unknown.

John Davidson

THE POET'S VOYAGE

From *Alastor*

THE day was fair and sunny; sea and sky
    Drank its inspiring radiance, and the
        wind
Swept strongly from the shore, blackening the
    waves.
Following his eager soul, the wanderer

THE SEA

Leaped in the boat; he spread his cloak aloft
On the bare mast, and took his lonely seat,
And felt the boat speed o'er the tranquil sea
Like a torn cloud before the hurricane.

   As one that in a silver vision floats
Obedient to the sweep of odorous winds
Upon resplendent clouds, so rapidly
Along the dark and ruffled waters fled
The straining boat. A whirlwind swept it on,
With fierce gust and precipitating force,
Through the white ridges of the chafèd sea.
The waves arose. Higher and higher still
Their fierce necks writhed beneath the tempest's
      scourge
Like serpents struggling in a vulture's grasp.
Calm and rejoicing in the fearful war
Of wave ruining on wave, and blast on blast
Descending, and black flood on whirlpool driven
With dark obliterating course, he sate:
As if their genii were the ministers
Appointed to conduct him to the light
Of those belovèd eyes, the Poet sate
Holding the steady helm. Evening came on,
The beams of sunset hung their rainbow hues
High 'mid the shifting domes of sheeted spray
That canopied his path o'er the waste deep;
Twilight, ascending slowly from the east,
Entwined in duskier wreaths her braided locks
O'er the fair front and radiant eyes of day;
Night followed, clad with stars. On every side
More horribly the multitudinous streams
Of ocean's mountainous waste to mutual war
Rushed in dark tumult thundering, as to mock
The calm and spangled sky. The little boat
Still fled before the storm; still fled, like foam
Down the steep cataract of a wintry river;

THE GYPSY TRAIL

Now pausing on the edge of the riven wave;
Now leaving far behind the bursting mass
That fell, convulsing ocean; safely fled —
As if that frail and wasted human form,
Had been an elemental god.
                              At midnight
The moon arose: and lo! the ethereal cliffs
Of Caucasus, whose icy summits shone
Among the stars like sunlight, and around
Whose caverned base the' whirlpools and the
      waves
Bursting and eddying irresistibly
Rage and resound forever.— Who shall save? —
The boat fled on,— the boiling torrent drove,—
The crags closed round with black and jagged
      arms,
The shattered mountain overhung the sea,
And faster still, beyond all human speed,
Suspended on the sweep of the smooth wave,
The little boat was driven. A cavern there
Yawned, and amid its slant and winding depths
Ingulfed the rushing sea. The boat fled on
With unrelaxing speed.—"Vision and Love!"
The Poet cried aloud, "I have beheld
The path of thy departure. Sleep and death
Shall not divide us long!"
                    Percy Bysshe Shelley

CORSAIRS' SONG

O'ER the glad waters of the dark blue sea,
    Our thoughts as boundless and our souls
      as free,
Far as the breeze can bear, the billows foam,
Survey our empire, and behold our home!
These are our realms, no limits to their sway —
Our flag the sceptre all who meet obey.

THE SEA

Ours the wild life in tumult still to range
From toil to rest, and joy in every change.
Ah, who can tell? not thou, luxurious slave!
Whose soul would sicken at the heaving wave;
Nor thou, vain lord of wantonness and ease!
Whom slumber sooths not — pleasure cannot
    please —
O, who can tell, save he whose heart has tried,
And danced in triumph o'er the waters wide,
The exulting sense — the pulse's maddening
    play —
That thrills the wanderer of that trackless way?
                       Lord Byron

THE OCEAN

THERE is a pleasure in the pathless woods,
    There is a rapture on the lonely shore,
There is society, where none intrudes,
By the deep Sea, and music in its roar:
I love not man the less, but Nature more,
From these our interviews, in which I steal
From all I may be, or have been before,
To mingle with the Universe, and feel
What I can ne'er express, yet cannot all conceal.

Roll on, thou deep and dark blue ocean — roll!
Ten thousand fleets sweep over thee in vain;
Man marks the earth with ruin — his control
Stops with the shore; — upon the watery plain
The wrecks are all thy deed, nor doth remain
A shadow of man's ravage, save his own,
When, for a moment, like a drop of rain,
He sinks into thy depth with bubbling groan,
Without a grave, unknelled, uncoffined, and un-
    known.

THE GYPSY TRAIL

His steps are not upon thy paths,— thy fields
Are not a spoil for him,— thou dost arise
And shake him from thee; the vile strength he
    wields
For earth's destruction thou dost all despise,
Spurning him from thy bosom to the skies,
And send'st him, shivering in thy playful spray,
And howling, to his Gods, where haply lies
His petty hope in some near port or bay,
And dashest him again to earth: — there let him
    lay.

      •   •   •   •

Thou glorious mirror, where the Almighty's
    form
Glasses itself in tempests; in all time,
Calm or convulsed — in breeze, or gale, or
    storm,
Icing the pole, or in the torrid clime
Dark-heaving; — boundless, endless, and sub-
    lime —
The image of Eternity — the throne
Of the Invisible; even from out thy slime
The monsters of the deep are made; each zone
Obeys thee; thou goest forth, dread, fathomless,
    alone.

And I have loved thee, Ocean! and my joy
Of youthful sports was on thy breast to be
Borne, like thy bubbles, onward: from a boy
I wantoned with thy breakers — they to me
Were a delight; and if the freshening sea
Made them a terror —'twas a pleasing fear,
For I was, as it were, a child of thee,
And trusted to thy billows far and near,
And laid my hand upon thy mane — as I do here.

                           Lord Byron

THE SEA

ON THE LIDO

FROM *Julian and Maddalo*

I RODE one evening with Count Maddalo
   Upon the bank of land which breaks the
     flow
Of Adria towards Venice. A bare strand
Of hillocks, heaped from ever-shifting sand,
Matted with thistles and amphibious weeds,
Such as from earth's embrace the salt ooze
   breeds,
Is this; an uninhabited sea-side,
Which the lone fisher, when his nets are dried
Abandons; and no other object breaks
The waste but one dwarf tree and some few
   stakes
Broken and unrepaired, and the tide makes
A narrow space of level sand thereon,
Where 'twas our wont to ride while day went
   down.
This ride was my delight. I love all waste
And solitary places; where we taste
The pleasure of believing what we see
Is boundless, as we wish our souls to be:
And such was this wide ocean, and this shore
More barren than its billows; and yet more
Than all, with a remembered friend I love
To ride as then I rode; — for the winds drove
The living spray along the sunny air
Into our faces; the blue heavens were bare,
Stripped to their depths by the awakening north;
And, from the waves, sound like delight broke
   forth
Harmonizing with solitude, and sent
Into our hearts aërial merriment.

Percy Bysshe Shelley

THE GYPSY TRAIL

DRIFTING

MY soul to-day
  Is far away
Sailing the Vesuvian Bay;
  My winged boat,
  A bird afloat,
Swims round the purple peaks remote:

  Round purple peaks
  It sails and seeks
Blue inlets and their crystal creeks,
  Where high rocks throw,
  Through deeps below,
A duplicated golden glow.

Far, vague, and dim,
  The mountains swim;
While on Vesuvius' misty brim
  With outstretched hands,
  The gray smoke stands
O'erlooking the volcanic lands.

  Here Ischia smiles
  O'er liquid miles;
And yonder, bluest of the isles,
  Calm Capri waits,
  Her sapphire gates
Beguiling to her bright estates.

  I heed not, if
  My rippling skiff
Float swift or slow from cliff to cliff:
  With dreamful eyes
  My spirit lies
Under the walls of Paradise.

THE SEA

Under the walls
Where swells and falls
The bay's deep breast at intervals,
At peace I lie,
Blown softly by,
A cloud upon the liquid sky.

The day so mild
Is Heaven's own child,
With Earth and Ocean reconciled;
The airs I feel
Around me steal
Are murmuring to the murmuring keel.

Over the rail
My hand I trail
Within the shadow of the sail;
A joy intense,
The cooling sense
Glides down my drowsy indolence.

With dreamful eyes
My spirit lies
Where summer sings and never dies;
O'erveiled with vines,
She glows and shines
Among her future oil and wines.

Her children, hid
The cliffs amid,
Are gambolling with the gambolling kid;
Or down the walls
With tipsy calls,
Laugh in the rocks like waterfalls.

The fisher's child,
With tresses wild,
Unto the smooth, bright sand beguiled,

THE GYPSY TRAIL

With glowing lips
Sings as she skips,
And gazes at the far-off ships.

Yon deep bark goes
Where traffic blows,
From lands of sun to lands of snows;
This happier one,
Its course is run
From lands of snow to lands of sun.

O happy ship,
To rise and dip,
With the blue crystal at your lip!
O happy crew,
My heart with you
Sails, and sails, and sings anew!

No more, no more
The worldly shore
Upbraids me with its loud uproar!
With dreamful eyes
My spirit lies
Under the walls of Paradise.
Thomas Buchanan Read

IN GUERNSEY

I

THE heavenly bay, ringed round with cliffs
and moors,
Storm-stain'd ravines, and crags that lawns in-
lay,
Soothes as with love the rocks whose guard se-
cures
The heavenly bay.

THE SEA

O friend, shall time take ever this away,
This blessing given of beauty that endures,
This glory shown us, not to pass but stay?

Though sight be changed for memory, love en-
    sures
What memory, changed by love to sight, would
    say —
The word that seals forever mine and yours
    The heavenly bay.

II

My mother sea, my fostress, what new strand,
What new delight of waters, may this be,
The fairest found since time's first breezes
    fanned
    My mother sea?

Once more I give me body and soul to thee,
Who hast my soul forever: cliff and sand
Recede, and heart to heart once more are we.

My heart springs first and plunges, ere my hand
Strike out from shore: more close it brings to
    me,
More near and dear than seems my fatherland,
    My mother sea.

III

Across and along, as the bay's breadth opens, and
    o'er us
Wild autumn exults in the wind, swift rapture
    and strong
Impels us, and broader the wide waves brighten
    before us
    Across and along.

THE GYPSY TRAIL

The whole world's heart is uplifted and knows
    not wrong;
The whole world's life is a chant to the sea-
    tide's chorus;
Are we not as waves of the water, as notes of
    the song?

Like children unworn of the passions and toils
    that wore us,
We breast for a season the breadth of the seas
    that throng,
Rejoicing as they, to be borne as of old they
    bore us
    Across and along.
       •   •   •

Algernon Charles Swinburne

TRISTRAM OF LYONESSE

BUT by the sea-banks where at morn their foes
   Might find them, lay those knightly name-
    fellows,
One sick with grief of heart and sleepless, one
With heart of hope triumphant as the sun
Dreaming asleep of love and fame and fight:
But sleep at last wrapped warm the wan young
    knight;
And Tristram with the first pale windy light
Woke ere the sun spake summons, and his ear
Caught the sea's call that fired his heart to hear,
A noise of waking waters: for till dawn
The sea was silent as a mountain lawn
When the wind speaks not, and the pines are
    dumb,
And summer takes her fill ere autumn comes
Of life more soft than slumber: but ere day

THE SEA

Rose, and the first beam smote the bounding bay,
Up sprang the strength of the dark East, and
   took
With its wide wings the waters as they shook,
And hurled them huddling on aheap, and cast
The full sea shoreward with a great glad blast,
Blown from the heart of morning: and with joy
Full-souled and perfect passion, as a boy
That leaps up light to wrestle with the sea
For pure heart's gladness and large ecstasy,
Up sprang the might of Tristram; and his soul
Yearned for delight within him, and waxed
   whole
As a young child's with rapture of the hour
That brought his spirit and all the world to
   flower,
And all the bright blood in his veins beat time
To the wind's clarion and the water's chime
That called him and he followed it and stood
On the sand's verge before the grey great flood
Where the white hurtling heads of waves that
   met
Rose unsaluted of the sunrise yet.
And from his heart's root outward shot the sweet
Strong joy that thrilled him to the hands and
   feet,
Filling his limbs with pleasure and glad might,
And his soul drank the immeasurable delight
That earth drinks in with morning, and the free
Limitless love that lifts the stirring sea
When on her bare bright bosom as a bride
She takes the young sun, perfect in his pride,
Home to his place with passion: and the heart
Trembled for joy within the man whose part
Was here not least in living; and his mind
Was rapt abroad beyond man's meaner kind

THE GYPSY TRAIL

And pierced with love of all things and with
    mirth
Moved to make one with heaven and heavenlike
    earth
And with the light live water. So awhile
He watched the dim sea with a deepening smile,
And felt the sound and savor and swift flight
Of waves that fled beneath the fading night
And died before the darkness, like a song
With harps between and trumpets blown along
Through the loud air of some triumphant day,
Sink through his spirit and purge all sense away
Save of the glorious gladness of his hour
And all the world about to break in flower
Before the sovereign laughter of the sun;
And he, ere night's wide work lay all undone,
As earth from her bright body casts off night,
Cast off his raiment for a rapturous flight
And stood between the sea's edge and the sea
Naked, and godlike of his mould as he
Whose swift foot's sound shook all the towers
    of Troy;
So clothed with might, so girt upon with joy,
As, ere the knife had shorn to feed the fire
His glorious hair before the unkindled pyre
Whereon the half of his great heart was laid,
Stood, in the light of his live limbs arrayed,
Child of heroic earth and heavenly sea,
The flower of all men; scarce less bright than
    he,
If any of all men latter-born might stand,
Stood Tristram, silent, on the glimmering strand.
Not long: but with a cry of love that rang
As from a trumpet golden-mouthed, he sprang,
As toward a mother's where his head might rest
Her child rejoicing, toward the strong sea's
    breast

THE SEA

That none may gird nor measure; and his heart
Sent forth a shout that bade his lips not part,
But triumphed in him silent; no man's voice,
No song, no sound of clarions that rejoice,
Can set that glory forth which fills with fire
The body and the soul that have their whole
    desire
Silent, and freer than birds or dreams are free
Take all their will of all the encountering sea.
And toward the foam he bent and forward smote,
Laughing, and launched his body like a boat
Full to the sea-breach, and against the tide
Struck strongly forth with amorous arms made
    wide
To take the bright breast of the wave to his
And on his lips the sharp sweet minute's kiss
Given of the wave's lip for a breath's space
    curled
And pure as at the daydawn of the world.
And round him all the bright rough shuddering
    sea
Kindled, as though the world were even as he,
Heart-stung with exultation of desire;
And all the life that moved him seemed to
    aspire,
As all the sea's life toward the sun; and still
Delight within him waxed with quickening will
More smooth and strong and perfect as a flame
That springs and spreads, till each glad limb be-
    came
A note of rapture in the tune of life,
Live music mild and keen as sleep and strife:
Till the sweet change that bids the sense grow
    sure
Of deeper depth and purity more pure
Wrapped him and lapped him round with clearer
    cold,

THE GYPSY TRAIL

And all the rippling green grew royal gold
Between him and the far sun's rising rim.
And like the sun his heart rejoiced in him,
And brightened with a broadening flame of mirth:
And hardly seemed its life a part of earth,
But the life kindled of a fiery birth
And passion of a new-begotten son
Between the live sea and the living sun.
And mightier grew the joy to meet full-faced
Each wave, and mount with upward plunge, and
    taste
The rapture of its rolling strength, and cross
Its flickering crown of snows that flash and toss
Like plumes in battle's blithest charge, and
    thence
To match the next with yet more strenuous
    sense;
Till on his eyes the light beat hard and bade
His face turn west and shoreward through the
    glad
Swift revel of the waters golden-clad,
And back with light reluctant heart he bore
Across the broad-backed rollers in to shore,
Strong-spirited for the chance and cheer of
    fight,
And donned his arms again, and felt the might
In all his limbs rejoice for strength, and praised
God for such life as that whereon he gazed,
And wist not surely its joy was even as fleet
As that which laughed and lapsed against his
    feet,
The bright thin grey foam-blossom, glad and
    hoar,
That flings its flower along the flowerless shore
On sand or shingle, and still with sweet strange
    snows
As where one great white storm-dishevelled rose

THE SEA

May rain her wild leaves on a windy land,
Strews for long leagues the sounding slope of
strand,
And flower on flower falls flashing and anew
A fresh light leaps up whence the last flash flew,
And casts its brief glad gleam of life away
To fade not flowerwise but as drops the day
Storm-smitten, when at once the dark devours
Heaven and the sea and earth with all their flow-
ers;
No star in heaven, on earth no rose to see,
But the white blown brief blossoms of the sea,
That make her green gloom starrier than the
sky,
Dance yet before the tempest's tune, and die.
And all these things he glanced upon, and knew
How fair they shone, from earth's least flake of
dew
To stretch of seas and imminence of skies,
Unwittingly, with unpresageful eyes,
For the last time. The world's half heavenly
face,
The music of the silence of the place,
The confluence and refluence of the sea,
The wind's note ringing over wold and lea,
Smote once more through him keen as fire that
smote,
Rang once more through him one reverberate
note,
That faded as he turned again and went,
Fulfilled by strenuous joy with strong content,
To take his last delight of labor done
That yet should be beholden of the sun.

•   •   •   •

Algernon Charles Swinburne

THE GYPSY TRAIL

SWIMMING AT SUNRISE

A S one that ere a June day rise
   Makes seaward for the dawn, and tries
  The water with delighted limbs
  That taste the sweet dark sea, and swims
Right eastward under strengthening skies,
  And sees the gradual rippling rims
Of waves whence day breaks blossom-wise
  Take fire ere light peer well above,
  And laughs from all his heart with love;

And softlier swimming with raised head
Feels the full flower of morning shed
  And fluent sunrise round him rolled
  That laps and laves his body bold
With fluctuant heaven in water's stead,
  And urgent through the growing gold
Strikes, and sees all the spray flash red,
  And his soul takes the sun, and yearns
  For joy wherewith the sea's heart burns;

So the soul seeking through the dark
Heavenward, a dove without an ark,
  Transcends the unnavigable sea
  Of years that wear out memory;
So calls, a sunward-singing lark,
  In the ear of souls that should be free;
So points them toward the sun for mark
  Who steer not for the stress of waves,
  And seek strange helmsmen, and are slaves.

For if the swimmer's eastward eye
Must see no sunrise — must put by
  The hope that lifted him and led
  Once, to have light about his head,
To see beneath the clear low sky

THE SEA

The green foam-whitened wave wax red
And all the morning's banner fly —
   Then, as earth's helpless hopes go down,
   Let earth's self in the dark tides drown.

Yea, if no morning must behold
Man, other than were they now cold,
   And other deeds than past deeds done,
   Nor any near or far-off sun
Salute him risen and sunlike-souled,
   Free, boundless, fearless, perfect, one,
Let man's world die like worlds of old,
   And here in heaven's sight only be
   The sole sun on a worldless sea.
Algernon Charles Swinburne

CHORUS

From *Hippolytus*

COULD I take me to some cavern for mine
  hiding,
  In the hill-tops where the Sun scarce hath
    trod;
Or a cloud make the home of mine abiding,
  As a bird among the bird-droves of God!
    Could I wing me to my rest amid the roar
    Of the deep Adriatic on the shore,
Where the water of Eridanus is clear,
  And Phaëthon's sad sisters by his grave
Weep into the river, and each tear
  Gleams, a drop of amber, in the wave.

To the strand of the Daughters of the Sunset,
  The Apple-tree, the singing and the gold;
Where the mariner must stay him from his on-
    set,
  And the red wave is tranquil as of old;

THE GYPSY TRAIL

Yea, beyond that Pillar of the End
That Atlas guardeth, would I wend;
Where a voice of living waters never ceaseth
In God's quiet garden by the sea,
And Earth, the ancient life-giver, increaseth
Joy among the meadows like a tree.

Euripides
Translation by Gilbert Murray

CHORUS

FROM *The Bacchae*

WHERE is the Home for me?
O Cyprus, set in the sea,
Aphrodite's home In the soft sea-foam,
Would I could wend to thee;
Where the wings of the Loves are furled,
And faint the heart of the world.

Aye, unto Paphos' isle,
Where the rainless meadows smile
With riches rolled From the hundred-fold
Mouths of the far-off Nile,
Streaming beneath the waves
To the roots of the sea-ward caves.

But a better land is there
Where Olympus cleaves the air,
The high still dell Where the Muses dwell,
Fairest of all things fair!
O there is Grace, and there is the Heart's De-
sire,
And peace to adore thee, thou Spirit of Guiding
Fire!

Euripides
Translation by Gilbert Murray
202

THE HILLS

Perchè non sali il dilettoso monte — ?

Dante

See, in the evening-glow,
How sharp the silver spear-heads charge
When Alp meets heaven in snow!

Browning

Thin, thin the pleasant human noises grow,
  And faint the city gleams;
Rare the lone pastoral huts — marvel not thou!
The solemn peaks but to the stars are known,
But to the stars and the cold lunar beams;
Alone the sun arises, and alone
  Spring the great streams.

Arnold

THE HILLS

THE SUMMONS

FROM *Monadnoc*

UP! — If thou knew'st who calls
    To twilight parks of beech and pine,
High o'er the river intervals,
Above the ploughman's highest line,
Over the owner's farthest walls!
Up! where the the airy citadel
O'erlooks the surging landscape's swell!
Let not unto the stones the Day
Her lily and rose, her sea and land display.
Read the celestial sign!
Lo! the south answers to the north;
Bookworm, break this sloth urbane;
A greater spirit bids thee forth
Than the gray dreams which thee detain.
Mark how the climbing Oreads
Beckon thee to their arcades;
Youth, for a moment free as they,
Teach thy feet to feel the ground,
Ere yet arrives the wintry day
When Time thy feet has bound
Take the bounty of thy birth,
Taste the lordship of the earth.
              Ralph Waldo Emerson

PARTING

YE storm-winds of Autumn!
    Who rush by, who shake
The window, and ruffle
The gleam-lighted lake;

205

THE GYPSY TRAIL

Who cross to the hillside
Thin-sprinkled with farms,
Where the high woods strip sadly
Their yellowing arms,—
Ye are bound for the mountains!
Ah! with you let me go
Where your cold, distant barrier,
The vast range of snow,
Through the loose clouds lifts dimly
Its white peaks in air,—
How deep is their stillness!
Ah! would I were there!

.   .   .   .

Hark! fast by the window
The rushing winds go,
To the ice-cumbered gorges,
The vast seas of snow!
There the torrents drive upward
Their rock-strangled hum;
There the avalanche thunders
The hoarse torrent dumb.
—I come, O ye mountains!
Ye torrents, I come!

.   .   .   .

Hark! the wind rushes past us!
Ah! with that let me go
To the clear, waning hill-side,
Unspotted by snow,
There to watch, o'er the sunk vale,
The frore mountain wall,
Where the niched snow-bed sprays down
Its powdery fall.
There its dusky blue clusters
The aconite spreads;
There the pines slope, the cloud-strips
Hung soft in their heads.

THE HILLS

No life but, at moments,
The mountain bee's hum.
— I come, O ye mountains!
Ye pine-woods, I come!

    .   .   .   .

Blow, ye winds! lift me with you!
  I come to the wild.
Fold closely, O Nature!
  Thine arms round thy child.

To thee only God granted
  A heart ever new —
To all always open,
  To all always true.

Ah! calm me, restore me;
  And dry up my tears
On thy high mountain-platforms,
  Where morn first appears;

Where the white mists, for ever,
  Are spread and unfurl'd —
In the stir of the forces
  Whence issued the world.

Matthew Arnold

MORGENLIED

AT Mürren let the morning lead thee out
    To walk upon the cold and cloven hills,
To hear the congregated mountains shout
  Their paean of a thousand foaming rills:
Raimented with intolerable light,
  The snow-peaks stand above thee, row on row
Arising, each a seraph in his might;
  An organ each of varied stop doth blow.

THE GYPSY TRAIL

Heaven's azure dome trembles through all her
    spheres,
  Feeling that music vibrate; and the sun
Raises his tenor as he upward steers;
  And all the glory-coated mists that run
Beneath him in the valley, hear his voice,
And cry unto the dewy fields: rejoice!
             John Addington Symonds

PASSAGE OF THE APENNINES

LISTEN, listen, Mary mine,
    To the whisper of the Apennine,
It bursts on the roof like the thunder's roar,
Or like the sea on a northern shore,
Heard in its raging ebb and flow
By the captives pent in the cave below.
The Apennine in the light of day
Is a mighty mountain dim and grey,
Which between the earth and sky doth lay;
But when night comes, a chaos dread
On the dim starlight then is spread,
And the Apennine walks abroad with the storm.
             Percy Bysshe Shelley

THE CLOUD

I BRING fresh showers for the thirsting flow-
   ers,
  From the seas and the streams;
I bear light shade for the leaves when laid
  In their noonday dreams.
From my wings are shaken the dews that waken
  The sweet buds every one,
When rocked to rest on their mother's breast,

THE HILLS

As she dances about the sun.
I wield the flail of the lashing hail,
    And whiten the green plains under,
And then again I dissolve it in rain,
    And laugh as I pass in thunder.

I sift the snow on the mountains below,
    And their great pines groan aghast;
And all the night 'tis my pillow white,
    While I sleep in the arms of the blast.
Sublime on the towers of my skyey bowers,
    Lightning my pilot sits,
In a cavern under is fettered the thunder,
    It struggles and howls at fits;
Over earth and ocean, with gentle motion,
    This pilot is guiding me,
Lured by the love of the genii that move
    In the depths of the purple sea;
Over the rills, and the crags, and the hills,
    Over the lakes and the plains,
Wherever he dream, under mountain or stream,
    The Spirit he loves remains;
And I all the while bask in heaven's blue smile,
    Whilst he is dissolving in rains.

The sanguine sunrise, with his meteor eyes,
    And his burning plumes outspread,
Leaps on the back of my sailing rack,
    When the morning star shines dead,
As on the jag of a mountain crag,
    Which an earthquake rocks and swings,
An eagle alit one moment may sit
    In the light of its golden wings.
And when sunset may breathe, from the lit sea
    beneath,
    Its ardors of rest and of love,
And the crimson pall of eve may fall

THE GYPSY TRAIL

From the depths of heaven above,
With wings folded I rest, on mine airy nest,
   As still as a brooding dove.

That orbèd maiden with white fire laden,
   Whom mortals call the moon,
Glides glimmering o'er my fleece-like floor,
   By the midnight breezes strewn;
And wherever the beat of her unseen feet,
   Which only the angels hear,
May have broken the woof of my tent's thin
     roof,
   The stars peep behind her and peer;
And I laugh to see them whirl and flee,
   Like a swarm of golden bees,
When I widen the rent in my wind-built tent,
   Till the calm rivers, lakes, and seas,
Like strips of the sky fallen thro' me on high,
   Are each paved with the moon and these.

I bind the sun's throne with a burning zone,
   And the moon's with a girdle of pearl;
The volcanoes are dim, and the stars reel and
     swim,
   When the whirlwinds my banner unfurl.
From cape to cape, with a bridge-like shape,
   Over a torrent sea,
Sunbeam-proof, I hang like a roof,
   The mountains its columns be.
The triumphal arch thro' which I march
   With hurricane, fire, and snow,
When the powers of the air are chained to my
     chair,
   Is the million-colored bow;
The sphere-fire above its soft colors wove,
   While the moist earth was laughing below.

THE HILLS

I am the daughter of earth and water,
    And the nursling of the sky;
I pass thro' the pores of the ocean and shores;
    I change, but I cannot die.
For after the rain when with never a stain,
    The pavilion of heaven is bare,
And the winds and sunbeams with their convex
       gleams,
    Build up the blue dome of air,
I silently laugh at my own cenotaph,
    And out of the caverns of rain,
Like a child from the womb, like a ghost from
    the tomb,
    I arise and unbuild it again.
Percy Bysshe Shelley

THE CHASE

I

THE stag at eve had drunk his fill,
    Where danced the moon on Monan's rill,
And deep his midnight lair had made
In lone Glenartney's hazel shade;
But, when the sun his beacon red
Had kindled on Benvoirlich's head,
The deep-mouthed bloodhound's heavy bay
Resounded up the rocky way,
And faint, from farther distance borne,
Were heard the clanging hoof and horn.

II

As chief who hears his warder call,
"To arms! the foemen storm the wall!"
The antlered monarch of the waste
Sprang from his heathery couch in haste.
But ere his fleet career he took,

THE GYPSY TRAIL

The dew-drops from his flanks he shook;
Like crested leader proud and high,
Tossed his beamed frontlet to the sky;
A moment gazed adown the dale,
A moment snuffed the tainted gale,
A moment listened to the cry,
That thickened as the chase drew nigh;
Then, as the headmost foes appeared,
With one brave bound the copse he cleared,
And, stretching forward free and far,
Sought the wild heaths of Uam-Var.

III

Yelled on the view the opening pack,
Rock, glen, and cavern paid them back;
To many a mingled sound at once
The awakened mountain gave response.
A hundred dogs bayed deep and strong,
Clattered a hundred steeds along,
Their peal the merry horns rang out,
A hundred voices joined the shout;
With hark, and whoop, and wild halloo,
No rest Benvoirlich's echoes knew.
Far from the tumult fled the roe,
Close in her covert cowered the doe,
The falcon from her cairn on high,
Cast on the rout a wondering eye,
Till far beyond her piercing ken,
The hurricane had swept the glen.
Faint, and more faint, its failing din
Returned from cavern, cliff, and linn,
And silence settled, wide and still,
On the lone wood and mighty hill.

IV

Less loud the sounds of silvan war
Disturbed the heights of Uam-Var,

THE HILLS

And roused the cavern where 'tis told
A giant made his den of old;
For ere that steep ascent was won,
High in his pathway hung the sun,
And many a gallant, stayed perforce,
Was fain to breathe his faltering horse;
And of the trackers of the deer,
Scarce half the lessening pack was near;
So shrewdly on the mountain side,
Had the bold burst their mettle tried.

V

The noble stag was pausing now
Upon the mountain's southern brow
Where broad extended far beneath,
The varied realms of fair Menteith.
With anxious eye he wandered o'er
Mountain and meadow, moss and moor,
And pondered refuge from his toil,
By far Lochard or Aberfoyle.
But nearer was the copsewood gray
That waved and wept on Loch-Achray,
And mingled with the pine-trees blue
On the bold cliffs of Benvenue.
Fresh vigor with the hope returned,
With flying foot the heath he spurned,
Held westward with unwearied race,
And left behind the panting chase.

VI

'Twere long to tell what steeds gave o'er,
As swept the hunt through Cambus-more;
What reins were tightened in despair,
When rose Benledi's ridge in air;
Who flagged upon Bochastle's heath,

THE GYPSY TRAIL

Who shunned to stem the flooded Teith,—
For twice that day, from shore to shore,
The gallant stag swam stoutly o'er.
Few were the stragglers, following far,
That reached the lake of Vennachar;
And when the Brigg of Turk was won,
The headmost horseman rode alone.

VII

Alone, but with unbated zeal,
That horseman plied the scourge and steel;
For, jaded now, and spent with toil,
Embossed with foam, and dark with soil,
While every gasp with sobs he drew,
The laboring stag strained full in view.
Two dogs of black St. Hubert's breed,
Unmatched for courage, breath, and speed,
Fast on his flying traces came,
And all but won that desperate game;
For, scarce a spear's length from his haunch,
Vindictive toiled the bloodhounds stanch;
Nor nearer might the dogs attain,
Nor farther might the quarry strain.
Thus up the margin of the lake,
Between the precipice and brake,
O'er stock and rock their race they take.

VIII

The hunter marked that mountain high,
The lone lake's western boundary,
And deemed the stag must turn to bay,
Where that huge rampart barred the way;
Already glorying in the prize,
Measured his antlers with his eyes;
For the death-wound and death-halloo,
Mustered his breath, his whinyard drew;

THE HILLS

But, thundering as he came prepared,
With ready arm and weapon bared,
The wily quarry shunned the shock,
And turned him from the opposing rock;
Then, dashing down a darksome glen,
Soon lost to hound and hunter's ken,
In the deep Trosach's wildest nook
His solitary refuge took.
There while close-couched the thicket shed
Cold dews and wild-flowers on his head,
He heard the baffled dogs in vain
Rave through the hollow pass amain,
Chiding the rocks that yelled again.

IX

Close on the hounds the hunter came,
To cheer them on the vanished game;
But, stumbling in the rugged dell,
The gallant horse, exhausted, fell.
The impatient rider strove in vain
To rouse him with the spur and rein,
For the good steed, his labors o'er,
Stretched his stiff limbs to rise no more;
Then, touched with pity and remorse,
He sorrowed o'er the expiring horse: —
" I little thought, when first thy rein
I slacked upon the banks of Seine,
That Highland eagle e'er should feed
On thy fleet limbs, my matchless steed!
Woe worth the chase, woe worth the day,
That costs thy life, my gallant gray!"

X

Then through the dell his horn resounds,
From vain pursuit to call the hounds.
Back limped, with slow and crippled pace,

THE GYPSY TRAIL

The sulky leaders of the chase:
Close to their master's side they pressed,
With drooping tail and humbled crest;
But still the dingle's hollow throat
Prolonged the swelling bugle-note.
The owlets started from their dream,
The eagles answered with their scream,
Round and around the sounds were cast,
Till echo seemed an answering blast;
And on the hunter hied his way,
To join some comrades of the day;
Yet often paused, so strange the road,
So wondrous were the scenes it showed.

XI

The western waves of ebbing day
Rolled o'er the glen their level way;
Each purple peak, each flinty spire,
Was bathed in floods of living fire.
But not a setting beam could glow
Within the dark ravines below,
Where twined the path in shadow hid,
Round many a rocky pyramid,
Shooting abruptly from the dell
Its thunder-splintered pinnacle;
Round many an insulated mass,
The native bulwarks of the pass,
Huge as the tower which builders vain
Presumptuous piled on Shinar's plain.
Their rocky summits, split and rent,
Formed turret, dome, or battlement,
Or seemed fantastically set
With cupola or minaret,
Wild crests as pagod ever decked,
Or mosque of Eastern architect.
Nor were these earth-born castles bare,

THE HILLS

Nor lacked they many a banner fair;
For, from their shivered brows displayed,
Far o'er the unfathomable glade,
All twinkling with the dew drops' sheen,
The brier-rose fell in streamers green,
And creeping shrubs of thousand dyes,
Waved in the west-wind's summer sighs.

XII

Boon Nature scattered, free and wild,
Each plant or flower, the mountain's child.
Here eglantine embalmed the air,
Hawthorn and hazel mingled there;
The primrose pale, and violet flower,
Found in each cliff a narrow bower;
Fox-glove and night-shade, side by side,
Emblems of punishment and pride,
Grouped their dark hues with every stain
The weather-beaten crags retain.
With boughs that quaked at every breath,
Gray birch and aspen wept beneath;
Aloft, the ash and warrior oak
Cast anchor in the rifted rock;
And, higher yet, the pine-tree hung
His shattered trunk, and frequent flung,
Where seemed the cliffs to meet on high,
His boughs athwart the narrowed sky.
Highest of all, where white peaks glanced,
Where glistening streamers waved and danced,
The wanderer's eye could barely view
The summer heaven's delicious blue;
So wondrous wild, the whole might seem
The scenery of a fairy dream.

THE GYPSY TRAIL

XIII

Onward, amid the copse 'gan peep
A narrow inlet, still and deep,
Affording scarce such breadth of brim,
As served the wild-duck's brood to swim.
Lost for a space, through thickets veering,
But broader when again appearing,
Tall rocks and tufted knolls their face
Could on the dark-blue mirror trace;
And farther as the hunter strayed,
Still broader sweep its channels made.
The shaggy mounds no longer stood,
Emerging from entangled wood,
But, wave-encircled, seemed to float,
Like castle girdled with its moat;
Yet broader floods extending still,
Divide them from their parent hill,
Till each, retiring, claims to be
An islet in an inland sea.

XIV

And now, to issue from the glen,
No pathway meets the wanderer's ken,
Unless he climb, with footing nice,
A far projecting precipice.
The broom's tough roots his ladder made,
The hazel saplings lent their aid;
And thus an airy point he won,
Where, gleaming with the setting sun,
One burnished sheet of living gold,
Loch Katrine lay beneath him rolled,
In all her length far winding lay,
With promontory, creek, and bay,
And islands that, empurpled bright,
Floated amid the livelier light;
And mountains, that like giants stand,

THE HILLS

To sentinel enchanted land.
High on the south, huge Benvenue
Down on the lake in masses threw
Crags, knolls, and mounds, confusedly hurled,
The fragments of an earlier world;
A wildering forest feathered o'er
His ruined sides and summit hoar,
While on the north, through middle air,
Ben-an heaved high his forehead bare.

Sir Walter Scott

DAWN ON THE ALPS

From *Prometheus Unbound*

BENEATH is a wide plain of billowy mist,
   As a lake, paving in the morning sky,
With azure waves which burst in silver light,
Some Indian vale. Behold it, rolling on
Under the curdling winds, and islanding
The peak whereon we stand, midway, around,
Encinctured by the dark and blooming forests,
Dim twilight-lawns, and stream-illumined caves,
And wind-enchanted shapes of wandering mist;
And far on high the keen sky-cleaving moun-
   tains
From icy spires of sun-like radiance fling
The dawn, as lifted Ocean's dazzling spray,
From some Atlantic islet scattered up,
Spangles the wind with lamp-like waterdrops.
The vale is girdled with their walls, a howl
Of cataracts from their thaw-cloven ravines,
Satiates the listening wind, continuous, vast,
Awful as silence. Hark! the rushing snow!
The sun-awakened avalanche! whose mass,
Thrice sifted by the storm, had gathered there
Flake after flake, in heaven-defying minds

As thought by thought is piled, till some **great**
    truth
Is loosened, and the nations echo round,
Shaken to their roots, as do the mountains **now.**

       .   .   .

Look how the gusty sea of mist is breaking
In crimson foam, even at our feet! it rises
As Ocean at the enchantment of the moon.
                      Percy Bysshe Shelley

MONT BLANC

I

THE everlasting universe of things
    Flows thro' the mind, and rolls its **rapid**
      waves,
Now   dark—now   glittering—now   reflecting
    gloom—
Now lending splendor, where from secret springs
The source of human thought its tribute brings
Of waters,— with a sound but half its own,
Such as a feeble brook will oft assume
In the wild woods, among the mountains lone,
Where waterfalls around it leap for ever,
Where woods and winds contend, and a **vast**
    river
Over its rocks ceaselessly bursts and raves.

II

Thus thou, Ravine of Arve—dark, deep Ra-
    vine—
Thou many-colored, many-voicèd vale,
Over whose pines, and crags, and caverns sail
Fast cloud-shadows and sunbeams: awful scene,
Where Power in likeness of the Arve comes
    down

THE HILLS

From the ice gulfs that gird his secret throne,
Bursting thro' these dark mountains like the
    flame
Of lightning thro' the tempest; — thou dost lie,
Thy giant brood of pines around thee clinging,
Children of elder time, in whose devotion
The chainless winds still come and ever came
To drink their odors, and their mighty swinging
To hear — an old and solemn harmony;
Thine earthly rainbows stretched across the
    sweep
Of the ethereal waterfall, whose veil
Robes some unsculptured image; the strange
    sleep
Which when the voices of the desert fail
Wraps all in its own deep eternity; —
Thy caverns echoing to the Arve's commotion,
A loud, lone sound no other sound can tame;
Thou art pervaded with that ceaseless motion,
Thou art the path of that unresting sound —
Dizzy Ravine! and when I gaze on thee
I seem as in a trance sublime and strange
To muse on my own separate fantasy,
My own, my human mind, which passively
Now renders and receives fast influencings,
Holding an unremitting interchange
With the clear universe of things around;
One legion of wild thoughts, whose wandering
    wings
Now float above thy darkness, and now rest
Where that or thou art no unbidden guest,
In the still cave of the witch Poesy,
Seeking among the shadows that pass by
Ghosts of all things that are, some shade of thee,
Some phantom, some faint image; till the breast
From which they fled recalls them, thou art there!

III

Some say that gleams of a remoter world
Visit the soul in sleep,— that death is slumber,
And that its shapes the busy thoughts outnumber
Of those who wake and live.— I look on high;
Has some unknown omnipotence unfurled
The veil of life and death? or do I lie
In dream, and does the mightier world of sleep
Spread far around and inaccessibly
Its circles? For the very spirit fails,
Driven like a homeless cloud from steep to steep
That vanishes among the viewless gales!
Far, far above, piercing the infinite sky,
Mont Blanc appears,— still, snowy, and serene —
Its subject mountains their unearthly forms
Pile around it, ice and rock; broad vales be-
    tween
Of frozen floods, unfathomable deeps,
Blue as the overhanging heaven, that spread
And wind among the accumulated steeps;
A desert peopled by the storms alone,
Save when the eagle brings some hunter's bone,
And the wolf tracks her there — how hideously

Its shapes are heaped around! rude, bare, and
    high,
Ghastly, and scarred, and riven.— Is this the
    scene
Where the old Earthquake-daemon taught her
    young
Ruin? Were these their toys? or did a sea
Of fire, envelop once this silent snow?
None can reply — all seems eternal now.
The wilderness has a mysterious tongue
Which teaches awful doubt, or faith so mild,
So solemn, so serene, that man may be
But for such faith with nature reconciled;

THE HILLS

Thou hast a voice, great Mountain, to repeal
Large codes of fraud and woe; not understood
By all, but which the wise and great and good
Interpret, or make felt, or deeply feel.

IV

The fields, the lakes, the forests, and the streams,
Ocean, and all the living things that dwell
Within the daedal earth; lightning and rain,
Earthquake and fiery flood and hurricane,
The torpor of the year when feeble dreams
Visit the hidden buds, or dreamless sleep
Holds every future leaf and flower; the bound
With which from that detested trance they leap;
The works and ways of men, their death and
    birth,
And that of him, and all that his may be;
All things that move and breathe with toil and
    sound
Are born and die, revolve, subside, and swell.
Power dwells apart in its tranquillity,
Remote, serene, and inaccessible:
And *this,* the naked countenance of earth
On which I gaze, even these primeval mountains,
Teach the adverting mind. The glaciers creep,
Like snakes that watch their prey, from their far
    fountains,
Slow rolling on; there, many a precipice,
Frost and the Sun in scorn of mortal power
Have piled — dome, pyramid, and pinnacle,
A city of death, distinct with many a tower
And wall impregnable of beaming ice.
Yet not a city, but a flood of ruin
Is there that from the boundaries of the skies
Rolls its perpetual stream; vast pines are strew-
    ing

Its destined path, or in the mangled soil
Branchless and shattered stand; the rocks, drawn
    down
From yon remotest waste, have overthrown
The limits of the dead and living world,
Never to be reclaimed. The dwelling-place
Of insects, beasts, and birds, becomes its spoil;
Their food and their retreat forever gone,
So much of life and joy is lost. The race
Of man flies far in dread; his work and dwelling
Vanish, like smoke before the tempest's stream,
And their place is not known. Below, vast caves
Shine in the rushing torrent's restless gleam,
Which from those secret chasms in tumult well-
    ing
Meet in the vale; and one majestic River,
The breath and blood of distant lands, forever
Rolls its loud waters to the ocean-waves,
Breathes its swift vapors to the circling air.

V

Mont Blanc yet gleams on high: the power is
    there,
The still and solemn power of many sights
And many sounds, and much of life and death.
In the calm darkness of the moonless nights,
In the lone glare of day, the snows descend
Upon that Mountain; none beholds them there,
Nor when the flakes burn in the sinking sun,
Or the star-beams dart through them:— Winds
    contend
Silently there, and heap the snow, with breath
Rapid and strong, but silently. Its home
The voiceless lightning in these solitudes
Keeps innocently, and like vapor broods
Over the snow. The secret strength of things,

Which governs thought, and to the infinite dome
Of heaven is as a law, inhabits thee.
And what wert thou and earth and stars and
     sea,
If to the human Mind's imaginings
Silence and Solitude were vacancy?

Percy Bysshe Shelley

ALPENJÄGER'S LIED

ES donnern die Höhen, es zittert der Steg,
   Nicht grauet dem Schützen auf schwind-
    lichtem Weg.
Er schreitet verwegen
Auf Feldern von Eis,
Da pranget kein Frühling,
Da grünet kein Reis;
Und unter den Füssen ein neblichtes Meer,
Erkennt er die Städte der Menschen nicht mehr;
Durch den Riss nur der Wolken
Erblickt er die Welt,
Tief unter den Wassern
Das grünende Feld.

Friedrich von Schiller

HYMN

BEFORE SUN-RISE, IN THE VALE OF CHAMOUNI

*Besides the rivers Arve and Arveiron, which
have their sources in the foot of Mont Blanc, five
conspicuous torrents rush down its sides; and
within a few paces of the Glaciers, the Gentiana
Major grows in immense numbers with its " flow-
ers of loveliest blue."*

THE GYPSY TRAIL

H AST thou a charm to stay the morning-star
    In his steep course? So long he seems to
        pause
On thy bald awful head, O sovran Blanc!
The Arve and Arveiron at thy base
Rave ceaselessly; but thou, most awful Form!
Risest from forth thy silent sea of pines,
How silently! Around thee and above
Deep is the air and dark, substantial, black,
An ebon mass: methinks thou piercest it,
As with a wedge! But when I look again,
It is thine own calm home, thy crystal shrine,
Thy habitation from eternity!
O dread and silent Mount! I gazed upon thee,
Till thou, still present to the bodily sense,
Didst vanish from my thought: entranced in
        prayer
I worshipped the Invisible alone.

    Yet, like some sweet beguiling melody,
So sweet, we know not we are listening to it,
Thou, the meanwhile, wast blending with my
        thought,
Yea, with my life and life's own secret joy:
Till the dilating Soul, enrapt, transfused,
Into the mighty vision passing — there
As in her natural form, swelled vast to Heaven!

    Awake, my soul! not only passive praise
Thou owest! not alone these swelling tears,
Mute thanks and secret ecstasy! Awake,
Voice of sweet song! Awake, my heart, awake,
Green vales and icy cliffs, all join my Hymn.

    Thou first and chief, sole sovran of the Vale!
O struggling with the darkness all the night,
And visited all night by troops of stars,

THE HILLS

Or when they climb the sky or when they sink:
Companion of the morning-star at dawn,
Thyself Earth's rosy star, and of the dawn
Co-herald: wake, O wake, and utter praise!
Who sank thy sunless pillars deep in Earth?
Who filled thy countenance with rosy light?
Who made thee parent of perpetual streams?

And you, ye five wild torrents fiercely glad!
Who called you forth from night and utter death,
From dark and icy caverns called you forth,
Down those precipitous, black, jagged Rocks,
Forever shattered and the same forever?
Who gave you your invulnerable life,
Your strength, your speed, your fury, and your
    joy,
Unceasing thunder and eternal foam?
And who commanded (and the silence came),
Here let the billows stiffen, and have rest?

Ye ice-falls! ye that from the mountain's brow
Adown enormous ravines slope amain —
Torrents, methinks, that heard a mighty voice,
And stopped at once amid their maddest plunge!
Motionless torrents! silent cataracts!
Who made you glorious as the gates of Heaven
Beneath the keen full moon? Who bade the sun
Clothe you with rainbows? Who, with living
    flowers
Of loveliest blue, spread garlands at your feet? —
God! let the torrents, like a shout of nations,
Answer! and let the ice-plains echo, God!
God! sing ye meadow-streams with gladsome
    voice!
Ye pine-groves, with your soft and soul-like
    sounds!
And they too have a voice, yon piles of snow,
And in their perilous fall shall thunder, God!

THE GYPSY TRAIL

Ye living flowers that skirt the eternal frost!
Ye wild goats sporting round the eagle's nest!
Ye eagles, play-mates of the mountain-storm!
Ye lightnings, the dread arrows of the clouds!
Ye signs and wonders of the element!
Utter forth God, and fill the hills with praise!

Thou too, hoar Mount! with thy sky-pointing
    peaks,
Oft from whose feet the avalanche, unheard,
Shoots downward, glittering through the pure
    serene
Into the depth of clouds that veil thy breast —
Thou too again, stupendous Mountain! thou
That as I raise my head, awhile bowed low
In adoration, upward from thy base
Slow travelling with dim eyes suffused with tears,
Solemnly seemest, like a vapory cloud,
To rise before me — Rise, O ever rise,
Rise like a cloud of incense, from the Earth!
Thou kingly Spirit throned among the hills,
Thou dread ambassador from Earth to Heaven,
Great hierarch! tell thou the silent sky,
And tell the stars, and tell yon rising sun,
Earth, with her thousand voices, praises God.
                        Samuel Taylor Coleridge

PSALM CXXI

I WILL lift up mine eyes unto the hills, from
    whence cometh my help.
My help cometh from the Lord, which made
    heaven and earth.
He will not suffer thy foot to be moved: he that
    keepeth thee will not slumber.

THE HILLS

Behold, he that keepeth Israel shall neither slumber nor sleep.

The Lord is thy keeper: the Lord is thy shade upon thy right hand.

The sun shall not smite thee by day, nor the moon by night.

The Lord shall preserve thee from all evil: he shall preserve thy soul.

The Lord shall preserve thy going out and thy coming in from this time forth and even for evermore.

THE ROAD TO ELFLAND

And see ye not yon bonny road
That winds about the ferny brae?
That is the road to fair Elfland
Where you and I this night maun gae.

Old Ballad

Aus alten Märchen winkt es
Hervor mit weisser Hand,
Da singt es und da klingt es
Von einem Zauberland.

Wo alle Bäume sprechen,
Und singen wie ein Chor,
Und laute Quellen brechen
Wie Tanzmusik hervor.

Heine

THE ROAD TO ELFLAND

THE HORNS OF ELFLAND

THE splendor falls on castle walls
And snowy summits old in story:
The long light shakes across the lakes
And the wild cataract leaps in glory.
Blow, bugle, blow, set the wild echoes flying,
Blow, bugle; answer, echoes, dying, dying, dying!

O hark, O hear! how thin and clear,
And thinner, clearer, farther going!
O sweet and far from cliff and scar
The horns of Elfland faintly blowing!
Blow, let us hear the purple glens replying:
Blow, bugle; answer, echoes, dying, dying, dying!

O love, they die in yon rich sky,
They faint on hill or field or river:
Our echoes roll from soul to soul,
And grow for ever and for ever.
Blow, bugle, blow, set the wild echoes flying,
And answer, echoes, answer, dying, dying, dying!
Alfred, Lord Tennyson

FROM THE HILLS OF DREAM

ACROSS the silent stream
Where the slumber-shadows go,
From the dim blue Hills of Dream
I have heard the west wind blow.

THE GYPSY TRAIL

Who hath seen that fragrant land,
  Who hath seen that unscanned west?
Only the listless hand
  And the unpulsing breast.

But when the west wind blows
  I see moon-lances gleam
Where the Host of Faerie flows
  Athwart the Hills of Dream.

And a strange song I have heard
  By a shadowy stream,
And the singing of a snow-white bird
  On the Hills of Dream.

Fiona Macleod

THE FAIRIES

UP the airy mountain,
  Down the rushy glen,
We daren't go a-hunting
  For fear of little men;
Wee folk, good folk,
  Trooping all together;
Green jacket, red cap,
  And white owl's feather!

Down along the rocky shore
  Some make their home,
They live on crispy pancakes
  Of yellow tide-foam;
Some in the reeds
  Of the black mountain lake,
With frogs for their watch-dogs,
  All night awake.

THE ROAD TO ELFLAND

High on the hill-top
  The old King sits;
He is now so old and gray
  He's nigh lost his wits.
With a bridge of white mist
  Columbkill he crosses,
On his stately journeys
  From Slieveleague to Rosses;
Or going up with music
  On cold starry nights
To sup with the Queen
  Of the gay Northern Lights.

They stole little Bridget
  For seven years long;
When she came down again
  Her friends were all gone.
They took her lightly back,
  Between the night and morrow,
They thought that she was fast asleep,
  But she was dead with sorrow.
They have kept her ever since
  Deep within the lake,
On a bed of flag-leaves,
  Watching till she wake.

By the craggy hill-side,
  Through the mosses bare,
They have planted thorn-trees
  For pleasure here and there.
If any man so daring
  As dig them up in spite,
He shall find their sharpest thorns
  In his bed at night.

Up the airy mountain,
  Down the rushy glen,

THE GYPSY TRAIL

We daren't go a-hunting
    For fear of little men;
Wee folk, good folk,
    Trooping all together;
Green jacket, red cap,
    And white owl's feather!

William Allingham

FAERIES' SONG

FROM *The Land Of Heart's Desire*

THE wind blows out of the gates of the day,
    The wind blows over the lonely of heart,
And the lonely of heart is withered away,
While the faeries dance in a place apart,
Shaking their milk-white feet in a ring,
Tossing their milk-white arms in the air;
For they hear the wind laugh and murmur **and**
    sing
Of a land where even the old are fair,
And even the wise are merry of tongue;
But I heard a reed of Coolaney say,
"When the wind has laughed and murmured
    and sung,
The lonely of heart is withered away."

William Butler Yeats

WHERE THE BEE SUCKS

WHERE the bee sucks, there suck I:
    In a cowslip's bell I lie;
There I couch when owls do cry.
On the bat's back I do fly
After summer merrily.
Merrily, merrily, shall I live now
Under the blossom that hangs on the bough.

Shakespeare

THE ROAD TO ELFLAND

OVER HILL, OVER DALE

OVER hill, over dale,
   Thorough bush, thorough brier,
Over park, over pale,
Thorough flood, thorough fire,
  I do wander everywhere,
  Swifter than the moon's sphere;
  And I serve the fairy queen,
  To dew her orbs upon the green:
  The cowslips tall her pensioners be;
  In their gold coats spots you see;
  Those be rubies, fairy favors,
  In those freckles live their savors:
I must go seek some dew-drops here,
And hang a pearl in every cowslip's ear.
                      Shakespeare

YOU SPOTTED SNAKES

YOU spotted snakes, with double tongue,
   Thorny hedgehogs, be not seen;
Newts and blind-worms, do no wrong;
  Come not near our fairy queen.

    Philomel, with melody
    Sing in our sweet lullaby;
  Lulla, lulla, lullaby; lulla, lulla, lullaby;
      Never harm,
      Nor spell nor charm,
    Come our lovely lady nigh;
    So good-night, with lullaby.

THE GYPSY TRAIL

Weaving spiders, come not here;
  Hence, you long-legg'd spinners, hence!
Beetles black, approach not near;
  Worm, nor snail, do no offence.

    Philomel, with melody
    Sing in our sweet lullaby;
Lulla, lulla, lullaby; lulla, lulla, lullaby:
    Never harm,
    Nor spell nor charm,
    Come our lovely lady nigh;
    So good-night, with lullaby.

Shakespeare

COME UNTO THESE YELLOW SANDS

COME unto these yellow sands,
  And then take hands:
Court'sied when you have and kiss'd,
  The wild waves whist,
Foot it featly here and there,
And, sweet sprites, the burthen bear:
    Hark, hark!
      Bow-wow.
    The watchdog's bark:
      Bow-wow.
Hark, hark! I hear
The strain of strutting chanticleer
  Cry, Cock-a-diddle-dow.

Shakespeare

THE ROAD TO ELFLAND

FULL FATHOM FIVE

FULL fathom five thy father lies;
    Of his bones are coral made;
Those are pearls that were his eyes:
    Nothing of him that doth fade,
But doth suffer a sea-change
Into something rich and strange.
Sea-nymphs hourly ring his knell:
                    Ding-dong.
    Hark! now I hear them —
                    Ding-dong, bell!
                        Shakespeare

THE LADY OF SHALOTT

I

ON either side the river lie
    Long fields of barley and of rye,
That clothe the wold and meet the sky;
And thro' the field the road runs by
        To many-tower'd Camelot;
And up and down the people go,
Gazing where the lilies blow
Round an island there below,
        The island of Shalott.

Willows whiten, aspens quiver,
Little breezes dusk and shiver
Thro' the wave that runs for ever
By the island in the river
        Flowing down to Camelot.
Four gray walls, and four gray towers,
Overlook a space of flowers,
And the silent isle imbowers
        The Lady of Shalott.

THE GYPSY TRAIL

By the margin, willow-veil'd,
Slide the heavy barges trail'd
By slow horses; and unhail'd
The shallop flitteth silken-sail'd
    Skimming down to Camelot:
But who hath seen her wave her hand?
Or at the casement seen her stand?
Or is she known in all the land,
    The Lady of Shalott?

Only reapers, reaping early
In among the bearded barley,
Hear a song that echoes cheerly
From the river winding clearly,
    Down to tower'd Camelot:
And by the moon the reaper weary,
Piling sheaves in uplands airy,
Listening, whispers " 'Tis the fairy
    Lady of Shalott."

II

There she weaves by night and day
A magic web with colors gay.
She has heard a whisper say,
A curse is on her if she stay
    To look down to Camelot.
She knows not what the curse may be,
And so she weaveth steadily,
And little other care hath she,
    The Lady of Shalott.

And moving thro' a mirror clear
That hangs before her all the year,
Shadows of the world appear.
There she sees the highway near
    Winding down to Camelot:

THE ROAD TO ELFLAND

There the river eddy whirls,
And there the surly village-churls,
And the red cloaks of market girls,
    Pass onward from Shalott.

Sometimes a troop of damsels glad,
An abbot on an ambling pad,
Sometimes a curly shepherd-lad,
Or long-hair'd page in crimson clad,
    Goes by to tower'd Camelot;
And sometimes thro' the mirror blue
The knights come riding two and two:
She hath no loyal knight and true,
    The Lady of Shalott.

But in her web she still delights
To weave the mirror's magic sights,
For often thro' the silent nights
A funeral, with plumes and lights,
    And music, went to Camelot:
Or when the moon was overhead,
Came two young lovers lately wed;
"I am half sick of shadows," said
    The Lady of Shalott.

III

A bow-shot from her bower-eaves,
He rode between the barley-sheaves,
The sun came dazzling thro' the leaves,
And flamed upon the brazen greaves
    Of bold Sir Lancelot.
A red-cross knight for ever kneel'd
To a lady in his shield,
That sparkled on the yellow field,
    Beside remote Shalott.

THE GYPSY TRAIL

The gemmy bridle glitter'd free,
Like to some branch of stars we see
Hung in the golden Galaxy.
The bridle bells rang merrily
  As he rode down to Camelot:
And from his blazon'd baldric slung
A mighty silver bugle hung,
And as he rode his armor rung,
  Beside remote Shalott.

All in the blue unclouded weather
Thick-jewell'd shone the saddle-leather,
The helmet and the helmet-feather
Burn'd like one burning flame together,
  As he rode down to Camelot.
As often thro' the purple night,
Below the starry clusters bright,
Some bearded meteor, trailing light,
  Moves over still Shalott.

His broad clear brow in sunlight glow'd;
On burnish'd hooves his war-horse trode;
From underneath his helmet flow'd
His coal-black curls as on he rode,
  As he rode down to Camelot.
From the bank and from the river
He flash'd into the crystal mirror,
"Tirra lirra," by the river
  Sang Sir Lancelot.

She left the web, she left the loom,
She made three paces thro' the room,
She saw the water-lily bloom,
She saw the helmet and the plume,
  She look'd down to Camelot.

THE ROAD TO ELFLAND

Out flew the web and floated wide;
The mirror crack'd from side to side;
"The curse is come upon me," cried
    The Lady of Shalott.

IV

In the stormy east-wind straining,
The pale yellow woods were waning,
The broad stream in his banks complaining,
Heavily the low sky raining
    Over tower'd Camelot;
Down she came and found a boat
Beneath a willow left afloat,
And round about the prow she wrote
    The Lady of Shalott.

And down the river's dim expanse —
Like some bold seer in a trance,
Seeing all his own mischance —
With a glassy countenance
    Did she look to Camelot.
And at the closing of the day
She loosed the chain, and down she lay;
The broad stream bore her far away,
    The Lady of Shalott.

Lying, robed in snowy white
That loosely flew to left and right —
The leaves upon her falling light —
Thro' the noises of the night
    She floated down to Camelot.
And as the boat-head wound along
The willowy hills and fields among,
They heard her singing her last song,
    The Lady of Shalott.

THE GYPSY TRAIL

Heard a carol, mournful, holy,
Chanted loudly, chanted lowly,
Till her blood was frozen slowly,
And her eyes were darken'd wholly,
    Turn'd to tower'd Camelot;
For ere she reach'd upon the tide
The first house by the water-side,
Singing in her song she died,
    The Lady of Shalott.

Under tower and balcony,
By garden-wall and gallery,
A gleaming shape she floated by,
Dead-pale between the houses high,
    Silent into Camelot.
Out upon the wharfs they came,
Knight and burgher, lord and dame,
And round the prow they read her name,
    The Lady of Shalott.

Who is this? and what is here?
And in the lighted palace near
Died the sound of royal cheer;
And they cross'd themselves for fear,
    All the knights at Camelot:
But Lancelot mused a little space;
He said, " She has a lovely face;
God in his mercy lend her grace,
    The Lady of Shalott."

        Alfred, Lord Tennyson

THOMAS THE RHYMER

TRUE Thomas lay on Huntlie bank;
  A ferlie he spied wi' his e'e;
And there he saw a ladye bright
  Come riding down by the Eildon Tree.

THE ROAD TO ELFLAND

Her skirt was o' the grass-green silk,
  Her mantle o' the velvet fyne;
At ilka tett o' her horse's mane,
  Hung fifty siller bells and nine.

True Thomas he pu'd aff his cap,
  And louted low down on his knee:
"Hail to thee, Mary, Queen of Heaven!
  For thy peer on earth could never be."

"O no, O no, Thomas," she said,
  "That name does not belang to me;
I'm but the Queen o' fair Elfland,
  That am hither come to visit thee.

"Harp and carp, Thomas," she said;
  "Harp and carp along wi' me;
And if ye dare to kiss my lips
  Sure of your bodie I will be."

"Betide me weal, betide me woe,
  That weird shall never daunten me."
Syne he has kissed her rosy lips,
  All underneath the Eildon Tree.

"Now ye maun go wi' me," she said,
  "True Thomas, ye maun go wi' me;
And ye maun serve me seven years,
  Thro' weal or woe as may chance to be."

She's mounted on her milk-white steed,
  She's ta'en true Thomas up behind;
And aye, whene'er her bridle rang,
  Her steed gaed swifter than the wind.

O they rade on, and farther on,
  The steed gaed swifter than the wind;
Until they reach'd a desert wide,
  And living land was left behind.

THE GYPSY TRAIL

"Light down, light down now, true Thomas,
　　And lean your head upon my knee;
Abide ye there a little space,
　　And I will show you ferlies three.

"O see ye not yon narrow road,
　　So thick beset wi' thorns and briers?
That is the Path of Righteousness,
　　Though after it but few inquires.

"And see ye not yon braid, braid road,
　　That lies across the lily leven?
That is the Path of Wickedness,
　　Though some call it the Road to Heaven.

"And see ye not yon bonny road
　　That winds about the fernie brae?
That is the Road to fair Elfland,
　　Where you and I this night maun gae.

"But, Thomas, ye sall haud your tongue,
　　Whatever ye may hear or see;
For speak ye word in Elflyn-land,
　　Ye'll ne'er win back to your ain countrie."

O, they rade on, and farther on,
　　And they waded rivers abune the knee;
And they saw neither sun nor moon,
　　But they heard the roaring of the sea.

It was mirk, mirk night, there was nae starlight,
　　They waded thro red blude to the knee;
For a' the blude that's shed on the earth
　　Rins through the springs o' that countrie.

Syne they came to a garden green,
　　And she pu'd an apple frae a tree:
"Take this for thy wages, true Thomas;
　　It will give thee the tongue that can never lee."

THE ROAD TO ELFLAND

"My tongue is my ain," true Thomas he said;
  "A gudely gift ye wad gie to me!
I neither dought to buy or sell
  At fair or tryst where I might be.

"I dought neither speak to prince or peer,
  Nor ask of grace from fair ladye!"
"Now haud thy peace, Thomas," she said,
  "For as I say, so must it be."

He has gotten a coat of the even cloth,
  And a pair o' shoon of the velvet green;
And till seven years were gane and past,
  True Thomas on earth was never seen.
                  Anonymous

LA BELLE DAME SANS MERCI

O WHAT can ail thee, knight-at-arms,
  Alone and palely loitering?
The sedge has wither'd from the lake,
  And no birds sing.

O what can ail thee, knight-at-arms,
  So haggard and so woe-begone?
The squirrel's granary is full,
  And the harvest's done.

I see a lily on thy brow
  With anguish moist and fever dew,
And on thy cheeks a fading rose
  Fast withereth too.—

I met a lady in the meads,
  Full beautiful — a faery's child,
Her hair was long, her foot was light,
  And her eyes were wild.

THE GYPSY TRAIL

I made a garland for her head,
  And bracelets too, and fragrant zone;
She look'd at me as she did love,
  And made sweet moan.

I set her on my pacing steed,
  And nothing else saw all day long,
For sidelong would she bend, and sing
  A faery's song.

She found me roots of relish sweet,
  And honey wild, and manna dew,
And sure in language strange she said —
  " I love thee true! "

She took me to her elfin grot,
  And there she wept and sigh'd full sore,
And there I shut her wild, wild eyes
  With kisses four.

And there she lulled me asleep,
  And there I dream'd — ah! woe betide!
The latest dream I ever dream'd
  On the cold hill's side.

I saw pale kings and princes too,
  Pale warriors, death-pale were they all;
They cried —" La Belle Dame sans Merci
  Hath thee in thrall! "

I saw their starved lips in the gloam,
  With horrid warning gaped wide,
And I awoke and found me here,
  On the cold hill's side.

And this is why I sojourn here,
  Alone and palely loitering,
Though the sedge is wither'd from the lake
  And no birds sing.   *John Keats*

THE ROAD TO ELFLAND

NIAMH

OH who is she, and what is she?
   A beauty born eternally
Of shimmering moonshine, sunset flame,
And rose-red heart of dawn;
None knows the secret ways she came —
Whither she journeys on.

I follow her, I follow her
By haunted pools with dreams astir,
And over blue unwearied tides
Of shadow-waves, where sleep
Old loves, old hates, whose doom derides
Vows we forgot to keep.

I send my cry, I send my cry
Adown the arches of the sky,
Along the pathway of the stars,
Through quiet and through stress;
I beat against the saffron bars
That guard her loveliness.

And low I hear, oh, low I hear,
Her cruel laughter, fluting clear,
I see far-off the drifted gold
Of wind-blown flying hair;
I stand without in dark and cold
And she is — Where? Where? Where?
Ethna Carbery

THE GYPSY TRAIL

LA SOURCE ENCHANTÉE

J'ERRAIS dans la montagne un jour de chaleur
   grande.
Une source s'offrit, claire, parmi les houx.
Comme les chevaliers dont parle la legende
Pour boire dans ma main je me mis à genoux.
"Quelqu'une qui passait un troupeau dans la
   lande
Me crie, mais hélas! trop tard: "Malheur à
   vous!"
J'avais bu, sans savoir, l'eau de Broceliande,
Ma lèvre en a gardé l'impérissable goût,
Et je vais, depuis lors, indifférent aux choses
Qui font les hommes gais ou qui les font moroses.
La source fée en moi luit sans les arbres verts;
Je suis le prisonnier de son eau diaphane,
Et je ne sais plus rien de l'immense univers
Que le reflèt changeant des yeux de Viviane.

Anatole Le Braz

KUBLA KHAN

IN Xanadu did Kubla Khan
   A stately pleasure-dome decree:
Where Alph, the sacred river, ran
Through caverns measureless to man
   Down to a sunless sea.
So twice five miles of fertile ground
With walls and towers were girdled round:
And there were gardens bright with sinuous rills
Where blossomed many an incense-bearing tree;
And here were forests ancient as the hills,
Enfolding sunny spots of greenery.

THE ROAD TO ELFLAND

But O! that deep romantic chasm which slanted
Down the green hill athwart a cedarn cover!
A savage place! as holy and enchanted
As e'er beneath a waning moon was haunted
By woman wailing for her demon-lover!
And from this chasm, with ceaseless turmoil
    seething,
As if this earth in fast thick pants were breath-
    ing,
A mighty fountain momently was forced:
Amid whose swift half-intermitted burst
Huge fragments vaulted like rebounding hail,
Or chaffy grain beneath the thresher's flail:
And 'mid these dancing rocks at once and ever
It flung up momently the sacred river.
Five miles meandering with a mazy motion
Through wood and dale the sacred river ran,
Then reached the caverns measureless to man,
And sank in tumult to a lifeless ocean:
And 'mid this tumult Kubla heard from far
Ancestral voices prophesying war!

    The shadow of the dome of pleasure
    Floated mid-way on the waves;
    Where was heard the mingled measure
    From the fountain and the caves.
It was a miracle of rare device,
A sunny pleasure-dome with caves of ice!
    A damsel with a dulcimer
    In a vision once I saw:
    It was an Abyssinian maid,
    And on her dulcimer she played,
    Singing of Mount Abora.
    Could I revive within me
    Her symphony and song,
    To such a deep delight 'twould win me

THE GYPSY TRAIL

That with music loud and long,
I would build that dome in air,
That sunny dome! those caves of ice!
And all who heard should see them there,
And all should cry, Beware! Beware!
His flashing eyes, his floating hair!
Weave a circle round him thrice,
And close your eyes with holy dread,
For he on honey-dew hath fed,
And drunk the milk of Paradise.

Samuel Taylor Coleridge

DER FISCHER

DAS Wasser rauscht', das Wasser schwoll,
    Ein Fischer sass daran,
Sah nach der Angel ruhevoll,
Kühl bis ans Herz hinan.
Und wie er sitzt und wie er lauscht,
Teilt sich die Flut empor;
Aus dem bewegten Wasser rauscht
Ein feuchtes Weib hervor.

Sie sang zu ihm, sie sprach zu ihm:
"Was lockst du meine Brut
Mit Menschenwitz und Menschenlist
Hinauf in Todesglut?
Ach wüsstest du, wie's Fischlein ist
So wohlig auf dem Grund,
Du stiegst herunter wie du bist,
Und würdest erst gesund.

"Labt sich die liebe Sonne nicht,
Der Mond sich nicht im Meer?
Kehrt wellenatmend ihr Gesicht
Nicht doppelt schöner her?

THE ROAD TO ELFLAND

Lockt dich der tiefe Himmel nicht,
Das feuchtverklärte Blau?
Lockt dich dein eigen Angesicht
Nicht her im ew'gen Tau? "

Das Wasser rauscht', das Wasser schwoll,
Netzt' ihm den nackten Fuss;
Sein Herz wuchs ihm so sehnsuchtsvoll
Wie bei der Liebsten Gruss.
Sie sprach zu ihm, sie sang zu ihm;
Da war's um ihn geschehn:
Halb zog sie ihn, halb sank er hin,
Und ward nicht mehr gesehn.
Johann Wolfgang von Goethe

FISCHERKNABE SINGT IM KAHN

ES lächelt der See, er ladet zum Bade,
  Der Knabe schlief ein am grünen Ges-
tade,
    Da hört er ein Klingen
    Wie Flöten so süss,
    Wie Stimmen der Engel
    Im Paradies.
Und wie er erwachet in seliger Lust,
Da spülen die Wasser ihm um die Brust,
    Und es ruft aus den Tiefen:
    Lieb Knabe, bist mein!
    Ich locke den Schläfer,
    Ich zieh' ihn herein.
Friedrich von Schiller

THE GYPSY TRAIL

SONG

FROM *Comus*

SABRINA fair,
  Listen where thou art sitting
Under the glassy, cool, translucent wave,
  In twisted braids of lilies knitting
The loose train of thy amber-dropping
      hair;
    Listen for dear honor's sake,
      Goddess of the silver lake,
        Listen and save.
Listen and appear to us
In name of great Oceanus,
By th' earth-shaking Neptune's mace
And Tethy's grave majestic pace,
By hoary Nereus' wrinkled look,
And the Carpathian wizard's hook,
By scaly Triton's winding shell,
And old sooth-saying Glaucus' spell,
By Leucothea's lovely hands,
And her son that rules the strands,
By Thetis' tinsel-slippered feet,
And the songs of Sirens sweet,
By dead Parthenope's dear tomb,
And fair Ligea's golden comb,
Wherewith she sits on diamond rocks
Sleeking her soft alluring locks,
By all the nymphs that nightly dance
Upon thy streams with wily glance
Rise, rise, and heave thy rosy head
From thy coral-paven bed,
And bridle in thy headlong wave,
Till thou our summons answered have.
     Listen and save.

THE ROAD TO ELFLAND

SABRINA SINGS

BY the rushy-fringed bank,
  Where grows the willow and the
    osier dank,
My sliding chariot stays,
Thick set with agate, and the azure sheen
Of turkis blue, and emerald green
  That in the channel strays;
Whilst from off the waters fleet
Thus I set my printless feet
O'er the cowslip's velvet head,
That bends not as I tread;
Gentle swain, at thy request
    I am here.

John Milton

THE FORSAKEN MERMAN

COME, dear children, let us away;
  Down and away below!
Now my brothers call from the bay,
Now the great winds shoreward blow,
Now the salt tides seaward flow;
Now the wild white horses play,
Champ and chafe and toss in the spray.
Children dear, let us away!
This way, this way!

Call her once before you go,—
Call once yet!
In a voice that she will know,—
" Margaret! Margaret! "
Children's voices should be dear
(Call once more) to a mother's ear;
Children's voices, wild with pain,—

255

THE GYPSY TRAIL

Surely she will come again!
Call her once, and come away;
This way, this way!
" Mother dear, we cannot stay!
The wild white lorses foam and fret."
Margaret! Margaret!

Come, dear children, come away down:
Call no more!
One last look at the white-walled town,
And the little grey church on the windy shore;
Then come down!
She will not come, though you call all day;
Come away, come away!

Children dear, was it yesterday
We heard the sweet bells over the bay,—
In the caverns where we lay,
Through the surf and through the swell,
The far-off sound of a silver bell?
Sand-strewn caverns, cool and deep,
Where the winds are all asleep;
Where the spent lights quiver and gleam,
Where the salt weed sways in the stream,
Where the sea-beasts, ranged all round,
Feed in the ooze of their pasture-ground;
Where the sea-snakes coil and twine,
Dry their mail and bask in the brine;
Where great whales come sailing by,
Sail and sail, with unshut eye,
Round the world for ever and aye?
When did music come this way?
Children dear, was it yesterday?

Children dear, was it yesterday
(Call yet once) that she went away?

THE ROAD TO ELFLAND

Once she sate with you and me,
On a red gold throne in the heart of the sea,
And the youngest sate on her knee.
She combed its bright hair, and she tended it well,
When down swung the sound of a far-off bell.
She sighed, she looked up through the clear green
    sea;
She said: " I must go, for my kinsfolk pray
In the little grey church on the shore to-day.
'Twill be Easter-time in the world — ah me!
And I lose my poor soul, Merman! here with
    thee."
I said: " Go up, dear heart, through the waves;
Say thy prayer, and come back to the kind sea-
    caves ! "
She smiled, she went up through the surf in the
    bay.
Children dear, was it yesterday?

Children dear, were we long alone?
" The sea grows stormy, the little ones moan;
Long prayers," I said, " in the world they say;
Come! " I said; and we rose through the surf in
    the bay.
We went up the beach, by the sandy down
Where the sea-stocks bloom, to the white-walled
    town;
Through the narrow paved streets, where all was
    still,
To the little grey church on the windy hill.
From the church came a murmur of folk at their
    prayers,
But we stood without in the cold blowing airs.
We climbed on the graves, on the stones worn
    with rains,
And we gazed up the aisle through the small
    leaded panes.

THE GYPSY TRAIL

She sate by the pillar; we saw her clear:
"Margaret, hist! come quick, we are here!
Dear heart," I said, "we are long alone;
The sea grows stormy, the little ones moan."
But, ah! she gave me never a look,
For her eyes were sealed to the holy book.
Loud prays the priest; shut stands the door.
Come away, children, call no more!
Come away, come down, call no more!

Down, down, down!
Down to the depths of the sea!
She sits at her wheel in the humming town,
Singing most joyfully.
Hark what she sings: "O joy, O joy,
For the humming street, and the child with its
        toy!
For the priest, and the bell, and the holy well;
For the wheel where I spun,
And the blessed light of the sun!"
And so she sings her fill,
Singing most joyfully,
Till the spindle drops from her hand,
And the whizzing wheel stands still.
She steals to the window, and looks at the sand,
And over the sand at the sea;
And her eyes are set in a stare;
And anon there breaks a sigh,
And anon there drops a tear,
From a sorrow-clouded eye,
And a heart sorrow-laden,
A long, long sigh,
For the cold strange eyes of a little Mermaiden,
And the gleam of her golden hair.

Come away, away, children;
Come, children, come down!

THE ROAD TO ELFLAND

The hoarse wind blows colder;
Lights shine in the town.
She will start from her slumber
When gusts shake the door:
She will hear the winds howling,
Will hear the waves roar.
We shall see, while above us
The waves roar and whirl,
A ceiling of amber,
A pavement of pearl;
Singing, "Here came a mortal,
But faithless was she!
And alone dwell forever
The kings of the sea."

But, children, at midnight,
When soft the winds blow,
When clear falls the moonlight,
When spring-tides are low;
When sweet airs come seaward
From heaths starred with broom,
And high rocks throw mildly
On the blanched sands a gloom;
Up the still, glistening beaches,
Up the creeks we will hie,
Over banks of bright seaweed
The ebb-tide leaves dry.
We will gaze, from the sand-hills,
At the white sleeping town;
At the church on the hill-side,
And then come back down,
Singing, "There dwells a loved one,
But cruel is she!
She left lonely forever
The kings of the sea."

Matthew Arnold

THE GYPSY TRAIL

THE BUGLES OF DREAMLAND

SWIFTLY the dews of the gloaming are fall-
ing:
Faintly the bugles of Dreamland are calling.
  O hearken, my darling, the elf-flutes are blow-
    ing
  The shining-eyed folk from the hill-side are
    flowing,
  I' the moonshine the wild-apple blossoms are
    snowing,
  And louder and louder where the white dews
    are falling
  The far-away bugles of Dreamland are calling.

O what are the bugles of Dreamland calling
There where the dews of the gloaming are fall-
    ing?
  Come away from the weary old world of tears,
  Come away, come away to where one never
    hears
  The slow weary drip of the slow weary years,
  But peace and deep rest till the white dews are
    falling
  And the blithe bugle-laughters through Dream-
    land are calling.

        .   .   .   .

                        Fiona Macleod

GREEK ECHOES

Not here, O Apollo!
Are haunts meet for thee.
But where Helicon breaks down
In cliff to the sea,

Where the moon-silver'd inlets
Send far their light voice
Up the still vale of Thisbe,
O speed and rejoice!

Arnold

GREEK ECHOES

ON FIRST LOOKING INTO CHAPMAN'S
HOMER

MUCH have I travell'd in the realms of gold,
    And many goodly states and kingdoms
        seen;
  Round many western islands have I been
Which bards in fealty to Apollo hold.
Oft of one wide expanse had I been told,
    That deep-brow'd Homer ruled as his demesne:
    Yet did I never breathe its pure serene
Till I heard Chapman speak out loud and bold:
Then felt I like some watcher of the skies
    When a new planet swims into his ken;
Or like stout Cortez when with eagle eyes
    He stared at the Pacific — and all his men
Look'd at each other with a wild surmise —
    Silent, upon a peak in Darien.
                                    John Keats

ON A GRECIAN URN

THOU still unravish'd bride of quietness!
    Thou foster-child of Silence and slow
        Time,
Sylvan historian, who canst thus express
    A flowery tale more sweetly than our rhyme:
What leaf-fringed legend haunts about thy shape
    Of deities or mortals, or of both,

THE GYPSY TRAIL

In Tempe or the dales of Arcady?
What men or gods are these   What maidens
  loath?
 What mad pursuit? What struggle to escape?
  What pipes and timbrels? What wild ec-
  stasy?

Heard melodies are sweet, but those unheard
 Are sweeter; therefore, ye soft pipes, play on;
Not to the sensual ear, but, more endear'd,
 Pipe to the spirit ditties of no tone:
Fair youth, beneath the trees, thou canst not
  leave
 Thy song, nor ever can those trees be bare;
  Bold Lover, never, never canst thou kiss,
Though winning near the goal — yet, do not
  grieve;
 She cannot fade, though thou hast not thy
  bliss,
  For ever wilt thou love, and she be fair!

Ah, happy, happy boughs! that cannot shed
 Your leaves, nor ever bid the Spring adieu;
And, happy melodist, unwearied,
 For ever piping songs for ever new;
More happy love! more happy, happy love!
 For ever warm and still to be enjoy'd,
  For ever panting and for ever young;
All breathing human passion far above,
 That leaves a heart high sorrowful and cloy'd,
  A burning forehead, and a parching tongue.

Who are these coming to the sacrifice?
 To what green altar, O mysterious priest,
Lead'st thou that heifer lowing at the skies,
 And all her silken flanks with garlands drest?

GREEK ECHOES

What little town by river or sea-shore,
  Or mountain-built with peaceful citadel,
    Is emptied of its folk, this pious morn?
And, little town, thy streets for evermore
  Will silent be; and not a soul to tell
    Why thou art desolate, can e'er return.

O Attic shape! Fair attitude! with brede
  Of marble men and maidens overwrought,
With forest branches and the trodden weed;
  Thou, silent form! dost tease us out of thought
As doth eternity: Cold Pastoral!
  When old age shall this generation waste,
    Thou shalt remain, in midst of other woe
Than ours, a friend to man, to whom thou say'st,
  " Beauty is truth, truth beauty,"— that is all
    Ye know on earth, and all ye need to know.
                                        John Keats

SONGS OF CALLICLES

I

THE track winds down to the clear stream,
    To cross the sparkling shallows; there
The cattle love to gather, on their way
To the high mountain-pastures, and to stay,
Till the rough cow-herds drive them past,
Knee-deep in the cool ford; for 'tis the last
Of all the woody, high, well-watered dells
On Etna; and the beam
Of noon is broken there by chestnut-boughs
Down its steep verdant sides; the air
Is freshened by the leaping stream, which throws
Eternal showers of spray on the mossed roots
Of trees, and veins of turf, and long dark shoots

265

Of ivy-plants, and fragrant hanging bells
Of hyacinths, and on late anemones,
That muffle its wet banks; but glade,
And stream, and sward, and chestnut-trees,
End here; Etna beyond, in the broad glare
Of the hot noon, without a shade,
Slope behind slope, up to the peak, lies bare,—
The peak, round which the white clouds play.

    In such a glen, on such a day,
    On Pelion, on the grassy ground,
    Chiron, the aged Centaur, lay,
    The young Achilles standing by.
    The Centaur taught him to explore
    The mountains; where the glens are dry,
    And the tired Centaurs come to rest,
    And where the soaking springs abound,
    And the straight ashes grow for spears,
    And where the hill-goats come to feed,
    And the sea-eagles build their nest.
    He showed him Phthia far away,
    And said, " O boy, I taught this lore
    To Peleus, in long-distant years! "
    He told him of the gods, the stars,
    The tides; and then of mortal wars,
    And of the life which heroes lead
    Before they reach the Elysian place,
    And rest in the immortal mead;
    And all the wisdom of his race.

II

FAR, far from here,
    The Adriatic breaks in a warm bay
Among the green Illyrian hills; and there
The sunshine in the happy glens is fair,
And by the sea, and in the brakes.

GREEK ECHOES

The grass is cool, the sea-side air
Buoyant and fresh, the mountain flowers
More virginal and sweet than ours.
And there, they say, two bright and aged snakes,
Who once were Cadmus and Harmonia,
Bask in the glens or on the warm sea-shore,
In breathless quiet, after all their ills;
Nor do they see their country, nor the place
Where the Sphinx lived among the frowning
    hills,
Nor the unhappy palace of their race,
Nor Thebes, nor the Ismenus, any more.

There those two live, far in the Illyrian brakes!
They had stayed long enough to see,
In Thebes, the billow of calamity
Over their own dear children rolled,
Curse upon curse, pang upon pang,
For years, they sitting helpless in their home,
A gray old man and woman; yet of old
The Gods had to their marriage come,
And at the banquet all the Muses sang.

Therefore they did not end their days
In sight of blood; but were rapt, far away,
To where the west-wind plays,
And murmurs of the Adriatic come
To those untrodden mountain lawns; and there
Placed safely in changed forms, the pair
Wholly forget their first sad life, and home,
And all that Theban woe, and stray
Forever through the glens, placid and dumb.

III

A S the sky-brightening south-wind clears the
  day,
And makes the massed clouds roll,

THE GYPSY TRAIL

The music of the lyre blows away
The clouds which wrap the soul.

Oh! that Fate had let me see
That triumph of the sweet persuasive lyre,
That famous, final victory
When jealous Pan with Marsyas did conspire;

When, from far Parnassus' side,
Young Apollo, all the pride
Of the Phrygian flutes to tame,
To the Phrygian highlands came;
Where the long green reed-beds sway
In the rippled waters gray
Of that solitary lake
Where Maeander's springs are born;
Whence the ridged pine-wooded roots
Of Messogis westward break,
Mounting westward, high and higher.
There was held the famous strife;
There the Phrygian brought his flutes,
And Apollo brought his lyre;
And, when now the westering sun
Touched the hills, the strife was done,
And the attentive Muses said,
"Marsyas, thou art vanquishèd!"
Then Apollo's minister
Hanged upon a branching fir
Marsyas, that unhappy Faun,
And began to whet his knife.
But the Maenads, who were there,
Left their friend, and with robes flowing
In the wind, and loose dark hair
O'er their polished bosoms blowing,
Each her ribboned tambourine
Flinging on the mountain-sod,

GREEK ECHOES

With a lovely frightened mien
Came about the youthful god.
But he turned his beauteous face
Haughtily another way,
From the grassy sun-warmed place
Where in proud repose he lay,
With one arm over his head,
Watching how the whetting sped.

But aloof, on the lake-strand,
Did the young Olympus stand,
Weeping at his master's end;
For the Faun had been his friend.
For he taught him how to sing,
And he taught him flute-playing.
Many a morning had they gone
To the glimmering mountain lakes,
And had torn up by the roots
The tall crested water-reeds
With long plumes and soft brown seeds,
And had carved them into flutes,
Sitting on a tabled stone
Where the shoreward ripple breaks.
And he taught him how to please
The red-snooded Phrygian girls,
Whom the summer evening sees
Flashing in the dance's whirls
Underneath the starlit trees
In the mountain villages.
Therefore now Olympus stands,
At his master's piteous cries
Pressing fast with both his hands
His white garment to his eyes,
Not to see Apollo's scorn.—
Ah, poor Faun, poor Faun! ah, poor Faun!

THE GYPSY TRAIL

IV

THROUGH the black, rushing
   smoke-bursts,
Thick breaks the red flame
All Etna heaves fiercely
Her forest-clothed frame.

Not here, O Apollo!
Are haunts meet for thee.
But where Helicon breaks down
In cliff to the sea,—

Where the moon-silvered inlets
Send far their light voice
Up the still vale of Thisbe,—
Oh, speed, and rejoice!

On the sward at the cliff-top
Lie strewn the white flocks:
On the cliff-side the pigeons
Roost deep in the rocks.

In the moonlight the shepherds,
Soft lulled by the rills,
Lie wrapt in their blankets
Asleep on the hills.

— What forms are these coming
So white through the gloom?
What garments out-glistening
The gold-flowered broom?

What sweet-breathing presence
Out-perfumes the thyme?
What voices enrapture
The night's balmy prime? —

GREEK ECHOES

'Tis Apollo comes leading
His choir, the Nine.
— The leader is fairest,
But all are divine.

They are lost in the hollows!
They stream up again!
What seeks on this mountain
The glorified train?

They bathe on this mountain,
In the spring by their road;
Then on to Olympus,
Their endless abode.

— Whose praise do they mention?
Of what is it told? —
What will be forever,
What was from of old.

First hymn they the Father
Of all things; and then,
The rest of immortals,
The action of men.

The day in his hotness,
The strife with the palm;
The night in her silence,
The stars in their calm.

Matthew Arnold

THE LOTOS-EATERS

"COURAGE!" he said, and pointed toward
the land,
"This mounting wave will roll us shoreward
soon."
In the afternoon they came unto a land
In which it seemed always afternoon.

THE GYPSY TRAIL

All round the coast the languid air did swoon,
Breathing like one that hath a weary dream.
Full-faced above the valley stood the moon;
And like a downward smoke, the slender stream
Along the cliff to fall and pause and fall did
    seem.

A land of streams! some, like a downward smoke,
Slow-dropping veils of thinnest lawn, did go;
And some thro' wavering lights and shadows
    broke,
Rolling a slumbrous sheet of foam below.
They saw the gleaming river seaward flow
From the inner land: far off, three mountain-
    tops,
Three silent pinnacles of aged snow,
Stood sunset-flush'd: and, dew'd with showery
    drops,
Up-clomb the shadowy pine above the woven
    copse.

The charmed sunset linger'd low adown
In the red West: thro' mountain clefts the dale
Was seen far inland, and the yellow down
Border'd with palm, and many a winding vale
And meadow, set with slender galingale;
A land where all things always seem'd the same!
And round about the keel with faces pale,
Dark faces pale against that rosy flame,
The mild-eyed melancholy Lotos-eaters came.

Branches they bore of that enchanted stem,
Laden with flower and fruit, whereof they gave
To each, but whoso did receive of them,
And taste, to him the gushing of the wave
Far far away did seem to mourn and rave

On alien shores; and if his fellow spake,
His voice was thin, as voices from the grave;
And deep-asleep he seem'd, yet all awake,
And music in his ears his beating heart did
make.

They sat them down upon the yellow sand,
Between the sun and moon upon the shore;
And sweet it was to dream of Fatherland,
Of child, and wife, and slave; but evermore
Most weary seem'd the sea, weary the oar,
Weary the wandering fields of barren foam.
Then some one said, "We will return no more;"
And all at once they sang, "Our island home
Is far beyond the wave; we will no longer roam."
Alfred, Lord Tennyson

CHORIC SONG OF THE LOTOS-EATERS

I

THERE is sweet music here that softer falls
Than petals from blown roses on the grass,
Or night-dews on still waters between walls
Of shadowy granite, in a gleaming pass;
Music that gentlier on the spirit lies,
Than tir'd eyelids upon tir'd eyes;
Music that brings sweet sleep down from the
blissful skies.
Here are cool mosses deep,
And thro' the moss the ivies creep,
And in the stream the long-leaved flowers weep,
And from the craggy ledge the poppy hangs in
sleep.

THE GYPSY TRAIL

II

Why are we weigh'd upon with heaviness,
And utterly consumed with sharp distress,
While all things else have rest from weariness?
All things have rest: why should we toil alone,
We only toil, who are the first of things,
And make perpetual moan,
Still from one sorrow to another thrown:
Nor ever fold our wings,
And cease from wanderings,
Nor steep our brows in slumber's holy balm;
Nor harken what the inner spirit sings,
" There is no joy but calm!"
Why should we only toil, the roof and crown of
        things?

III

Lo! in the middle of the wood,
The folded leaf is woo'd from out the bud
With winds upon the branch, and there
Grows green and broad, and takes no care,
Sun-steep'd at noon, and in the moon
Nightly dew-fed; and turning yellow
Falls, and floats adown the air.
Lo! sweeten'd with the summer light,
The full-juiced apple, waxing over-mellow,
Drops in a silent autumn night.
All its allotted length of days,
The flower ripens in its place,
Ripens and fades, and falls, and hath no toil,
Fast-rooted in the fruitful soil.

IV

Hateful is the dark-blue sky,
Vaulted o'er the dark-blue sea.

GREEK ECHOES

Death is the end of life; ah, why
Should life all labor be?
Let us alone. Time driveth onward fast,
And in a little while our lips are dumb.
Let us alone. What is it that will last?
All things are taken from us, and become
Portions and parcels of the dreadful Past.
Let us alone. What pleasure can we have
To war with evil? Is there any peace
In ever climbing up the climbing wave?
All things have rest, and ripen toward the grave
In silence; ripen, fall and cease:
Give us long rest or death, dark death, or dream-
    ful ease.

V

How sweet it were, hearing the downward
    stream,
With half-shut eyes ever to seem
Falling asleep in a half-dream!
To dream and dream, like yonder amber light,
Which will not leave the myrrh-bush on the
    height;
To hear each other's whisper'd speech;
Eating the Lotos day by day,
To watch the crisping ripples on the beach,
And tender curving lines of creamy spray;
To lend our hearts and spirits wholly
To the influence of mild-minded melancholy;
To muse and brood and live again in memory,
With those old faces of our infancy
Heap'd over with a mound of grass,
Two handfuls of white dust, shut in an urn of
    brass!

THE GYPSY TRAIL

VI

Dear is the memory of our wedded lives,
And dear the last embraces of our wives
And their warm tears: but all hath suffer'd
    change;
For surely now our household hearths are cold:
Our sons inherit us: our looks are strange:
And we should come like ghosts to trouble joy.
Or else the island princes over-bold
Have eat our substance, and the minstrel sings
Before them of the ten-years' war in Troy,
And our great deeds, as half-forgotten things.
Is there confusion in the little isle?
Let what is broken so remain.
The Gods are hard to reconcile:
'Tis hard to settle order once again.
There *is* confusion worse than death,
Trouble on trouble, pain on pain,
Long labor unto aged breath,
Sore task to hearts worn out by many wars
And eyes grown dim with gazing on the pilot-
    stars.

VII

But, propt on beds of amaranth and moly,
How sweet (while warm airs lull us, blowing
    lowly)
With half-dropt eyelids still,
Beneath a heaven dark and holy,
To watch the long bright river drawing slowly
His waters from the purple hill —
To hear the dewy echoes calling
From cave to cave thro' the thick-twined vine —
To watch the emerald-color'd water falling
Thro' many a wov'n acanthus-wreath divine!

GREEK ECHOES

Only to hear and see the far-off sparkling brine,
Only to hear were sweet, stretch'd out beneath
the pine.

VIII

The Lotos blooms beneath the barren peak:
The Lotos blows by every winding creek:
All day the wind breathes low with mellower
tone:
Thro' every hollow cave and alley lone
Round and round the spicy downs the yellow
Lotos-dust is blown.
We have had enough of action, and of motion
we,
Roll'd to starboard, roll'd to larboard, when the
surge was seething free,
Where the wallowing monster spouted his foam-
fountains in the sea.

Let us swear an oath, and keep it with an equal
mind,
In the hollow Lotos-land to live and lie reclined
On the hills like Gods together, careless of man-
kind.
For they lie beside their nectar, and the bolts are
hurl'd
Far below them in the valleys, and the clouds are
lightly curl'd
Round their golden houses, girdled with the
gleaming world:
Where they smile in secret, looking over wasted
lands,
Blight and famine, plague and earthquake, roar-
ing deeps and fiery sands,
Clanging fights, and flaming towns, and sinking
ships, and praying hands.

But they smile, they find a music centred in a
doleful song
Steaming up, a lamentation and an ancient tale of
wrong,
Like a tale of little meaning tho' the words are
strong;
Chanted from an ill-used race of men that cleave
the soil,
Sow the seed, and reap the harvest with enduring
toil,
Storing yearly little dues of wheat, and wine and
oil;

Till they perish and they suffer — some, 'tis
whisper'd — down in hell
Suffer endless anguish, others in Elysian valleys
dwell,
Resting weary limbs at last on beds of asphodel.
Surely, surely, slumber is more sweet than toil,
the shore
Than labor in the deep mid-ocean, wind and
wave and oar;
O rest ye, brother mariners, we will not wander
more.

Alfred, Lord Tennyson

HYLAS

DEAR to the sailor-kings,
    Bronze-bearded, steadfast-hearted,
Oars' dash, when galley swings
    Black through the grey waves parted.
But they said: "Make the cove
Where breathes a moonless grove,
    And larks hang glad

278

GREEK ECHOES

O'er pebbly pools and sweet;
He sickens with the heat,
   Our little lad."

So they call, the gold-browed kings,
  Hylas, Hylas, Hylas! clear;
And Alcides' great voice rings,—
  For he loved the brown child dear.

He left the blue profound
  To follow winding valleys;
He lost the surf's faint sound
  In aspen-shivering alleys.
Beside the freshes cold
He found white fingers hold
   His brown hand hot;
The dark kings waited long,
   But he came not.

Yet they call him from the shore,
  Hylas, Hylas, Hylas! thrice;
But Alcides sails no more
  Remembering the drowned child's eyes.
          Georgiana Goddard King

ORPHEUS

ORPHEUS with his lute made trees
   And the mountain tops that freeze
  Bow themselves when he did sing:
To his music plants and flowers
Ever sprung; as sun and showers
  There had made a lasting spring.

Every thing that heard him play,
Even the billows of the sea,

Hung their heads and then lay by.
In sweet music is such art,
Killing care and grief of heart
    Fall asleep, or hearing, die.
                        Shakespeare?

HYMN OF PAN

FROM the forests and highlands
    We come, we come;
From the river-girt islands,
    Where loud waves are dumb
Listening to my sweet pipings.
    The wind in the reeds and the rushes,
        The bees on the bells of thyme,
    The birds on the myrtle bushes,
        The cicale above in the lime,
And the lizards below in the grass,
Were as silent as ever old Tmolus was,
    Listening to my sweet pipings.

    Liquid Peneus was flowing,
        And all dark Tempe lay
    In Pelion's shadow, outgrowing
        The light of the dying day,
    Speeded by my sweet pipings.
        The Sileni, and Sylvans, and Fauns,
            And the nymphs of the wood and waves,
        To the edge of the moist river-lawns,
            And the brink of the dewy caves.
And all that did then attend and follow,
Were silent with love,— as you now, Apollo,
    With envy of my sweet pipings.

GREEK ECHOES

I sang of the dancing stars,
    I sang of the daedal earth,
And of heaven, and the giant wars,
    And love, and death, and birth.
And then I changed my pipings,—
    Singing how down the vale of Maenalus
      I pursued a maiden, and clasp'd a reed:
Gods and men, we are all deluded thus:
    It breaks in our bosom and then we bleed.
All wept — as I think both ye now would,
If envy or age had not frozen your blood —
    At the sorrow of my sweet pipings.
                Percy Bysshe Shelley

PHILOMELA

HARK! ah, the nightingale —
    The tawny-throated!
Hark! from that moonlit cedar what a burst!
What triumph! hark! — what pain!

O wanderer from a Grecian shore,
Still, after many years, in distant lands,
Still nourishing in thy bewildered brain
That wild, unquenched, deep-sunken, old-world
    pain —
Say, will it never heal?
And can this fragrant lawn
With its cool trees, and night,
And the sweet, tranquil Thames,
And moonshine, and the dew,
To thy racked heart and brain
Afford no balm?

THE GYPSY TRAIL

Dost thou to-night behold,
Here, through the moonlight on this English
    grass,
The unfriendly palace in the Thracian wild?
Dost thou again peruse
With hot cheeks and seared eyes
The too clear web, and thy dumb sister's shame?
Dost thou once more assay
Thy flight, and feel come over thee,
Poor fugitive, the feathery change
Once more, and once more seem to make re-
    sound
With love and hate, triumph and agony,
Lone Daulis, and the high Cephissian vale?
Listen, Eugenia,—
How thick the bursts come crowding through
    the leaves!
Again — thou hearest?
Eternal passion!
Eternal pain!

Matthew Arnold

THE ISLES OF GREECE

THE isles of Greece, the isles of Greece!
    Where burning Sappho loved and sung,
Where grew the arts of war and peace,
Where Delos rose, and Phoebus sprung!
Eternal summer gilds them yet,
But all, except their sun, is set.

The Scian and the Teian muse,
The hero's harp, the lover's lute,
Have found the fame your shores refuse;
Their place of birth alone is mute

GREEK ECHOES

To sounds which echo further west
Than your sires' "Islands of the Blest."

The mountains look on Marathon —
And Marathon looks on the sea;
And musing there an hour alone,
I dreamed that Greece might still be free;
For, standing on the Persian's grave,
I could not deem myself a slave.

A king sate on the rocky brow
Which looks o'er sea-born Salamis;
And ships, by thousands, lay below,
And men in nations; — all were his!
He counted them at break of day —
And when the sun set, where were they?

And where are they? and where art thou,
My country? On thy voiceless shore
The heroic lay is tuneless now —
The heroic bosom beats no more!
And must thy lyre, so long divine,
Degenerate into hands like mine?

'Tis something, in the dearth of fame,
Though linked among a fettered race,
To feel at least a patriot's shame,
Even as I sing, suffuse my face;
For what is left the poet here?
For Greeks a blush — for Greece a tear.

Must *we* but weep o'er days more blest
Must *we* but blush? — Our fathers bled.
Earth! render back from out thy breast
A remnant of our Spartan dead!
Of the three hundred grant but three,
To make a new Thermopylae!

THE GYPSY TRAIL

What, silent still? and silent all?
Ah! no; — the voices of the dead
Sound like a distant torrent's fall,
And answer, "Let one living head,
But one arise,—we come, we come!"
'Tis but the living who are dumb.

In vain — in vain: strike other chords;
Fill high the cup with Samian wine!
Leave battle to the Turkish hordes,
And shed the blood of Scio's vine!
Hark! rising to the ignoble call —
How answers each bold Bacchanal!

You have the Pyrrhic dance as yet,
Where is the Pyrrhic phalanx gone?
Of two such lessons, why forget
The nobler and the manlier one?
You have the letters Cadmus gave —
Think ye he meant them for a slave?

Fill high the bowl with Samian wine!
We will not think of themes like these!
It made Anacreon's song divine:
He served — but served Polycrates —
A tyrant; but our masters then
Were still at least our countrymen.

The tyrant of the Chersonese
Was freedom's best and bravest friend;
That tyrant was Miltiades!
Oh! that the present hour would lend
Another despot of the kind!
Such chains as his were sure to bind.

GREEK ECHOES

Fill high the bowl with Samian wine!
On Suli's rock and Parga's shore,
Exists the remnant of a line
Such as the Doric mothers bore;
And there, perhaps, some seed is sown,
The Heracleidan blood might own.

Trust not for freedom to the Franks —
They have a king who buys and sells:
In native swords, and native ranks,
The only hope of courage dwells:
But Turkish force and Latin fraud,
Would break your shield, however broad.

Fill high the bowl with Samian wine!
Our virgins dance beneath the shade —
I see their glorious black eyes shine;
But gazing on each glowing maid,
My own the burning tear-drop laves,
To think such breasts must suckle slaves.

Place me on Sunium's marbled steep,
Where nothing, save the waves and I,
May hear our mutual murmurs sweep;
There, swan-like, let me sing and die:
A land of slaves shall ne'er be mine —
Dash down yon cup of Samian wine!

Lord Byron

CHORUS

From *Hellas*

THE world's great age begins anew,
The golden years return,
The earth doth like a snake renew
Her winter weeds outworn:

THE GYPSY TRAIL

Heaven smiles, and faiths and empires
    gleam,
Like wrecks of a dissolving dream.

A brighter Hellas rears its mountains
    From waves serener far;
A new Peneus rolls his fountains
    Against the morning star.
Where fairer Tempes bloom, there sleep
Young Cyclads on a sunnier deep.

A loftier Argo cleaves the main,
    Fraught with a later prize;
Another Orpheus sings again,
    And loves, and weeps, and dies.
A new Ulysses leaves once more
Calypso for his native shore.

O, write no more the tale of Troy,
    If earth Death's scroll must be!
Nor mix with Laian rage the joy
    Which dawns upon the free:
Although a subtler Sphinx renew
Riddles of death Thebes never knew.

Another Athens shall arise,
    And to remoter time
Bequeath, like sunset to the skies,
    The splendor of its prime;
And leave, if naught so bright may live,
All earth can take or Heaven can give.

Saturn and Love their long repose
    Shall burst, more bright and good
Than all who fell, than One who rose,
    Than many unsubdued:
Not gold, not blood, their altar dowers,
But votive tears and symbol flowers.

GREEK ECHOES

O, cease! must hate and death return?
  Cease! must men kill and die?
Cease! drain not to its dregs the urn
  Of bitter prophecy.
The world is weary of the past,
O, might it die or rest at last!

Percy Bysshe Shelley

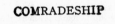

COMRADESHIP

I will sing the song of Companionship —
Whitman

Camerado! I give you my hand!
I give you my love, more precious than money,
I give you myself, before preaching or law;
Will you give me yourself? will you come travel with
   me?
Shall we stick by each other as long as we live?
Whitman

COMRADESHIP

FORBEARANCE

HAST thou named all the birds without a
    gun;
Loved the wood-rose, and left it on its stalk;
At rich men's tables eaten bread and pulse;
Unarmed, faced danger with a heart of trust;
And loved so well a high behavior
In man or maid, that thou from speech refrained,
Nobility more nobly to repay? —
O be my friend, and teach me to be thine!

Ralph Waldo Emerson

FRIENDSHIP

A RUDDY drop of manly blood
    The surging sea outweighs,
The world uncertain comes and goes;
The lover rooted stays.
I fancied he was fled,—
And after many a year,
Glowed unexhausted kindliness
Like daily sunrise there.
My careful heart was free again,
O friend, my bosom said,
Through thee alone the sky is arched,
Through thee the rose is red;
All things through thee take nobler form,
And look beyond the earth,
The mill-round of our fate appears

THE GYPSY TRAIL

A sun-path in thy worth.
Me too thy nobleness has taught
To master my despair;
The fountains of my hidden life
Are through thy friendship fair.

Ralph Waldo Emerson

THE APOCRYPHA

Ecclesiasticus, ch. vi.

A FAITHFUL friend is a strong defence;
And he that hath found him hath found a
treasure.
There is nothing that can be taken in exchange
for a faithful friend;
And his excellency is beyond price.
A faithful friend is a medicine of life;
And they that fear the Lord shall find him.
He that feareth the Lord directeth his friendship
aright;
For as he is, so is his neighbor also.

.   .   .

Change not a friend for a thing indifferent;
Neither a true brother for the gold of Ophir.

ETIENNE DE LA BOÈCE

I SERVE you not, if you I follow.
Shadow-like, o'er hill and hollow,
And bend my fancy to your leading,
All too nimble for my treading.
When the pilgrimage is done,
And we've the landscape overrun,
I am bitter, vacant, thwarted,

COMRADESHIP

And your heart is unsupported.
Vainly valiant, you have missed
The manhood that should yours resist,—
Its complement; but if I could,
In severe or cordial mood,
Lead you rightly to my altar,
Where the wisest muses falter,
And worship that world-warming spark
Which dazzles me in midnight dark,
Equalizing small and large,
While the soul it doth surcharge,
Till the poor is wealthy grown,
And the hermit never alone,—
The traveller and the road seem one
With the errand to be done; —
That were a man's and lover's part,
That were Freedom's whitest chart.
Ralph Waldo Emerson

PHILOLÄUS TO DIOCLES

HOW often at dusk, dear friend, when thou
art absent,
Sitting alone I wonder of what thou doest,
And dream, and wait of thee.

All the sweet noons and moons we have spent
together;
All the glad interchange of laughter and love,
And thoughts, so grave, or fanciful:
What can compare with these, or what surpass
them?
All the unbroken faith and steadfast reliance —
nigh twenty years twining the roots of life
far down;

THE GYPSY TRAIL

And not a mistrustful hour between us — or
    moment of anger:
What can surpass all this, or what compare?
Could riches or fame?
Or if the Thebans honor me for their lawgiver,
Or thou, Diocles, in Olympic fields art victor
    beloved and crowned,
What are these things to that?

And still thou growest upon me, as a mountain,
Seen from another mountain-summit, rises
Clearer, more grand, more beautiful than ever;
And still within thine eyes, and ever plainer,
I see my own soul sleeping.

.   .

Edward Carpenter

FROM FAR

FROM far, from eve and morning,
    And yon twelve-winded sky,
The stuff of life to knit me
    Blew hither: here am I.

Now — for a breath I tarry,
    Nor yet disperse apart —
Take my hand quick and tell me,
    What have you in your heart?

Speak now, and I will answer;
    How shall I help you, say;
Ere to the wind's twelve quarters
    I take my endless way?

A. E. Housman

COMRADESHIP

DER GUTE KAMERAD

ICH hatt' einen Kameraden,
    Einen bessern findst du nit.
Die Trommel schlug zum Streite,
Er ging an meiner Seite
In gleichem Schritt und Tritt.

Eine Kugel kam geflogen,
Gilt's mir oder gilt es dir?
Ihn hat es weggerissen,
Er liegt mir vor den Füssen,
Als wär's ein Stück von mir.

Will mir die Hand noch reichen,
Derweil ich eben lad':
"Kann dir die Hand nicht geben,
Bleib du im ew'gen Leben
Mein guter Kamerad!"

Ludwig Uhland

THYRSIS

HOW changed is here each spot man makes
    or fills!
In the two Hinkseys nothing keeps the same;
    The village street its haunted mansion lacks,
And from the sign is gone Sibylla's name,
    And from the roofs the twisted chimney-
        stacks —
    Are ye too changed, ye hills?
See, 'tis no foot of unfamiliar men
    To-night from Oxford up your pathway
       strays!
Here came I often, often, in old days,—
Thyrsis and I; we still had Thyrsis then.

THE GYPSY TRAIL

Runs it not here, the track by Childsworth
    Farm,
  Past the high wood, to where the elm-tree
    crowns
    The hill behind whose ridge the sunset
    flames?
  The signal-elm, that looks on Ilsley Downs,
    The Vale, the three lone weirs, the youthful
    Thames?
    This winter-eve is warm;
  Humid the air; leafless, yet soft as spring,
    The tender purple spray on copse and briers;
    And that sweet city with her dreaming spires,
She needs not June for beauty's heightening.

Lovely all times she lies, lovely to-night! —
  Only, methinks, some loss of habit's power
    Befalls me wandering through this upland
    dim.
  Once passed I blindfold here, at any hour;
    Now seldom come I, since I came with him.
    That single elm-tree bright
Against the west — I miss it! is it gone?
    We prized it dearly; while it stood, we said,
    Our friend the Gipsy-Scholar was not dead;
While the tree lived, he in these fields lived on.

Too rare, too rare, grow now my visits here,
  But once I knew each field, each flower, each
    stick;
    And with the country-folk acquaintance made
By barn in threshing-time, by new-built rick.
    Here, too, our shepherd-pipes we first as-
    sayed.
    Ah me! this many a year

COMRADESHIP

My pipe is lost, my shepherd's-holiday!
　Needs must I lose them, needs with heavy
　　heart
　Into the world and wave of men depart.
But Thyrsis of his own will went away.

It irked him to be here, he could not rest.
　He loved each simple joy the country yields,
　　He loved his mates; but yet he could not
　　　keep,
　For that a shadow lowered on the fields,
　　Here with the shepherds and the silly sheep.
　　　Some life of men unblest
　He knew, which made him droop, and filled
　　his head.
　　He went; his piping took a troubled sound
　　Of storms that rage outside our happy
　　　ground;
　He could not wait their passing; he is dead.

So, some tempestuous morn in early June,
　When the year's primal burst of bloom is o'er,
　　Before the roses and the longest day,—
　When garden-walks, and all the grassy floor,
　　With blossoms red and white of fallen May,
　　And chestnut-flowers, are strewn,—
　So have I heard the cuckoo's parting cry,
　　From the wet field, through the vexed gar-
　　　den-trees,
　　Come with the volleying rain and tossing
　　　breeze:
　The bloom is gone, and with the bloom go I!

Too quick despairer, wherefore wilt thou go?
　Soon will the high midsummer pomps come on,
　　Soon will the musk carnations break and
　　　swell,

THE GYPSY TRAIL

Soon shall we have gold-dusted snapdragon,
  Sweet-william with his homely cottage-smell,
    And stocks in fragrant blow;
Roses that down the alleys shine afar,
    And open, jasmine-muffled lattices,
    And groups under the dreaming garden-
      trees,
And the full moon, and the white evening-
    star.

He hearkens not! light comer, he is flown!
  What matters it? next year he will return,
    And we shall have him in the sweet spring-
      days,
  With whitening hedges, and uncrumpling fern,
    And bluebells trembling by the forest-ways,
    And scent of hay new-mown.
But Thyrsis never more we swains shall see,—
  See him come back, and cut a smoother reed,
    And blow a strain the world at last shall
      heed;
For Time, not Corydon, hath conquered thee!

Alack, for Corydon no rival now! —
  But when Sicilian shepherds lost a mate,
    Some good survivor with his flute would go,
  Piping a ditty sad for Bion's fate;
    And cross the unpermitted ferry's flow,
    And relax Pluto's brow,
  And make leap up with joy the beauteous head
    Of Proserpine, among whose crownèd hair
    Are flowers first opened on Sicilian air,
  And flute his friend, like Orpheus, from the
    dead.

COMRADESHIP

O easy access to the hearer's grace
 When Dorian shepherds sang to Proserpine!
  For she herself had trod Sicilian fields,
 She knew the Dorian water's gush divine,
   She knew each lily white which Enna yields,
   Each rose with blushing face;
  She loved the Dorian pipe, the Dorian strain.
   But ah! of our poor Thames she never
    heard;
   Her foot the Cumner cowslips never stirred;
  And we should tease her with our plaint in
   vain.

Well! wind-dispersed and vain the words will
  be;
 Yet, Thyrsis, let me give my grief its hour
  In the old haunt, and find our tree-topped
   hill!
 Who, if not I, for questing here hath power?
  I know the wood which hides the daffodil;
  I know the Fyfield tree;
 I know what white, what purple fritillaries
  The grassy harvest of the river-fields,
  Above by Ensham, down by Sandford,
   yields;
 And what sedged brooks are Thames's tribu-
  taries;

I know these slopes: who knows them if not I?
 But many a dingle on the loved hillside,
  With thorns once studded, old white-blos-
   somed trees,
 Where thick the cowslips grew, and far de-
  scried
  High towered the spikes of purple orchises,
  Hath since our day put by

299

THE GYPSY TRAIL

The coronals of that forgotten time;
  Down each green bank hath gone the plough-
      boy's team,
  And only in the hidden brookside gleam
Primroses, orphans of the flowery prime.

Where is the girl, who by the boatman's door,
  Above the locks, above the boating throng,
    Unmoored our skiff when through the
        Wytham flats,
  Red loosestrife and blond meadow-sweet
      among,
    And darting swallows and light water-gnats,
      We tracked the shy Thames shore?
  Where are the mowers, who, as the tiny swell
    Of our boat passing heaved the river-grass,
    Stood with suspended scythe to see us
        pass? —
They all are gone, and thou art gone as well!

Yes, thou art gone! and round me too the night
  In ever-nearing circle weaves her shade
    I see her veil draw soft across the day,
  I feel her slowly chilling breath invade
    The cheek grown thin, the brown hair sprent
        with gray;
      I feel her finger light
  Laid pausefully upon life's headlong train,—
    The foot less prompt to meet the morning
        dew,
    The heart less bounding at emotion new,
And hope, once crushed, less quick to spring
    again.

300

COMRADESHIP

And long the way appears, which seemed so
short
To the less practised eye of sanguine youth;
And high the mountain tops, in cloudy air,—
The mountain tops where is the throne of
Truth,
Tops in life's morning-sun so bright and
bare!
Unbreachable the fort
Of the long-battered world uplifts its wall;
And strange and vain the earthly turmoil
grows,
And near and real the charm of thy repose,
And night as welcome as a friend would fall.

But hush! the upland hath a sudden loss
Of quiet! Look, adown the dusk hillside,
A troop of Oxford hunters going home,
As in old days, jovial and talking, ride!
From hunting with the Berkshire hounds
they come.
Quick! let me fly, and cross
Into yon farther field! 'Tis done; and see,
Backed by the sunset, which doth glorify
The orange and pale violet evening-sky,
Bare on its lonely ridge, the Tree! the Tree!

I take the omen! Eve lets down her veil,
The white fog creeps from bush to bush about,
The west unflushes, the high stars grow
bright,
And in the scattered farms the lights come out.
I cannot reach the signal-tree to-night,
Yet, happy omen, hail!
Hear it from thy broad lucent Arno-vale

THE GYPSY TRAIL

(For there thine earth-forgetting eyelids
    keep
The morningless and unawakening sleep
Under the flowery oleanders pale),

Hear it, O Thyrsis, still our tree is there! —
    Ah, vain! These English fields, this upland
        dim,
        These brambles pale with mist engarlanded,
    That lone, sky-pointing tree, are not for him:
        To a boon southern country he is fled,
            And now in happier air,
    Wandering with the great Mother's train di-
        vine
        (And purer or more subtle soul than thee,
        I trow the mighty Mother doth not see)
    Within a folding of the Apennine,—

Thou hearest the immortal chants of old!
    Putting his sickle to the perilous grain
        In the hot cornfield of the Phrygian king,
    For thee the Lityerses-song again
        Young Daphnis with his silver voice doth
            sing;
        Sings his Sicilian fold,
    His sheep, his hapless love, his blinded eyes;
        And how a call celestial round him rang,
        And heavenward from the fountain-brink
            he sprang,
    And all the marvel of the golden skies.

There thou art gone, and me thou leavest here
Sole in these fields! yet will I not despair.
    Despair I will not, while I yet descry
    'Neath the soft canopy of English air
        That lonely tree against the western sky.

302

COMRADESHIP

Still, still these slopes, 'tis clear,
Our Gipsy-Scholar haunts, outliving thee!
Fields where soft sheep from cages pull the
hay,
Woods with anemones in flower till May,
Know him a wanderer still; then why not me?

A fugitive and gracious light he seeks,
Shy to illumine; and I seek it too.
This does not come with houses or with gold,
With place, with honor, and a flattering crew;
'Tis not in the world's market bought and
sold:
But the smooth-slipping weeks
Drop by, and leave its seeker still untired;
Out of the heed of mortals he is gone,
He wends unfollowed, he must house alone;
Yet on he fares, by his own heart inspired.

Thou too, O Thyrsis, on like quest wast bound!
Thou wanderedst with me for a little hour.
Men gave thee nothing; but this happy
quest,
If men esteemed thee feeble, gave thee power,
If men procured thee trouble, gave thee rest.
And this rude Cumner ground,
Its fir-topped Hurst, its farms, its quiet fields,
Here cam'st thou in thy jocund youthful
time,
Here was thine height of strength, thy golden
prime!
And still the haunt beloved a virtue yields.

What though the music of thy rustic flute
Kept not for long its happy, country tone;
Lost it too soon and learnt a stormy note

THE GYPSY TRAIL

Of men contention-tost, of men who groan,
  Which task'd thy pipe too sore, and tired thy
      throat—
    It fail'd, and thou wast mute!
Yet hadst thou alway visions of our light,
  And long with men of care thou couldst not
     stay,
  And soon thy foot resumed its wandering
     way,
Left human haunt, and on alone till night.

Too rare, too rare, grow now my visits here!
  'Mid city-noise, not, as with thee of yore,
    Thyrsis! in reach of sheep-bells is my home.
Then through the great town's harsh, heart-
     wearying roar,
    Let in thy voice a whisper often come,
     To chase fatigue and fear:
Why faintest thou? I wandered till I died.
  Roam on! The light we sought is shining
    still.
  Dost thou ask proof? Our tree yet crowns
    the hill,
Our Scholar travels yet the loved hill-side.
             Matthew Arnold

VIGIL STRANGE I KEPT ON THE FIELD ONE NIGHT

VIGIL strange I kept on the field one night:
  When you, my son and my comrade, dropt
    at my side that day,
One look I but gave, which your dear eyes re-
  turn'd, with a look I shall never forget;
One touch of your hand to mine, O boy, reach'd
  up as you lay on the ground;

COMRADESHIP

Then onward I sped in the battle, the even-con-
    tested battle;
Till late in the night reliev'd, to the place at last
    again I made my way;
Found you in death so cold, dear comrade —
    found your body, son of responding kisses
    (never again on earth responding;)
Bared your face in the starlight — curious the
    scene — cool blew the moderate night-wind;
Long there and then in vigil I stood, dimly
    around me the battle-field spreading;
Vigil wondrous and vigil sweet, there in the
    fragrant silent night;
But not a tear fell, not even a long-drawn sigh
    — Long, long I gazed;
Then on the earth partially reclining, sat by
    your side, leaning my chin in my hands;
Passing sweet hours, immortal and mystic hours
    with you, dearest comrade — Not a tear, not
    a word;
Vigil of silence, love and death — vigil for you,
    my son and my soldier,
As onward silently stars aloft, eastward new
    ones upward stole;
Vigil final for you, brave boy (I could not save
    you, swift was your death,
I faithfully loved you and cared for you living
    I think we shall surely meet again;)
Till at latest lingering of the night, indeed just
    as the dawn appear'd,
My comrade I wrapt in his blanket, envelop'd
    well his form,
Folded the blanket well, tucking it carefully over
    head, and carefully under feet;
And there and then, and bathed by the rising

sun, my son in his grave, in his rude-dug
  grave I deposited;
Ending my vigil strange with that — vigil of
  night and battle-field dim;
Vigil for boy of responding kisses (never again
  on earth responding;)
Vigil for comrade swiftly slain — vigil I never
  forget, how as day brighten'd,
I rose from the chill ground, and folded my sol-
  dier well in his blanket,
And buried him where he fell.

Walt Whitman

KNOWN AND UNKNOWN

FROM *In Memoriam*

D EAR friend, far off, my lost desire,
    So far, so near in woe and weal;
    O loved the most, when most I feel
There is a lower and a higher;

Known and unknown, human, divine;
    Sweet human hand and lips and eye;
    Dear heavenly friend that canst not **die**
Mine, mine, for ever, ever mine!

Strange friend, past, present, and to be,
    Loved deeplier, darklier understood;
    Behold, I dream a dream of good
And mingle all the world with thee.

Thy voice is on the rolling air;
    I hear thee where the waters **run**;
    Thou standest in the rising **sun,**
And in the setting thou art fair.

306

COMRADESHIP

What art thou then? I cannot guess;
　　But tho' I seem in star and flower
　　To feel thee some diffusive power,
I do not therefore love thee less:

My love involves the love before;
　　My love is vaster passion now;
　　Tho' mix'd with God and Nature thou,
I seem to love thee more and more.

Far off thou art, but ever nigh;
　　I have thee still, and I rejoice;
　　I prosper, circled with thy voice;
I shall not lose thee tho' I die.

Alfred, Lord Tennyson.

WAITING

SERENE, I fold my hands and wait,
　　Nor care for wind, or tide, or sea;
I rave no more 'gainst time or fate,
　　For, lo! my own shall come to me.

I stay my haste, I make delays,
　　For what avails this eager pace?
I stand amid the eternal ways,
　　And what is mine shall know my face.

Asleep, awake, by night or day,
　　The friends I seek are seeking me;
No wind can drive my bark astray,
　　Nor change the tide of destiny.

What matter if I stand alone?
　　I wait with joy the coming years;
My heart shall reap where it has sown,
　　And garner up its fruit of tears.

THE GYPSY TRAIL

The waters know their own and draw
  The brook that springs in yonder height;
So flows the good with equal law
  Unto the soul of pure delight.

The stars come nightly to the sky;
  The tidal wave unto the sea;
Nor time, nor space, nor deep, nor high,
  Can keep my own away from me.
John Burroughs

THE PILGRIM'S SCRIP

Give me solitude — give me Nature — give me again
O Nature, your primal sanities.

Whitman

So did Guy betimes discover
Fortune was his guard and lover;
In strange junctures, felt, with awe
His own symmetry with law.

Emerson

The rules to men made evident
By Him who built the day,
The columns of the firmament
Not firmer based than they.

Emerson

THE PILGRIM'S SCRIP

INFLUENCE OF NATURAL OBJECTS

IN CALLING FORTH AND STRENGTHENING THE IMAGINATION IN BOYHOOD AND EARLY YOUTH

WISDOM and Spirit of the Universe!
    Thou Soul, that art the Eternity of
      thought!
And giv'st to forms and images a breath
And everlasting motion! not in vain,
By day or starlight, thus from my first dawn
Of childhood didst thou intertwine for me
The passions that build up our human soul;
Not with the mean and vulgar works of Man;
But with high objects, with enduring things,
With life and nature; purifying thus
The elements of feeling and of thought,
And sanctifying by such discipline
Both pain and fear,— until we recognize
A grandeur in the beatings of the heart.
               William Wordsworth

ODE

INTIMATIONS OF IMMORTALITY
FROM RECOLLECTIONS OF EARLY CHILDHOOD

I

THERE was a time when meadow, grove, and
    stream,
    The earth, and every common sight,
      To me did seem
    Apparell'd in celestial light,

THE GYPSY TRAIL

The glory and the freshness of a dream.
It is not now as it hath been of yore; —
    Turn wheresoe'er I may
      By night or day,
The things which I have seen I now can see no
      more.

II

    The rainbow comes and goes,
    And lovely is the rose;
    The moon doth with delight
Look round her when the heavens are bare;
      Waters on a starry night
      Are beautiful and fair;
    The sunshine is a glorious birth;
    But yet I know, where'er I go,
That there hath passed away a glory from the
      earth.

III

Now, while the birds thus sing a joyous song,
  And while the young lambs bound
    As to the tabor's sound,
To me alone there came a thought of grief:
A timely utterance gave that thought relief,
    And I again am strong:
The cataracts blow their trumpets from the
       steep;
No more shall grief of mine the season wrong:
I hear the echoes through the mountains throng,
The winds come to me from the fields of sleep,
    And all the earth is gay;
      Land and sea
  Give themselves up to jollity,
    And with the heart of May

THE PILGRIM'S SCRIP

Doth every beast keep holiday!
  Thou Child of Joy,
Shout round me, let me hear thy shouts, thou
   happy Shepherd boy!

IV

Ye blessed creatures, I have heard the call
 Ye to each other make; I see
The heavens laugh with you in your jubilee;
  My heart is at your festival,
   My head hath its coronal,
The fulness of your bliss, I feel — I feel it all.
   O evil day! if I were sullen
   While Earth herself is adorning,
    This sweet May-morning;
    And the children are culling
     On every side,
    In a thousand valleys far and wide,
    Fresh flowers; while the sun shines warm,
And the babe leaps up on his mother's arm: —
    I hear, I hear, with joy I hear!
   — But there's a tree, of many, one
A single field which I have looked upon,
Both of them speak of something that is gone:
    The pansy at my feet
    Doth the same tale repeat:
Whither is fled the visionary gleam?
Where is it now, the glory and the dream?

V

Our birth is but a sleep and a forgetting:
The Soul that rises with us, our life's Star,
   Hath had elsewhere its setting,
    And cometh from afar:
   Not in entire forgetfulness,
   And not in utter nakedness,

But trailing clouds of glory do we come
    From God, who is our home:
Heaven lies about us in our infancy!
Shades of the prison-house begin to close
    Upon the growing Boy,
But he beholds the light, and whence it flows,
    He sees it in his joy;
The Youth, who daily further from the east
    Must travel, still is Nature's priest,
      And by the vision splendid
      Is on his way attended;
At length the Man perceives it die away,
And fade into the light of common day.

VI

Earth fills her lap with pleasures of her own;
Yearnings she hath in her own natural kind,
And even with something of a mother's mind,
    And no unworthy aim,
    The homely Nurse doth all she can
To make her foster-child, her inmate Man,
    Forget the glories he hath known,
And that imperial palace whence he came.

VII

Behold the Child among his new-born blisses,
A six years' darling of a pigmy size!
See where 'mid work of his own hand he lies,
Fretted by sallies of his mother's kisses,
With light upon him from his father's eyes!
See, at his feet, some little plan or chart,
Some fragment from his dream of human life
Shaped by himself with newly-learned art;
    A wedding or a festival,
    A mourning or a funeral;

THE PILGRIM'S SCRIP

And this hath now his heart,
And unto this he frames his song:
Then will he fit his tongue
To dialogues of business, love or strife;
But it will not be long
Ere this be thrown aside,
And with new joy and pride
The little actor cons another part;
Filling from time to time his "humorous stage"
With all the persons, down to palsied age,
That Life brings with her in her equipage;
As if his whole vocation
Were endless imitation.

VIII

Thou, whose exterior semblance doth belie
Thy Soul's immensity;
Thou best Philosopher, who yet dost keep
Thy heritage, thou Eye among the blind,
That, deaf and silent, read'st the eternal deep,
Haunted forever by the eternal mind,—
Mighty Prophet! Seer blest!
On whom those truths do rest,
Which we are toiling all our lives to find,
In darkness lost, the darkness of the grave;
Thou, over whom thy Immortality
Broods like the day, a Master o'er a Slave,
A Presence which is not to be put by;
Thou little Child, yet glorious in the might
Of heaven-born freedom on thy being's height,
Why with such earnest pains dost thou provoke
The years to bring the inevitable yoke,
Thus blindly with thy blessedness at strife?
Full soon thy Soul shall have her earthly freight,
And custom lie upon thee with a weight
Heavy as frost, and deep almost as life!

IX

O joy! that in our embers
Is something that doth live,
That nature yet remembers
What was so fugitive!
The thought of our past years in me doth breed
Perpetual benediction: not indeed
For that which is most worthy to be blest;
Delight and liberty, the simple creed
Of childhood, whether busy or at rest,
With new-fledged hope still fluttering in his
      breast : —
    Not for these I raise
    The song of thanks and praise:
    But for those obstinate questionings
    Of sense and outward things,
    Fallings from us, vanishings;
    Blank misgivings of a Creature
Moving about in worlds not realized,
High instincts before which our mortal nature
Did tremble like a guilty thing surprised:
    But for those first affections,
    Those shadowy recollections,
      Which, be they what they may,
Are yet the fountain light of all our day,
Are yet a master light of all our seeing;
    Uphold us, cherish, and have power to make
Our noisy years seem moments in the being
Of the eternal Silence: truths that wake,
      To perish never;
Which neither listlessness, nor mad endeavor,
      Nor Man nor Boy,
Nor all that is at enmity with joy,
Can utterly abolish or destroy!
    Hence in a season of calm weather,
      Though inland far we be,

THE PILGRIM'S SCRIP

Our Souls have sight of that immortal sea
    Which brought us hither,
    Can in a moment travel thither,
And see the Children sport upon the shore,
And hear the mighty waters rolling evermore.

X

Then sing, ye Birds, sing, sing a joyous song!
    And let the young Lambs bound
    As to the tabor's sound!
  We in thought will join your throng,
    Ye that pipe and ye that play,
    Ye that through your hearts to-day
    Feel the gladness of the May!
What though the radiance which was once so
       bright
Be now forever taken from my sight,
   Though nothing can bring back the hour
Of splendor in the grass, of glory in the flower;
    We will grieve not, rather find
    Strength in what remains behind;
    In the primal sympathy
    Which having been must ever be;
    In the soothing thoughts that spring
    Out of human suffering;
    In the faith that looks through death,
In years that bring the philosophic mind.

XI

And O, ye Fountains, Meadows, Hills, and
      Groves,
Forebode not any severing of our loves!
Yet in my heart of hearts I feel your might;
I only have relinquished one delight
To live beneath your more habitual sway.

THE GYPSY TRAIL

I love the brooks which down their channels
      fret,
Even more than when I tripped lightly as they;
The innocent brightness of a new-born day
      Is lovely yet;
The clouds that gather round the setting sun
Do take a sober coloring from an eye
That hath kept watch o'er man's mortality;
Another race hath been, and other palms are
      won.
Thanks to the human heart by which we live,
Thanks to its tenderness, its joys, and fears,
To me the meanest flower that blows can give
Thoughts that do often lie too deep for tears.
              William Wordsworth

LINES

COMPOSED A FEW MILES ABOVE TINTERN ABBEY, ON REVISITING THE BANKS OF THE WYE

FIVE years have past; five summers, with
    the length
Of five long winters! and again I hear
These waters, rolling from their mountain-
    springs
With a soft inland murmur.— Once again
Do I behold these steep and lofty cliffs,
That on a wild secluded scene impress
Thoughts of more deep seclusion; and connect
The landscape with the quiet of the sky.
The day is come when I again repose
Here, under this dark sycamore, and view
These plots of cottage-ground, these orchard-
    tufts,
Which at this season with their unripe fruits,

Are clad in one green hue, and lose themselves
'Mid groves and copses. Once again I see
These hedge-rows, hardly hedge-rows, little
    lines
Of sportive wood run wild: these pastoral farms,
Green to the very door; and wreaths of smoke
Sent up in silence from among the trees!
With some uncertain notice, as might seem
Of vagrant dweller's in the houseless woods,
Or of some Hermit's cave, where by his fire
The Hermit sits alone.
                These beauteous forms,
Through a long absence, have not been to me
As is a landscape to a blind man's eye:
But oft, in lonely rooms, and 'mid the din
Of towns and cities, I have owed to them
In hours of weariness, sensations sweet,
Felt in the blood, and felt along the heart;
And passing even into my purer mind,
With tranquil restoration: — feelings too
Of unremembered pleasure: such, perhaps,
As have no slight or trivial influence
On that best portion of a good man's life,
His little, nameless, unremembered acts
Of kindness and of love. Nor less, I trust,
To them I may have owed another gift,
Of aspect more sublime; that blessed mood,
In which the burthen of the mystery,
In which the heavy and the weary weight
Of all this unintelligible world
Is lightened: — that serene and blessed mood,
In which the affections gently lead us on,—
Until, the breath of this corporeal frame
And even the motion of our human blood
Almost suspended, we are laid asleep
In body, and become a living soul:

THE GYPSY TRAIL

While with an eye made quiet by the power
Of harmony, and the deep power of joy,
We see into the life of things.

                           If this
Be but a vain belief, yet, O, how oft,
In darkness, and amid the many shapes
Of joyless daylight; when the fretful stir
Unprofitable, and the fever of the world,
Have hung upon the beatings of my heart,
How oft, in spirit, have I turned to thee,
O sylvan Wye! thou wanderer thro' the woods,
How often has my spirit turned to thee!
And now with gleams of half-extinguished
    thought,
With many recognitions dim and faint,
And somewhat of a sad perplexity,
The picture of the mind revives again:
While here I stand, not only with the sense
Of present pleasure, but with pleasing thoughts
That in this moment there is life and food
For future years. And so I dare to hope,
Though changed, no doubt, from what I was
    when first
I came among these hills; when like a roe
I bounded o'er the mountains, by the sides
Of the deep rivers, and the lonely streams,
Wherever Nature led: more like a man
Flying from something that he dreads, than one
Who sought the thing he loved. For Nature
    then
(The coarser pleasures of my boyish days,
And their glad animal movements all gone by)
To me was all in all. I cannot paint
What then I was. The sounding cataract
Haunted me like a passion: the tall rock,
The mountain, and the deep and gloomy wood,

THE PILGRIM'S SCRIP

Their colors and their forms, were then to me
An appetite; a feeling and a love,
That had no need of a remoter charm,
By thought supplied, nor any interest
Unborrowed from the eye. That time is past,
And all its aching joys are now no more,
And all its dizzy raptures. Not for this
Faint I, nor mourn nor murmur; other gifts
Have followed; for such loss, I would believe,
Abundant recompense. For I have learned
To look on Nature, not as in the hour
Of thoughtless youth; but hearing oftentimes
The still, sad music of humanity,
Nor harsh nor grating, though of ample power
To chasten and subdue. And I have felt
A presence that disturbs me with the joy
Of elevated thoughts: a sense sublime
Of something far more deeply interfused,
Whose dwelling is the light of setting suns,
And the round ocean and the living air,
And the blue sky, and in the mind of man:
A motion and a spirit, that impels
All thinking things, all objects of all thought,
And rolls through all things. Therefore am I
     still
A lover of the meadows and the woods,
And mountains; and of all that we behold
From this green earth; of all the mighty world
Of eye and ear,— both what they half create,
And what perceive; well pleased to recognize
In nature and the language of the sense,
The anchor of my purest thoughts, the nurse,
The guide, the guardian of my heart, and soul
Of all my moral being.
                    Nor perchance,
If I were not thus taught, should I the more

THE GYPSY TRAIL

Suffer my genial spirits to decay:
For thou art with me here upon the banks
Of this fair river; thou, my dearest Friend,
My dear, dear Friend; and in thy voice I catch
The language of my former heart, and read
My former pleasures in the shooting lights
Of thy wild eyes. O! yet a little while
May I behold in thee what I was once,
My dear, dear Sister! and this prayer I make
Knowing that Nature never did betray
The heart that loved her; 'tis her privilege
Through all the years of this our life, to lead
From joy to joy: for she can so inform
The mind that is within us, so impress
With quietness and beauty, and so feed
With lofty thoughts, that neither evil tongues,
Rash judgments, nor the sneers of selfish men,
Nor greetings where no kindness is, nor all
The dreary intercourse of daily life,
Shall e'er prevail against us, or disturb
Our cheerful faith, that all which we behold
Is full of blessings. Therefore let the moon
Shine on thee in thy solitary walk;
And let the misty mountain winds be free
To blow against thee: and in after years,
When these wild ecstasies shall be matured
Into a sober pleasure; when thy mind
Shall be a mansion for all lovely forms,
Thy memory be as a dwelling-place
For all sweet sounds and harmonies; O! then,
If solitude, or fear, or pain, or grief,
Should be thy portion, with what healing
  thoughts
Of tender joy wilt thou remember me,
And these my exhortations! Nor, perchance —
If I should be where I no more can hear

THE PILGRIM'S SCRIP

Thy voice, nor catch from thy wild eyes these
    gleams
Of past existence,— wilt thou then forget
That on the banks of this delightful stream
We stood together; and that I, so long
A worshipper of Nature, hither came
Unwearied in that service: rather say
With warmer love — O! with far deeper zeal
Of holier love. Nor wilt thou then forget,
That after many wanderings, many years
Of absence, these steep woods and lofty cliffs,
And this green pastoral landscape, were to me
More dear, both for themselves and for thy
    sake!

William Wordsworth

THE WORLD IS TOO MUCH WITH US

THE world is too much with us; late and
    soon,
Getting and spending, we lay waste our powers:
Little we see in Nature that is ours;
We have given our hearts away, a sordid boon!
The Sea that bares her bosom to the moon;
The winds that will be howling at all hours,
And are up-gathered now like sleeping flowers;
For this, for everything, we are out of tune;
It moves us not.— Great God! I'd rather be
A Pagan suckled in a creed outworn;
So might I, standing on this pleasant lea,
Have glimpses that would make me less for-
    lorn,
Have sight of Proteus rising from the sea,
Or hear old Triton blow his wreathèd horn.

William Wordsworth

THE GYPSY TRAIL

DAYS

DAUGHTERS of Time, the hypocritic Days,
  Muffled and dumb like barefoot dervishes,
And marching single in an endless file,
Bring diadems and fagots in their hands.
To each they offer gifts after his will,
Bread, kingdoms, stars, and sky that holds them
  all.
I, in my pleached garden, watched the pomp,
Forgot my morning wishes, hastily
Took a few herbs and apples, and the Day
Turned and departed silent. I, too late,
Under her solemn fillet saw the scorn.
                    Ralph Waldo Emerson

EACH AND ALL

LITTLE thinks, in the field, yon red-cloaked
  clown
Of thee from the hill-top looking down;
The heifer, that lows in the upland farm,
Far-heard, lows not thine ear to charm;
The sexton, tolling his bell at noon,
Deems not that great Napoleon
Stops his horse, and lists with delight,
Whilst his files sweep round yon Alpine height;
Nor knowest thou what argument
Thy life to thy neighbor's creed has lent:
All are needed by each one,
Nothing is fair or good alone.
I thought the sparrow's note from heaven,
Singing at dawn on the alder bough;
I brought him home in his nest at even;
He sings the song, but it cheers not now;
For I did not bring home the river and sky;

THE PILGRIM'S SCRIP

He sang to my ear; they sang to my eye.
The delicate shells lay on the shore;
The bubbles of the latest wave
Fresh pearls to their enamel gave;
And the bellowing of the savage sea
Greeted their safe escape to me.
I wiped away the weeds and foam,
I fetched my sea-born treasures home;
But the poor, unsightly, noisome things
Had left their beauty on the shore
With the sun, and the sand, and the wild up-
    roar.
The lover watched his graceful maid
As 'mid the virgin train she strayed,
Nor knew her beauty's best attire
Was woven still by the snow-white choir.
At last she came to his hermitage,
Like the bird from the woodlands to the cage,—
The gay enchantment was undone,
A gentle wife, but fairy none.
Then I said, "I covet Truth;
Beauty is unripe childhood's cheat,
I leave it behind with the games of youth."
As I spoke, beneath my feet
The ground-pine curled its pretty wreath,
Running over the club-moss burrs;
I inhaled the violet's breath;
Around me stood the oaks and firs;
Pine cones and acorns lay on the ground;
Over me soared the eternal sky,
Full of light and of deity;
Again I saw, again I heard,
The rolling river, the morning bird; —
Beauty through my senses stole,
I yielded myself to the perfect whole.

                              Ralph Waldo Emerson

THE GYPSY TRAIL

SAADI

. . .

A ND thus to Saadi said the Muse:
  "Eat thou the bread which men re-
      fuse;
Flee from the goods which from thee flee;
Seek nothing,— Fortune seeketh thee.
Nor mount, nor dive; all good things keep
The midway of the eternal deep.
Wish not to fill the isles with eyes
To fetch thee birds of paradise;
On thine orchard's edge belong
All the brags of plumes and song;
Wise Ali's sunbright sayings pass
For proverbs in the market-place;
Through mountains bored by regal art
Toil whistles as he drives his cart.
Nor scour the seas, nor sift mankind,
A poet or a friend to find;
Behold, he watches at the door,
Behold his shadow on the floor.
Open innumerable doors
The heaven where unveiled Allah pours
The flood of truth, the flood of good,
The Seraph's and the Cherub's food;
Those doors are men; the Pariah hind
Admits thee to the perfect Mind.
Seek not beyond thy cottage wall
Redeemers that can yield thee all.
While thou sittest at thy door,
On the desert's yellow floor,
Listening to the gray-haired crones,
Foolish gossips, ancient drones,
Saadi, see! they rise in stature
To the height of mighty Nature,

And the secret stands revealed
Fraudulent Time in vain concealed,—
That blessed gods in servile masks
Plied for thee thy household tasks."
                              Ralph Waldo Emerson

WILT THOU NOT OPE THY HEART

FROM *Threnody*

WILT thou not ope thy heart to know
    What rainbows teach and sunsets
      show?
Verdict which accumulates
From lengthening scroll of human fates,
Voice of earth to earth returned,
Prayers of saints that inly burned,—
Saying, *what is excellent,*
As God lives, is permanent;
Hearts are dust, hearts' loves remain,
Heart's love will meet thee again.
Revere the Maker; fetch thine eye
Up to His style, and manners of the sky.
Not of adamant and gold
Built He heaven stark and cold,
No, but a nest of bending reeds,
Flowering grass and scented weeds,
Or like a traveller's fleeing tent,
Or bow above the tempest bent;
Built of tears and sacred flames,
And virtue reaching to its aims;
Built of furtherance and pursuing,
Not of spent deeds, but of doing.
Silent rushes the swift Lord
Through ruined systems still restored,
Broad-sowing, bleak and void to bless,
Plants with worlds the wilderness,

THE GYPSY TRAIL

Waters with tears of ancient sorrow
Apples of Eden ripe to-morrow;
House and tenant go to ground,
Lost in God, in Godhead found.

Ralph Waldo Emerson

THREE YEARS SHE GREW

THREE years she grew in sun and shower,
    Then Nature said, " A lovelier flower
On earth was never sown;
This Child I to myself will take;
She shall be mine, and I will make
A Lady of my own.

" Myself will to my darling be
Both law and impulse: and with me
The Girl, in rock and plain,
In earth and heaven, in glade and bower,
Shall feel an overseeing power
To kindle or restrain.

" She shall be sportive as the fawn
That wild with glee across the lawn,
Or up the mountain springs;
And hers shall be the breathing balm,
And hers the silence and the calm
Of mute insensate things.

" The floating clouds their state shall lend
To her; for her the willow bend;
Nor shall she fail to see
Even in the motions of the Storm
Grace that shall mould the Maiden's form
By silent sympathy.

THE PILGRIM'S SCRIP

"The stars of midnight shall be dear
To her; and she shall lean her ear
In many a secret place
Where rivulets dance their wayward round,
And beauty born of murmuring sound
Shall pass into her face.

"And vital feelings of delight
Shall rear her form to stately height,
Her virgin bosom swell;
Such thoughts to Lucy I will give
While she and I together live
Here in this happy dell."

Thus Nature spake — The work was done —
How soon my Lucy's race was run!
She died, and left to me
This heath, this calm and quiet scene;
The memory of what has been,
And nevermore will be.

William Wordsworth

GUY

MORTAL mixed of middle clay,
  Attempered to the night and day,
Interchangeable with things,
Needs no amulets nor rings.
Guy possessed the talisman
That all things from him began;
And as, of old, Polycrates
Chained the sunshine and the breeze,
So did Guy betimes discover
Fortune was his guard and lover;
In strange junctures, felt with awe
His own symmetry with law;

329

THE GYPSY TRAIL

That no mixture could withstand
The virtue of his lucky hand.
He gold or jewel could not lose,
Nor not receive his ample dues.
In the street, if he turned round,
His eye the eye 'twas seeking found.
It seemed his Genius discreet
Worked on the Maker's own receipt.
And made each tide and element
Stewards of stipend and of rent;
So that the common waters fell
As costly wine into his well.
He had so sped his wise affairs
That he caught Nature in his snares:
Early or late, the falling rain
Arrived in time to swell his grain;
Stream could not so perversely wind,
But corn of Guy's was there to grind;
The siroc found it on its way
To speed his sails, to dry his hay;
And the world's sun seemed to rise
To drudge all day for Guy the wise.
In his rich nurseries, timely skill
Strong crab with nobler blood did fill;
The zephyr in his garden rolled
From plum-trees vegetable gold;
And all the hours of the year
With their own harvest honored were.
There was no frost but welcome came,
Nor freshet, nor midsummer flame;
Belonged to wind and world the toil
And venture, and to Guy the oil.

                            Ralph Waldo Emerson

SWEET CONTENT

ART thou poor, yet hast thou golden slum-
bers?
O sweet content!
Art thou rich, yet is thy mind perplex'd?
O punishment!
Dost thou laugh to see how fools are vex'd
To add to golden numbers, golden numbers?
O sweet content! O sweet, O sweet con-
tent!
Work apace, apace, apace, apace;
Honest labor bears a lovely face;
Then hey nonny, nonny — hey nonny, nonny!

Canst drink the waters of the crispèd spring?
O sweet content!
Swim'st thou in wealth, yet sink'st in thine own
tears?
O punishment!
Then he that patiently want's burden bears,
No burden bears, but is a king, a king!
O sweet content! O sweet, O sweet con-
tent!
Work apace, apace, apace, apace;
Honest labor bears a lovely face;
Then hey nonny, nonny — hey nonny, nonny!

Thomas Dekker

EVENING

Eve lets down her veil,
The white fog creeps from bush to bush about,
   The west unflushes, the high stars grow bright,
And in the scattered farms the lights come out.
                                              Arnold

The moving Moon went up the sky
And nowhere did abide;
Softly she was going up,
And a star or two beside —

                              Coleridge

EVENING

ÜBER ALLEN GIPFELN

Ü̈BER allen Gipfeln
   Ist Ruh,
In allen Wipfeln
Spürest du
Kaum einen Hauch;
Die Vöglein schweigen in Walde.
Warte nur, balde
Ruhest du auch.
          Johann Wolfgang von Goethe

IT IS A BEAUTEOUS EVENING, CALM AND FREE

IT is a beauteous evening, calm and free;
   The holy time is quiet as a Nun,
Breathless with adoration; the broad sun
Is sinking down in its tranquillity;
The gentleness of heaven broods o'er the Sea:
Listen! the mighty Being is awake,
And doth with his eternal motion make
A sound like thunder — everlastingly.
Dear Child! dear Girl! that walkest with me
   here,
If thou appear untouched by solemn thought,
Thy nature is not therefore less divine:
Thou liest in Abraham's bosom all the year;
And worship'st at the Temple's inner shrine,
God being with thee when we know it not.
          William Wordsworth

THE GYPSY TRAIL

THE GREAT BREATH

ITS edges foamed with amethyst and rose,
    Withers once more the old blue flower of
      day:
There where the ether like a diamond glows
    Its petals fade away.

A shadowy tumult stirs the dusky air;
Sparkle the delicate dews, the distant snows;
The great deep thrills, for through it every-
    where
      The breath of Beauty blows.

I saw how all the trembling ages past,
Moulded to her by deep and deeper breath,
Neared to the. hour when Beauty breathes her
    last
      And knows herself in death.
              George William Russell

TO THE EVENING STAR

THOU fair-haired Angel of the Evening,
    Now, whilst the sun rests on the mountains,
      light
Thy bright torch of love — thy radiant crown
Put on, and smile upon our evening bed!
Smile on our loves; and while thou drawest the
Blue curtains of the sky, scatter thy silver dew
On every flower that shuts its sweet eyes
In timely sleep. Let thy west wind sleep on
The lake; speak silence with thy glimmering
    eyes,

EVENING

And wash the dusk with silver.— Soon, full
  soon,
Dost thou withdraw; then the wolf rages wide,
And the lion glares through the dun forest.
The fleeces of our flocks are covered with
Thy sacred dew: protect them with thy influ-
  ence!

William Blake

NIGHT

THE sun descending in the west,
  The evening star does shine;
The birds are silent in their nest,
And I must seek for mine.
  The moon, like a flower
  In heaven's high bower,
  With silent delight,
  Sits and smiles on the night.

Farewell, green fields and happy grove,
Where flocks have ta'en delight.
Where lambs have nibbled, silent move
The feet of angels bright;
  Unseen, they pour blessing,
  And joy without ceasing,
  On each bud and blossom,
  And each sleeping bosom.

They look in every thoughtless nest
Where birds are covered warm;
They visit caves of every beast,
To keep them all from harm:

THE GYPSY TRAIL

If they see any weeping
That should have been sleeping,
They pour sleep on their head,
And sit down by their bed.

.   .   .

William Blake

ABSCHIED

ABENDLICH schon rauscht der Wald
    Aus den tiefen Gründen,
Droben wird der Herr nun bald
An die Sterne zünden,
Wie so stille in den Schlünden,
Abendlich nur rauscht der Wald.

Alles geht zu seiner Ruh,
Wald und Welt versausen,
Schauernd hört der Wandrer zu,
Sehnt sich recht nach Hause,
Hier in Waldes grüner Klause,
Herz, geh' endlich auch zur Ruh!

Joseph von Eichendorff

SWEET AND LOW

SWEET and low, sweet and low,
    Wind of the western sea,
Low, low, breathe and blow,
    Wind of the western sea!
Over the rolling waters go,
Come from the dying moon, and blow,
    Blow him again to me;
While my little one, while my pretty
      one, sleeps.

EVENING

Sleep and rest, sleep and rest,
  Father will come to thee soon;
Rest, rest, on mother's breast,
  Father will come to thee soon;
Father will come to his babe in the nest,
Silver sails all out of the west
  Under the silver moon:
Sleep, my little one, sleep, my pretty
      one, sleep.

Alfred, Lord Tennyson

CROSSING THE BAR

SUNSET and evening star,
  And one clear call for me!
And may there be no moaning of the bar,
  When I put out to sea,

But such a tide as moving seems asleep,
  Too full for sound and foam,
When that which drew from out the boundless
      deep
  Turns again home.

Twilight and evening bell,
  And after that the dark!
And may there be no sadness of farewell,
  When I embark;

For tho' from out our bourne of Time and
      Place
  The flood may bear me far,
I hope to see my Pilot face to face
  When I have crost the bar.

Alfred, Lord Tennyson
339

NIGHT

Teach me your mood, O patient stars,
  Who climb each night the ancient sky,
Leaving on space no shade, no scars,
  No trace of age, no fear to die.

Emerson

The wonder of an ancient awe
Takes hold upon him when he sees
In the cold autumn dusk arise
Orion and the Pleiades;

Or when along the southern rim
Of the mysterious summer night
He marks, above the sleeping world,
Antares with his scarlet light.

Bliss Carman

The stars are forth, the moon above the tops
Of the snow-shining mountains.— Beautiful!
I linger yet with Nature, for the night
Hath been to me a more familiar face
Than that of man: and in her starry shade
Of dim and solitary loveliness,
I learned the language of another world.

Byron

NIGHT

A CLEAR MIDNIGHT

THIS is thy hour, O Soul, thy free flight into
    the wordless,
Away from books, away from art, the day erased,
    the lesson done,
Thee fully forth emerging, silent, gazing, pon-
    dering the themes thou lovest best,
Night, sleep, death, and the stars.

Walt Whitman

TO NIGHT

I

SWIFTLY walk over the western wave,
    Spirit of Night!
Out of the misty eastern cave,
Where all the long and lone daylight,
Thou wovest dreams of joy and fear,
Which make thee terrible and dear,—
    Swift be thy flight!

II

Wrap thy form in a mantle gray,
    Star-inwrought!
Blind with thine hair the eyes of Day;
Kiss her until she be wearied out,
Then wander o'er city, and sea, and land,
Touching all with thine opiate wand —
    Come, long sought!

343

THE GYPSY TRAIL

III

When I arose and saw the dawn,
     I sighed for thee;
When light rode high, and the dew was gone,
And noon lay heavy on flower and tree,
And the weary day turned to his rest,
Lingering like an unloved guest,
     I sighed for thee.

IV

Thy brother Death came, and cried,
     Wouldst thou me?
Thy sweet child Sleep, the filmy-eyed,
Murmured like a noontide bee,
Shall I nestle near thy side?
Wouldst thou me? — And I replied,
     No, not thee!

V

Death will come when thou art dead,
     Soon, too soon —
Sleep will come when thou art fled;
Of neither would I ask the boon
I ask of thee, belovèd Night —
Swift be thine approaching flight,
     Come soon, soon!

                    Percy Bysshe Shelley

NIGHT

MYSTERIOUS Night! when our first parent knew
Thee, from report divine, and heard thy name,
Did he not tremble for this lovely Frame,
This glorious canopy of Light and Blue?

344

NIGHT

Yet, 'neath a curtain of translucent dew,
Bathed in the rays of the great setting Flame,
Hesperus, with the Host of Heaven, came,
And lo! Creation widened on Man's view.
Who could have thought such darkness lay concealed
Within thy beams, O Sun! or who could find,
Whilst flower and leaf and insect stood revealed,
That to such countless Orbs thou mad'st us blind!
Why do we then shun Death with anxious strife?
If Light can thus deceive, wherefore not Life?
                              Joseph Blanco White

THE SPACIOUS FIRMAMENT ON HIGH

THE spacious firmament on high,
    And all the blue ethereal sky,
And spangled heavens, a shining frame,
Their great Original proclaim.
Th' unwearied Sun from day to day,
Does his Creator's power display,
And publishes to every land
The work of an Almighty hand.

Soon as the evening shades prevail,
The Moon takes up the wondrous tale,
And nightly to the listening Earth
Repeats the story of her birth;
Whilst all the stars that round her burn,
And all the planets in their turn,
Confirm the tidings as they roll,
And spread the truth from pole to pole.

THE GYPSY TRAIL

What though in solemn silence all
Move round the dark terrestrial ball;
What though no real voice nor sound
Amid their radiant orbs be found;
In Reason's ear they all rejoice,
And utter forth a glorious voice,
Forever singing as they shine,
The Hand that made us is divine.

Joseph Addison

LUCIDA TEMPLA DEORUM

IN caeloque deum sedes et templa locarunt,
  Per caelum volvi quia nox et luna videtur,
Luna dies et nox et noctis signa severa
Noctivagaeque faces caeli flammaeque volantes,
Nubila sol imbres nix venti fulmina grando
Et rapidi fremitus et murmura magna minarum.

Lucretius

LUCIFER IN STARLIGHT

ON a starred night Prince Lucifer uprose.
  Tired of his dark dominion swung the fiend
Above the rolling ball in cloud part screened,
Where sinners hugged their spectre of repose.
Poor prey to his hot fit of pride were those.
And now upon his western wing he leaned,
Now his huge bulk o'er Afric's sands careened,
Now the black planet shadowed Arctic snows.
Soaring through wider zones that pricked his
    scars
With memory of the old revolt from Awe,
He reached a middle height, and at the stars,

346

NIGHT

Which are the brain of heaven, he looked, and
    sank.
Around the ancient track marched, rank on rank,
The army of unalterable law.
George Meredith

THE STAR SIRIUS

BRIGHT Sirius! that when Orion pales
    To dotlings under moonlight still art keen
With cheerful fervor of a warrior's mien
Who holds in his great heart the battle-scales;
Unquenched of flame though swift the flood as-
    sails,
Reducing many lustrous to the lean:
Be thou my star, and thou in me be seen
To show what source divine is, and prevails.
Long watches through, at one with godly night,
I mark thee planting joy in constant fire;
And thy quick beams, whose jets of life inspire
Life to the spirit, passion for the light,
Dark Earth since first she lost her lord from
    sight
Has viewed and felt them sweep her as a lyre.
George Meredith

WINTER HEAVENS

SHARP is the night, but stars with frost alive,
    Leap off the rim of earth across the dome.
It is a night to make the heavens our home
More than the nest whereto apace we strive.
Lengths down our road each fir-tree seems a
    hive,
In swarms outrushing from the golden comb.

THE GYPSY TRAIL

They waken waves of thoughts that burst to
    foam:
The living throb in me, the dead revive.
Yon mantle clothes us: there, past mortal
    breath,
Life glistens on the river of the death.
It folds us flesh and dust; and have we knelt,
Or never knelt, or eyed as kine the springs
Of radiance, the radiance enrings:
And this is the soul's haven to have felt.

George Meredith

WHEN I HEARD THE LEARN'D
ASTRONOMER

WHEN I heard the learn'd astronomer;
    When the proofs, the figures, were
    ranged in columns before me;
When I was shown the charts and the diagrams,
    to add, divide, and measure them;
When I, sitting, heard the astronomer, where
    he lectured with much applause in the lec-
    ture-room,
How soon, unaccountable, I became tired and
    sick;
Till rising and gliding out, I wander'd off by my-
    self,
In the mystical moist night-air, and from time
    to time,
Look'd up in perfect silence at the stars.

Walt Whitman

NIGHT

THE AUGUST SKY

SPARKLING in splendor the Kite and the
　Dipper
Crossed the black welkin, and Scorpio's star
　　Lit on the runway stag, herdsman, and skip-
　　　per
　　When I was dust, perhaps, bed-rock or spar.

Dust, fire, or dew, or the wind of the morning,
　　Foam of some sea-coast unknown, on the
　　　deep,
　　Somewhere I lived in creation's adorning
　　Still, on the nights when Joan walked with
　　　her sheep.

What was I dreaming or where did I wander
　　All through the Augusts before I could
　　　know?
　　Crystal the Archer swept high over yonder:
　　Close to the zenith burned Vega's blue snow.

Glory on glory the night's coronation
　　Circled the heavens before I was born —
　　Shone while I slept in the soul of creation
　　Somewhere when Ruth wept for home in
　　　the corn.

Glory on glory the night's coronation
　　Throbbed in a beauty past dream or desire,
　　Proud as I slept in the soul of creation —
　　Breath of the morning or bed-rock or fire.
　　　　　　　　　　Edith Wyatt

349

THE GYPSY TRAIL

NIGHT BEFORE TROY

FROM *The Iliad*

A S when in heaven the stars about the moon
Look beautiful, when all the winds are laid,
And every height comes out, and jutting peak
And valley, and the immeasurable heavens
Break open to their highest, and all the stars
Shine, and the Shepherd gladdens in his heart:
So many a fire between the ships and stream
Of Xanthus blazed before the towers of Troy,
A thousand on the plain; and close by each
Sat fifty in the blaze of burning fire;
And eating hoary grain and pulse the steeds,
Fixt by their cars, waited the golden dawn.

Translation by Tennyson

NOX ET AURORA

FROM *The Aeneid*

N ECDUM orbem medium Nox horis acta
subibat:
Haud segnis strato surgit Palinurus et omnes
Explorat ventos, atque auribus aëra captat;
Sidera cuncta notat tacito labentia caelo,
Arcturum pluviasque Hyadas geminosque Tri-
ones,
Armatumque auro circumspicit Oriona.
Postquam cuncta videt caelo constare sereno,
Dat clarum e puppi signum; nos castra movemus,
Temptamusque viam et velorum pandimus alas.
Iamque rubescebat stellis Aurora fugatis,
Cum procul obscuros colles humilemque videmus
Italiam.

Vergil

350

NIGHT

THE INFINITE SHINING HEAVENS

THE infinite shining heavens
   Rose and I saw in the night
Uncountable angel stars
   Showering sorrow and light.

I saw them distant as heaven,
   Dumb and shining and dead,
And the idle stars of the night
   Were dearer to me than bread.

Night after night in my sorrow
   The stars stood over the sea,
Till lo! I looked in the dusk
   And a star had come down to me.
Robert Louis Stevenson

LAST SONNET

BRIGHT star! would I were steadfast as thou
   art —
  Not in lone splendor hung aloft the night,
And watching, with eternal lids apart,
  Like Nature's patient sleepless Eremite,
The moving waters at their priestlike task
  Of pure ablution round earth's human shores,
Or gazing on the new soft fallen mask
  Of snow upon the mountains and the moors —
No — yet still steadfast, still unchangeable,
  Pillow'd upon my fair love's ripening breast,
To feel for ever its soft fall and swell,
  Awake for ever in a sweet unrest,
Still, still to hear her tender-taken breath,
And so live ever — or else swoon to death.
John Keats

THE GYPSY TRAIL

HYMN TO CYNTHIA

QUEEN and huntress, chaste and fair,
  Now the sun is laid to sleep,
  Seated in thy silver chair,
State in wonted manner keep:
Hesperus entreats thy light,
Goddess excellently bright!

Earth, let not thy envious shade
Dare itself to interpose;
Cynthia's shining orb was made
Heaven to clear when day did close:
Bless us then with wishèd sight,
Goddess excellently bright!

Lay thy bow of pearl apart
And thy crystal-shining quiver;
Give unto the flying hart
Space to breathe, how short soever:
Thou that mak'st a day of night,
Goddess excellently bright!

Ben Jonson

AN APRIL NIGHT

O CLIMB with me, this April night,
  The silver ladder of the moon —
All dew and danger and delight:
Above the poplars soon,

Into the lilac-scented sky,
Shall mount her maiden horn,
Frail as a spirit to the eye —
O climb with me till morn!

Richard Le Gallienne

NIGHT

MONDNACHT

ES war, als hätt' der Himmel
   Die Erde still geküsst,
Dass sie im Blütenschimmer
Von ihm nun träumen müsst'.

Die Luft ging durch die Felder,
Die Aehren wogten sacht,
Es rauschten leis' die Wälder,
So sternklar war die Nacht.

Und meine Seele spannte
Weit ihre Flügel aus,
Flog durch die stillen Lande,
Als flöge sie nach Haus.

Joseph von Eichendorff

AN DEN MOND

FÜLLEST wieder Busch und Thal
   Still mit Nebelglanz,
Lösest endlich auch einmal
Meine Seele ganz;

Breitest über mein Gefild
Lindernd deinen Blick,
Wie des Freundes Auge mild
Uber mein Geschick.

.   .   .

Johann Wolfgang von Goethe

THE GYPSY TRAIL

I AM HE THAT WALKS WITH THE TENDER
AND GROWING NIGHT

I AM he that walks with the tender and grow-
    ing night;
I call to the earth and sea, half-held by the night.

Press close, bare-bosom'd night! Press close,
    magnetic, nourishing night!
Night of south winds! night of the large few
    stars!
Still, nodding night! mad, naked, Summer night.

Smile, O voluptuous, cool-breath'd earth!
Earth of the slumbering and liquid trees;
Earth of departed sunset! earth of the mountains,
    misty-topt!
Earth of the vitreous pour of the full moon,
    just tinged with blue!
Earth of shine and dark, mottling the tide of the
    river!
Earth of the limpid gray of clouds, brighter and
    clearer for my sake!
Far-swooping elbow'd earth! rich, apple-blos-
    som'd earth!
Smile for your lover comes!

Prodigal, you have given me love! Therefore I
    to you give love!
O unspeakable, passionate love!
Walt Whitman

NIGHT

EVENING AT PALERMO

NOW night descends with darkness: summer
 swoons
 Through the wide temples of the windless sky;
And on the mirrors of the waves, like moons,
 The breathing stars dilated languid lie:
 How cool to throbbing pulse and heated eye
Are those smooth silver curves that round the
 bay
Upon their sandy margent rest from play!

How sweet it were on this mysterious night
 Of pulsing stars and splendors, from the shore
Knee-deep to wade, and from the ripples bright
 To brush the phosphorescent foam-flowers
  hoar;
 Then with broad breast to cleave the watery
  floor,
And floating, dreaming, through the sphere to
 swim
Of silvery skies and silvery billows dim.

What if the waves of dreamless Death, like these,
 Should soothe our senses aching with the
  shine
Of Life's long radiance? O primeval ease,
 That wast and art and art to be divine,
 Thou shalt receive into the crystalline
These souls o'erburdened with mortality!
       John Addington Symonds

THE GYPSY TRAIL

TO A NIGHTINGALE

MY heart aches, and a drowsy numbness pains
My sense, as though of hemlock I had
drunk,
Or emptied some dull opiate to the drains
One minute past, and Lethe-wards had sunk:
'Tis not through envy of thy happy lot,
But being too happy in thy happiness,—
That thou, light-winged Dryad of the trees,
In some melodious plot
Of beechen green, and shadows numberless,
Singest of summer in full-throated ease.

O for a draught of vintage, that hath been
Cool'd a long age in the deep-delved earth,
Tasting of Flora and the country green,
Dance, and Provençal song, and sun-burnt
mirth!
O for a beaker full of the warm South,
Full of the true, the blushful Hippocrene,
With beaded bubbles winking at the brim,
And purple-stained mouth;
That I might drink and leave the world un-
seen,
And with thee fade away into the forest dim:

Fade far away, dissolve, and quite forget
What thou among the leaves hast never known,
The weariness, the fever, and the fret
Here, where men sit and hear each other
groan;
Where palsy shakes a few, sad, last gray hairs,
Where youth grows pale, and spectre-thin, and
dies;

NIGHT

Where but to think is to be full of sorrow
  And leaden-eyed despairs;
Where Beauty cannot keep her lustrous eyes,
  Or new Love pine at them beyond to-mor-
    row.

Away! away! for I will fly to thee,
  Not charioted by Bacchus and his pards,
But on the viewless wings of Poesy,
  Though the dull brain perplexes and retards:
Already with thee! tender is the night,
  And haply the Queen-Moon is on her throne,
    Cluster'd around by all her starry Fays;
      But here there is no light,
  Save what from heaven is with the breezes
      blown
    Through verdurous glooms and winding
      mossy ways.

I cannot see what flowers are at my feet,
  Nor what soft incense hangs upon the boughs,
But, in embalmed darkness, guess each sweet
  Wherewith the seasonable month endows
The grass, the thicket, and the fruit-tree wild;
  White hawthorn, and the pastoral eglantine;
    Fast-fading violets cover'd up in leaves;
      And mid-May's eldest child,
  The coming musk-rose, full of dewy wine,
    The murmurous haunt of flies on Summer
      eves.

Darkling I listen; and for many a time
  I have been half in love with easeful Death,
Call'd him soft names in many a mused rhyme,
  To take into the air my quiet breath;
Now more than ever seems it rich to die,

THE GYPSY TRAIL

To cease upon the midnight with no pain,
  While thou art pouring forth thy soul
     abroad
    In such an ecstasy!
Still wouldst thou sing, and I have ears in
     vain —
  To thy high requiem become a sod.

Thou wast not born for death, immortal Bird!
  No hungry generations tread thee down;
The voice I hear this passing night was heard
  In ancient days by emperor and clown:
Perhaps the self-same song that found a path

  Through the sad heart of Ruth, when, sick for
     home,
    She stood in tears amid the alien corn;
     The same that oft-times hath
    Charm'd magic casements, opening on the
     foam
Of perilous seas, in faery lands forlorn.

Forlorn! the very word is like a bell
  To toll me back from thee to my sole self!
Adieu! the fancy cannot cheat so well
  As she is famed to do, deceiving elf.
Adieu! adieu! thy plaintive anthem fades
  Past the near meadows, over the still stream,
    Up the hill-side; and now 'tis buried deep
    In the next valley-glades:
  Was it a vision or a waking dream?
    Fled is that music: — do I wake or sleep?
                 John Keats

NIGHT

WHEN LILACS LAST IN THE DOORYARD BLOOM'D

.   .   .   .

THEN with the knowledge of death as walk-
ing one side of me,
And the thought of death close-walking the other
side of me,
And I in the middle, as with companions and
as holding the hands of companions,
I fled forth to the hiding receiving night, that
talks not,
Down to the shores of the water, the path by the
swamp in the dimness,
To the solemn shadowy cedars, and ghostly pines
so still.
And the singer so shy to the rest receiv'd me;
The gray-brown bird I know receiv'd us com-
rades three;
And he sang what seem'd the carol of death,
and a verse for him I love.

From deep secluded recesses,
From the fragrant cedars, and the ghostly pines
so still,
Came the carol of the bird.

And the charm of the carol rapt me,
As I held, as if by their hands, my comrades in
the night;
And the voice of my spirit tallied the song of the
bird.

Come, lovely and soothing Death,
Undulate round the world, serenely arriving,
arriving,

THE GYPSY TRAIL

In the day, in the night, to all, to each,
Sooner or later, delicate Death.

Prais'd be the fathomless universe,
For life and joy, and for objects and knowl-
     edge curious;
And for love, sweet love — But praise!
     praise! praise!
For the sure-enwinding arms of cool-enfold-
     ing Death.

Dark Mother, always gliding near, with soft
     feet,
Have none chanted for thee a chant of ful-
     lest welcome?

Then I chant it for thee — I glorify thee
     above all;
I bring thee a song that when thou must in-
     deed come, come unfalteringly.

Approach, strong Deliveress!
When it is so — when thou hast taken them,
     I joyously sing the dead,
Lost in the loving floating ocean of thee,
Laved in the flood of thy bliss, O Death.

From me to thee, glad serenades,
Dances for thee I propose, saluting thee —
     adornments and feastings for thee;
And the sights of the open landscape, and the
     high-spread sky, are fitting,
And life and the fields, and the huge and
     thoughtful night.

NIGHT

The night in silence under many a star;
The ocean shore, and the husky whispering
    wave, whose voice I know;
And the soul turning to thee, O vast and
    well-veiled Death,
And the body gratefully nestling close to
    thee.
Over the tree-tops I float thee a song!
Over the rising and sinking waves — over
    the myriad fields, and the prairies wide;
Over the dense-pack'd cities all, and the
    teeming wharves and ways,
I float this carol with joy, with joy to thee,
    O Death!

                       Walt Whitman

JOY, SHIPMATE, JOY!

JOY, shipmate, joy!
    (Pleas'd to my soul at death I cry,)
Our life is closed, our life begins,
The long, long anchorage we leave,
The ship is clear at last, she leaps!
She swiftly courses from the shore,
Joy, shipmate, joy!

                       Walt Whitman

THE GYPSY TRAIL

REQUIEM

U NDER the wide and starry sky,
     Dig the grave and let me lie.
Glad did I live and gladly die,
     And I laid me down with a will.

This be the verse you grave for me:
Here he lies where he longed to be;
Home is the sailor, home from sea,
     And the hunter home from the hill.

                    Robert Louis Stevenson

AUTUMN

— When the sound of dropping nuts is heard, though
  all the trees are still,
And twinkle in the smoky light the waters of the rill —
Bryant

The day becomes more solemn and serene
  When noon is past — there is a harmony
  In Autumn, and a lustre in its sky,
Which thro' the Summer is not heard or seen.
Shelley

Earth knows no desolation.
She smells regeneration
In the moist breath of decay.
Meredith

O wind,
If Winter comes, can Spring be far behind?
Shelley

AUTUMN

HIRT AUF DEM BERGE

IHR Matten, lebt wohl!
  Ihr sonnigen Weiden!
Der Senne muss scheiden,
Der Sommer ist hin.
Wir fahren zu Berg, wir kommen wieder,
Wenn der Kuckuck ruft, wenn erwachen die
          Lieder,
Wenn mit Blumen die Erde sich kleidet neu,
Wenn die Brünnlein fliessen im lieblichen Mai.
    Ihr Matten, lebt wohl!
    Ihr sonnigen Weiden!
    Der Senne muss scheiden,
    Der Sommer ist hin.
                    Friedrich von Schiller

AUTUMN FIRES

IN the other gardens
  And all up the vale,
From the autumn bonfires
See the smoke trail!

Pleasant summer over
And all the summer flowers,
The red fire blazes,
The gray smoke towers.

THE GYPSY TRAIL

Sing a song of seasons!
Something bright in all!
Flowers in the summer,
Fires in the fall!

Robert Louis Stevenson

AT THE YELLOW OF THE LEAF

THE falling leaf is at the door;
　　The autumn wind is on the hill;
Footsteps I have heard before
Loiter at my cabin sill.

Full of crimson and of gold
Is the morning in the leaves;
And a stillness pure and cold
Hangs about the frosty eaves.

The mysterious autumn haze
Steals across the blue ravine,
Like an Indian ghost that strays
Through his olden lost demesne.

Now the goldenrod invades
Every clearing in the hills;
The dry glow of August fades,
And the lonely cricket shrills.

Yes, by every trace and sign
The good roving days are here.
Mountain peak and river line
Float the scarlet of the year.

Lovelier than ever now
Is the world I love so well.
Running water, waving bough,
And the bright wind's magic spell

AUTUMN

Rouse the taint of migrant blood
With the fever of the road,—
Impulse older than the flood
Lurking in its last abode.

Did I once pursue your way,
Litttle brothers of the air,
Following the vernal ray?
Did I learn my roving there?

Was it on your long spring rides,
Little brothers of the sea,
In the dim and peopled tides,
That I learned this vagrancy?

Now the yellow of the leaf
Bids away by hill and plain,
I shall say good-bye to grief,
Wayfellow with joy again.

The glamour of the open door
Is on me, and I would be gone,—
Speak with truth or speak no more,
House with beauty or with none.

Great and splendid, near and far,
Lies the province of desire;
Love the only silver star
Its discoverers require.

I shall lack nor tent nor food,
Nor companion in the way,
For the kindly solitude
Will provide for me to-day.

THE GYPSY TRAIL

Few enough have been my needs;
Fewer now they are to be;
Where the faintest follow leads,
There is heart's content for me.

Leave the bread upon the board;
Leave the book beside the chair;
With the murmur of the ford,
Light of spirit I shall fare.

Leave the latch-string in the door,
And the pile of logs to burn;
Others may be here before
I have leisure to return.

Bliss Carman

A VAGABOND SONG

THERE is something in the Autumn that is
native to my blood —
Touch of manner, hint of mood;
And my heart is like a rhyme,
With the yellow and the purple and the crimson
keeping time.

The scarlet of the maples can shake me like a cry
Of bugles going by,
And my lonely spirit thrills
To see the frosty asters like a smoke upon the
hills.

There is something in October sets the gypsy
blood astir;
We must rise and follow her,
When from each hill of flame
She calls and calls each vagabond by name.

Bliss Carman

AUTUMN

THE JOYS OF THE ROAD

NOW the joys of the road are chiefly these:
  A crimson touch on the hard-wood trees;

A vagrant's morning wide and blue,
In early fall, when the wind walks, too;

A shadowy highway cool and brown,
Alluring up and enticing down

From rippled water to dappled swamp,
From purple glory to scarlet pomp;

The outward eye, the quiet will,
And the striding heart from hill to hill;

The tempter apple over the fence;
The cobweb bloom on the yellow quince;

The palish asters along the wood,—
A lyric touch in the solitude;

An open hand, an easy shoe,
And a hope to make the day go through,—

Another to sleep with, and a third
To wake me up at the voice of a bird;

The resonant far-listening morn,
And the hoarse whisper of the corn;

The crickets mourning their comrades lost,
In the night's retreat from the gathering frost;

THE GYPSY TRAIL

(Or is it their slogan, plaintive and shrill,
As they beat on their corselets, valiant still?)

A hunger fit for the kings of the sea,
And a loaf of bread for Dickon and me;

A thirst like that of the Thirsty Sword,
And a jug of cider on the board;

An idle noon, a bubbling spring,
The sea in the pine-tops murmuring;

A scrap of gossip at the ferry;
A comrade neither glum nor merry,

Asking nothing, revealing naught,
But minting his words from a fund of thought,

A keeper of silence eloquent,
Needy, yet royally well content,

Of the mettled breed, yet abhorring strife,
And full of the mellow juice of life,

A taster of wine, with an eye for a maid,
Never too bold, and never afraid,

Never heart-whole, never heart-sick,
(These are the things I worship in Dick)

No fidget and no reformer, just
A calm observer of ought and must,

A lover of books, but a reader of man,
No cynic and no charlatan,

AUTUMN

Who never defers and never demands,
But, smiling, takes the world in his hands,—

Seeing it good as when God first saw
And gave it the weight of his will for law.

And O the joy that is never won,
But follows and follows the journeying sun,

By marsh and tide, by meadow and stream,
A will-o'-the-wind, a light-o'-dream,

Delusion afar, delight anear,
From morrow to morrow, from year to year,

A jack-o'-lantern, a fairy fire,
A dare, a bliss, and a desire!

The racy smell of the forest loam,
When the stealthy, sad-heart leaves go home;

(O leaves, O leaves, I am one with you,
Of the mould and the sun and the wind and the
    dew!)

The broad gold wake of the afternoon;
The silent fleck of the cold new moon;

The sound of the hollow sea's release
From stormy tumult to starry peace;

With only another league to wend;
And two brown arms at the journey's end!

These are the joys of the open road —
For him who travels without a load.

Bliss Carman

THE GYPSY TRAIL

AMONG THE ROCKS

OH, good gigantic smile o' the brown old
earth,
This autumn morning! How he sets his bones
To bask i' the sun, and thrusts out knees and
feet
For the ripple to run over in its mirth;
Listening the while, where on the heap of
stones
The white breast of the sea-lark twitters sweet.

That is the doctrine, simple, ancient, true;
Such is life's trial, as old earth smiles and
knows.
If you loved only what were worth your love,
Love were clear gain, and wholly well for you:
Make the low nature better by your throes!
Give earth yourself, go up for gain above!
Robert Browning

TO AUTUMN

SEASON of mists and mellow fruitfulness!
Close bosom-friend of the maturing sun;
Conspiring with him how to load and bless
With fruit the vines that round the thatch-
eaves run.
To bend with apples the moss'd cottage-trees,
And fill all fruit with ripeness to the core;
To swell the gourd, and plump the hazel
shells
With a sweet kernel; to set budding more,
And still more, later flowers for the bees,
Until they think warm days will never cease, •
For Summer has o'er-brimm'd their clammy
cells.

AUTUMN

Who hath not seen thee oft amid thy store?
  Sometimes whoever seeks abroad may find
Thee sitting careless on a granary floor,
  Thy hair soft-lifted by the winnowing wind;
Or on a half-reap'd furrow sound asleep,
  Drowsed with the fumes of poppies, while thy
    hook
    Spares the next swath and all its twined
      flowers;
And sometimes like a gleaner thou dost keep
  Steady thy laden head across a brook;
  Or by a cider-press, with patient look,
    Thou watchest the last oozings, hours by
      hours.

Where are the songs of Spring? Ay, where are
    they?
  Think not of them, thou hast thy music too,
    While barred clouds bloom the soft-dying
      day,
And touch the stubble-plains with rosy hue;
  Then in a wailful choir the small gnats mourn
  Among the river sallows, borne aloft
    Or sinking as the light wind lives or dies;
And full-grown lambs loud bleat from hilly
    bourn;
  Hedge-crickets sing; and now with treble soft
  The redbreast whistles from a garden-croft,
    And gathering swallows twitter in the skies.
                                        John Keats

THE GYPSY TRAIL

AN AUTUMN DAY

A SOUL is in the sunlight. Not one breath
Troubles the stainless and translucent sky.
Methinks the spirits of the mountain fly
Heavenward like flames. Blue air encompass-
eth
The congregated Alps that lift on high
Their crowned brows, to hear what Summer
saith.
She, having whispered, will depart; and death
Comes in the clasp of Winter by and by.
Hushed are the pines. There is no stir, no
strife,
No fretful wailing of frore winds that blow
Earth's winding-sheet of cold uncolored snow.
This morn, upon the brink of dying, Life
Draws a deep draft of peace, and rapture thrills
Thro' all the pulses of the impassioned hills.
                    John Addington Symonds

ODE TO THE SPIRIT OF EARTH IN AUTUMN

F AIR Mother Earth lay on her back last night,
To gaze her fill on Autumn's sunset skies,
When at a waving of the fallen light,
Sprang realms of rosy fruitage o'er her eyes.
A lustrous heavenly orchard hung the West,
Wherein the bloom of Eden bloomed again:
Red were the myriad cherub-mouths that pressed,
Among the clusters, rich with song, full fain,
But dumb, because that overmastering spell
Of rapture held them dumb: then, here and there,
A golden harp lost strings; a crimson shell
Burnt gray; and sheaves of lustre fell to air.
The illimitable eagerness of hue

374

AUTUMN

Bronzed, and the beamy winged bloom that flew
'Mid those bunched fruits and thronging figures
    failed.
A green-edged lake of saffron touched the blue,
With isles of fireless purple lying through:
And Fancy on that lake to seek lost treasures
    sailed.

    Not long the silence followed:
  The voice that issues from thy breast,
    O glorious South-west,
  Along the gloom-horizon halloa'd;
Warning the valleys with a mellow roar
Through flapping wings; then sharp the wood-
    land bore
  A shudder and a noise of hands:
  A thousand horns from some far vale
  In ambush sounding on the gale.
  Forth from the cloven sky came bands
Of revel-gathering spirits; trooping down,
Some rode the tree-tops; some on torn cloud-
    strips
  Burst screaming through the lighted town:
And scudding sea-ward, some fell on big ships:
  Or mounting the sea-horses blew
  Bright foam-flakes on the black review
  Of heaving hulls and burying beaks.

Still on the farthest line, with outpuffed cheeks,
'Twixt dark and utter dark, the great wind drew
From heaven that disenchanted harmony
To join earth's laughter in the midnight blind:
Booming a distant chorus to the shrieks
    Preluding him: then he,
His mantle streaming thunderingly behind,
Across the yellow realm of stiffened Day,

THE GYPSY TRAIL

Shot through the woodland alleys signals three;
   And with the pressure of a sea,
Plunged broad upon the vale that under lay.

   Night on the rolling foliage fell:
   But I, who love old hymning night,
   And know the Dryad voices well,
   Discerned them as their leaves took flight,
   Like souls to wander after death:
   Great armies in imperial dyes,
   And mad to tread the air and rise,
   The savage freedom of the skies
   To taste before they rot. And here,
   Like frail white-bodied girls in fear,
   The birches swung from shrieks to sighs;
   The aspens, laughers at a breath,
   In showery spray-falls mixed their cries,
   Or raked a savage ocean-strand
   With one incessant drowning screech
   Here stood a solitary beech,
   That gave its gold with open hand,
   And all its branches, toning chill,
   Did seem to shut their teeth right fast
   To shriek more mercilessly shrill,
   And match the fierceness of the blast.

   But heard I a low swell that noised
   Of far-off ocean, I was 'ware
   Of pines upon their wide roots poised,
   Whom never madness in the air
   Can draw to more than loftier stress
   Of mournfulness not mournfulness,
   Not mournfulness but Joy's excess,
That singing, on the lap of sorrow faints:
And Peace, as in the hearts of saints
   Who chant unto the Lord their God;
Deep Peace below upon the muffled sod,

AUTUMN

The stillness of the sea's unswaying floor.
　Could I be sole there not to see
　The life within the life awake;
　The spirit bursting from the tree,
　And rising from the troubled lake?
　Pour, let the wines of Heaven pour!
　The Golden Harp is struck once more,
　And all its music is for me!
　Pour, let the wines of Heaven pour!
　And, ho, for a night of Pagan glee!

　　There is a curtain o'er us.
　For once, good souls, we'll not pretend
　To be aught better than she who bore us,
　And is our only visible friend.
　Hark to her laughter! who laughs like this,
　Can she be dead, or rooted in pain?
　She has been slain by the narrow brain,
　But for us who love her she lives again.
　　Can she die? O, take her kiss!

The crimson-footed nymph is panting up the
　　　glade,
With the wine-jar at her arm-pit, and the
　　　drunken ivy-braid　　　'
Round her forehead, breasts, and thighs: starts
　　　a Satyr, and they speed:
Hear the crushing of the leaves: hear the crack-
　　　ing of the bough!
And the whistling of the bramble, the piping of
　　　the weed!

　　But the bull-voiced oak is battling now:
　　The storm has seized him half-asleep,
　　And round him the wild woodland throngs
　　To hear the fury of his songs,
　　The uproar of an outraged deep.

THE GYPSY TRAIL

He wakes to find a wrestling giant
Trunk to trunk and limb to limb,
And on his rooted force reliant,
He laughs and grasps the broadened giant,
And twist and roll the Anakim;
And multitudes acclaiming to the cloud,
    Cry which is breaking, which is bowed.

    Away, for the cymbals clash aloft
In the circles of pine, on the moss-floor soft.
The nymphs of the woodland are gathering
        there,
They huddle the leaves, and trample, and toss;
They swing in the branches, they roll in the
        moss,
    They blow the seed on the air.
Back to back they stand and blow
The winged seed on the cradling air,
A fountain of leaves over bosom and back.
The pipe of the Faun comes on their track,
And the weltering alleys overflow
With musical shrieks and wind-wedded hair.
The riotous companies melt to a pair.
    Bless them, mother of kindness!

A star has nodded through
The depths of the flying blue.
Time only to plant the light
Of a memory in the blindness.
But time to show me the sight
Of my life thro' the curtain of night;
Shining a moment, and mixed
With the onward-hurrying stream,
Whose pressure is darkness to me;
Behind the curtain, fixed,
Beams with endless beam
That star on the changing sea.

AUTUMN

Great Mother Nature! teach me, like thee,
To kiss the season and shun regrets.
And am I more than the mother who bore,
Mock me not with thy harmony!
    Teach me to blot regrets,
    Great Mother! me inspire
    With faith that forward sets
    But feeds the living fire.
    Faith that never frets
    For vagueness in the form.
    In life, O keep me warm!

    For what is human grief?
    And what do men desire?
Teach me to feel myself the tree,
    And not the withered leaf.
Fixed am I and await the dark to-be!

    And O, green bounteous Earth!
Bacchante Mother! stern to those
Who live not in thy heart of mirth;
Death shall I shrink from, loving thee?
Into the breast that gives the rose,
    Shall I with shuddering fall?

    Earth, the mother of all,
    Moves on her steadfast way,
    Gathering, flinging, sowing.
    Mortals, we live in her day,
    She in her children is growing.

She can lead us, only she,
Unto God's footstool, whither she reaches:
Loved, enjoyed, her gifts must be,
Reverenced the truths she teaches,
Ere a man may hope that he

THE GYPSY TRAIL

Ever can attain the glee
Of things without a destiny!

She knows not loss:
She feels but her need,
Who the winged seed
With the leaf doth toss.

And may not men to this attain?
That the joy of motion, the rapture of being,
Shall throw strong light when our season is flee-
ing,
Nor quicken aged blood in vain,
At the gates of the vault, on the verge of the
plain?
Life thoroughly lived is a fact in the brain,
While eyes are left for seeing.
Behold, in yon stripped Autumn, shivering grey,
Earth knows no desolation.
She smells regeneration
In the moist breath of decay.

Prophetic of the coming joy and strife,
Like the wild western war-chief sinking
Calm to the end he eyes unblinking,
Her voice is jubilant in ebbing life.
He for his happy hunting-fields,
Forgets the droning chant, and yields
His numbered breaths to exultation
In the proud anticipation:
Shouting the glories of his nation,
Shouting the grandeur of his race,
Shouting his own great deeds of daring:
And when at last death grasps his face,
And stiffened on the ground in peace
He lies with all his painted terrors glaring;
Hushed are the tribe to hear a threading cry

AUTUMN

Not from the dead man;
Not from the standers-by:
The spirit of the red man
Is welcomed by his fathers up on high.
                              George Meredith

ODE TO THE WEST WIND

I

O WILD West Wind, thou breath of Autumn's being,
Thou, from whose unseen presence the leaves dead
Are driven, like ghosts from an enchanter fleeing,

Yellow, and black, and pale, and hectic red,
Pestilence-stricken multitudes: O thou
Who chariotest to their dark wintry bed

The wingèd seeds, where they lie cold and low,
Each like a corpse within its grave, until
Thine azure sister of the Spring shall blow

Her clarion o'er the dreaming earth, and fill
(Driving sweet buds like flocks to feed in air)
With living hues and odors plain and hill:

Wild Spirit, which art moving everywhere;
Destroyer and preserver; hear, O hear!

THE GYPSY TRAIL

Thou on whose stream, mid the steep sky's com-
      motion,
Loose clouds like earth's decaying leaves are
      shed,
Shook from the tangled boughs of Heaven and
      Ocean,

Angels of rain and lightning: there are spread
On the blue surface of thine airy surge,
Like the bright hair uplifted from the head

Of some fierce Maenad, even from the dim verge
Of the horizon to the zenith's height
The locks of the approaching storm. Thou dirge

Of the dying year, to which this closing night
Will be the dome of a vast sepulchre,
Vaulted with all thy congregated might

Of vapors, from whose solid atmosphere
Black rain, and fire, and hail will burst: O hear!

III

Thou who didst waken from his summer dreams
The blue Mediterranean, where he lay,
Lulled by the coil of his crystalline streams,

Beside a pumice isle in Baiae's bay,
And saw in sleep old palaces and towers
Quivering within the wave's intenser day,

All overgrown with azure moss and flowers
So sweet, the sense faints picturing them! Thou
For whose path the Atlantic's level powers

AUTUMN

Cleave themselves into chasms, while far below
The sea-blooms and the oozy woods which wear
The sapless foliage of the ocean, know

Thy voice, and suddenly grow gray with fear,
And tremble and despoil themselves: O hear!

IV

If I were a dead leaf thou mightest bear;
If I were a swift cloud to fly with thee;
A wave to pant beneath thy power, and share

The impulse of thy strength, only less free
Than thou, O uncontrollable! If even
I were as in my boyhood, and could be

The comrade of thy wanderings over heaven,
As then, when to outstrip thy skyey speed
Scarce seemed a vision; I would ne'er have
        striven

As thus with thee in prayer in my sore need.
Oh lift me as a wave, a leaf, a cloud!
I fall upon the thorns of life! I bleed!

A heavy weight of hours has chained and bowed
One too like thee: tameless, and swift, and proud.

V

Make me thy lyre, even as the forest is:
What if my leaves are falling like its own!
The tumult of thy mighty harmonies

Will take from both a deep autumnal tone,
Sweet tho' in sadness. Be thou, spirit fierce,
My spirit! Be thou me, impetuous one!

THE GYPSY TRAIL

Drive my dead thoughts over the universe
Like withered leaves to quicken a new birth!
And, by the incantation of this verse,

Scatter, as from an unextinguished hearth
Ashes and sparks, my words among mankind!
Be thro' my lips to unawakened earth

The trumpet of a prophecy! O, wind,
If Winter comes, can Spring be far behind?
                    Percy Bysshe Shelley

PALLADIUM

SET where the upper streams of Simois flow,
  Was the Palladium, high 'mid rock and
    wood;
And Hector was in Ilium, far below,
And fought, and saw it not; but there it stood!

It stood, and sun and moonshine rained their
    light
On the pure columns of its glen-built hall.
Backward and forward rolled the waves of fight
Round Troy; but while this stood, Troy could
    not fall.

So, in its lovely moonlight, lives the soul.
Mountains surround it, and sweet virgin air;
Cold plashing, past it, crystal waters roll:
We visit it by moments, ah, too rare!

We shall renew the battle in the plain
To-morrow: red with blood will Xanthus be;
Hector and Ajax will be there again,
Helen will come upon the wall to see.

Then we shall rust in shade, or shine in strife,
And fluctuate 'twixt blind hopes and blind de-
    spairs,
And fancy that we put forth all our life,
And never know how with the soul it fares.

Still doth the soul, from its lone fastness high,
Upon our life a ruling effluence send;
And when it fails, fight as we will, we die;
And, while it lasts, we cannot wholly end.

Matthew Arnold

INDEX OF AUTHORS

INDEX OF AUTHORS

INDEX OF AUTHORS

INDEX OF AUTHORS

INDEX OF AUTHORS

INDEX OF AUTHORS

INDEX OF AUTHORS

INDEX OF AUTHORS

INDEX OF AUTHORS

INDEX OF AUTHORS